Current Paleoethnobotany

Prehistoric Archeology and Ecology
A Series Edited by Karl W. Butzer and Leslie G. Freeman

Current Paleoethnobotany

Analytical Methods and Cultural Interpretations of Archaeological Plant Remains

Edited by
Christine A. Hastorf and
Virginia S. Popper

The University of Chicago Press
Chicago and London

The University of Chicago Press, Chicago 60637
The University of Chicago Press, Ltd., London

Printed in the United States of America
97 96 95 94 93 92 91 5 4 3 2

Library of Congress Cataloging in Publication Data

Current paleoethnobotany : analytical methods and cultural
interpretations of archaeological plant remains / edited by
Christine A. Hastorf and Virginia S. Popper
p. cm. -- (Prehistoric archeology and ecology)
Bibliography: p.
Includes index.
1. Plant remains (Archaeology) I. Hastorf, Christine Ann, 1950-
II. Popper, Virginia S. III. Series.
CC79.5.P5C87 1988 88-20467
930.1--dc19 CIP
ISBN 0-226-31892-3
ISBN 0-226-31893-1 (pbk.)

Contents

Acknowledgments

Many people have helped with the completion of this book. Specific work on individual papers is mentioned in each chapter, but here we would like to give special thanks to those who worked on the final draft of the camera ready copy: Lisa Beyer, Virginia Card, Renee Holoien, Sissel Johannessen, and Heidi Lennstrom. Support for production of the manuscript was provided in part by the National Science Foundation Grant BNS8451369.

Series Editors' Foreword

Paleoethnobotany refers to the analysis and interpretation of archeobotanical remains to elucidate the interaction between human populations and plants. The papers assembled here by Christine Hastorf and Virginia Popper were originally presented at a special symposium on the occasion of the 1985 meetings of the Society for American Archaeology. In the interim, this nucleus of manuscripts has been transformed into a coherent whole, the chapters of which complement each other well, share a common theme, yet avoid redundancy. The resulting effort is a state-of-the-art volume about analytical methods and the cultural interpretations of archeological plant remains.

General works on archeobotanical research go back to Geoffrey Dimbleby's 1967 *Plants and Archeology* and Jane Renfrew's 1973 *Paleoethnobotany,* but flotation techniques have yielded vast samples for innumerable sites during the last fifteen years. As a result, the study of what have euphemistically been called macrobotanical remains has moved from qualitative or semiqualitative lists of species, into a truly quantitative realm where statistical concerns can be seriously discussed, and where far more detailed matters of interpretation can finally be raised. This is a particularly active research frontier, represented in Britain by Renfrew and Robin Dennell, and in the Netherlands by Willem Van Zeist. The contributors to this volume represent another strong group, of United States scholars, who have primarily been engaged in research in the Midwest, the Southwest, as well as Latin

America. Richard Ford, in 1985, assembled a volume entitled *Prehistoric Food Production in North America,** that marked a quantum jump in our understanding of food-gathering and agricultural activities in different American regions and time ranges. *Current Paleoethnobotany* complements Ford's monograph by focusing on methodologies and problems of interpretation.

The introduction, by the volume editors, reviews the subfield and discusses the role of cultural and noncultural patterning of archeobotanical data, and the attendant questions of accumulation and preservation. The various contributions are then discussed according to the primary thematic concerns of the book: sample collecting and processing, classification of the materials, quantification and statistical manipulating of the results, and interpretation of their significance. Gail Wagner's chapter (chap. 2) is directed to the problems of comparability of results generated by different recovery techniques—dry or water screening, hand or machine-operated flotation. In chapter 3, Mollie Toll addresses this issue with specific flotation results from southwestern sites, to argue that excavation resources should not be exclusively expended on the most productive sites. Low-frequency or negative data from a broad regional cross-section of sites, many of them eroded or structureless, help identify levels of uncertainty and also illuminate the horizontal variability essential to understandinbg a regional site complex.

Popper's specific paper (chap. 4) turns to measures that illustrate cultural and noncultural patterning, namely the different insights provided by absolute counts, "ubiquity" (presence analyses), ranking techniques, and diversity indices. Each method yields different insights, and its suitability varies according to the nature of the sample. There is then no ideal technique; the research question itself determines the most appropriate measures. The matter of ubiquity is explored in greater detail in chapter 5, by Naomi Miller, who evaluates different types of ratios, based on proportions, percentages, or densities, as means to effectively characterize an archeobotanical assemblage. David Asch and Nancy Sidell (chap. 6) show how botanical, faunal, and geochemical criteria can (and should) complement the use of diagnostic lithics in establishing site microstratigraphies.

The range of problems encountered within a single Peruvian cave site and its external slope is explored in chapter 7, by Deborah Pearsall. Plant matter was introduced as food, fuel, camelid dung, or matting; most was charred in cooking fires, and much was eventually cleared out onto the

*University of Michigan, Museum of Anthropology, Anthropological Paper no. 75.

slope. Although there was less difference in micropatterning across the site than there was change through time (related to varying intensity of site use), Pearsall's analyses allow useful inferences as to microactivities. Hastorf (chap. 8) follows up these questions in a Peruvian regional study, including a larger number of sites; she applies ethnographic evidence on plant production, processing, and consumption to the botanical results, to explore how well specific economic activities can be inferred from macrobotanical remains. Stable carbon isotope ratios on human bone, in comparison with isotopic values for available foods, suggest a need for an alternative statistical organization of plant results.

Chapter 9, by Sissel Johannessen, covers a large range of botanical data from some eighty sites that span 4,000 years in the American Bottom of Illinois. This is one of the most impressive quantitative studies yet provided for subsistence change over time. During the Early and Middle Woodland periods, starchy seeds replaced nuts as major plant foods, while maize, long present in minor quantities, became the major staple during the Woodland-Mississippian transition (a span of about 200 calibrated radiocarbon years). Settlement had switched from floodplain to upland sites during the Middle Woodland but, not long after the maize "revolution," began to concentrate once again on the more fertile floodplain soils. It is an unusually strong, standardized data base emerging from a comprehensive research plan. The results provide remarkably good information on how this important agricultural transition took place.

The final substantive chapter, by Tristine Smart and Ellen Hoffman (chap. 10), deals with charcoal of woody taxa as a source of information on local vegetation. The discussion ranges from wood uses, natural means of introduction, burning and preservation, recovery techniques, sampling and identification, to presentation methods that elucidate plant diversity, habitats, probable locations, and vegetation change over time.

The volume is concluded by three evaluations offering very different perspectives (chaps. 11-13). The first, by Joseph Kadane, a statistician, raises some thoughtful questions about ubiquity measures and ratios that suggest that paleobotanical data have become sufficiently rich and diversified to allow serious statistical manipulation. The second is by Richard Ford, one of the most influential proponents of paleoethnobotany. His thoughtful comments sketch a conceptual overview that pulls together ideas, suggests stimulating new points, and notes issues that require more attention, as for example, the geochemical and other processes that control preservation. The third evaluation is by an archeologist, William Marquart, who draws more specific attention to the linkages between paleoethnobotany and archeology, in terms of problem formulation, research design, and comprehensive interpretation.

Hastorf and Popper's volume exemplifies the wealth of information and unexpected insights that botanical studies can provide. But although some projects have had the foresight to emphasize such work, the majority of well-funded excavations include research by archeobotanists, zooarcheologists, and geoarcheologists as no more than adjunct components, insofar as they incorporate them at all.

Current Paleoethnobotany fills a yawning void in the literature. There is no single source where students or professional archeologists can find such a comprehensive overview of sampling, collection methods, analysis, and interpretation. The materials are presented with adequate explanations and good examples or illustrations, that can serve the nonspecialist well. But the book is far more than a compendium of tried and true methods. It both challenges and stimulates the reader by constantly questioning traditional assumptions.

Among earlier volumes of the Prehistoric Archeology and Ecology series, Anna Behrensmeyer and Andrew Hill provided a timely overview of taphonomy with their *Fossils in the Making*, and Richard Kleinand Kathryn Cruz-Uribe contributed a solid framework for zooarcheological research with *The Analysis of Animal Bones from Archeological Sites*. We believe that Christine Hastorf and Virginia Popper's *Current Paleoethnobotany* represents another such volume of major methodological and theoretical significance for a rapidly developing subfield of archeology.

Karl W. Butzer
Leslie G. Freeman

1

Introduction

Virginia S. Popper and Christine A. Hastorf

Paleoethnobotany is the study of past cultures by an examination of human populations' interactions with the plant world. People have relied on plants to fulfill a variety of their needs. Plants have satisfied the basic needs of food, fuel, shelter, clothing, and tools. Plants have been important to social and religious activities, such as exchange, status differentiation, ritual, and mythology. Examining the relationships between humans and plants within a past culture provides important information about the culture.

Human-plant relationships are dynamic. The natural environment affects cultural development by providing a human population with a particular set of resources. Plant resources have certain ecological limits and exploitation potential. In turn, humans alter the natural environment, for example by clearing land or extending the range where a plant grows. And humans' cultural perceptions, beliefs, and rules determine how humans will use the environment (e.g., which plants to collect, where, how, and how often to clear a field). Paleoethnobotanists study both cultural development and environmental change, keeping in mind the limitations and effects of one on the other.

The study of plant remains from archaeological sites provides information for a number of disciplines. For instance, ecologists and botanists may use plant remains to reconstruct past environments and to study morphological changes in plants due to plant domestication. Archaeologists may use them to examine how cultural groups provided for their basic needs, how extractive strategies (e.g., plant collecting and agriculture) changed over time, or how remains of plant offerings from burials help signal social status. Art historians may look for evidence of plants' symbolic meanings from depictions on artifacts and their presence in archaeological sediments.

Because plant remains from archaeological sites provide information in part related and in part unrelated to human activity, the study of these remains falls within two disciplines: archaeobotany and paleoethnobotany. Ford (1979:299) defines archaeobotany as "the study of plant remains from archaeological contexts. . . Archaeobotany refers to the *recovery* and *identification* of plants by specialists regardless of discipline." In other words, the data, the methods for collecting and analyzing the data, and data interpetation that do not involve human activity would fall within archaeobotany. Paleoethnobotany was defined by Renfrew (1973:1) as "the study of remains of plants cultivated or utilized by man in ancient times, which have survived in archaeological contexts." This definition adds the human element that differentiates archaeobotany from paleoethnobotany. Renfrew's definition differs, however, from Ford's (1979:299) definition of paleoethnobotany and that used in this volume, which include an ecological and anthropological approach. Here paleoethnobotany means the analysis and interpretation of archaeobotanical remains to provide information about the interaction of human populations and plants. [1]

The many shades of meaning of archaeobotany and paleoethnobotany are evidenced in this volume. Different authors use these terms differently and sometimes interchangeably, which reflects the lack of a consensus on the distinction between the terms. As the editors would articulate the difference, archaeobotany refers to the plant remains themselves, the methods for collecting, identifying, and recording the data, and noncultural interpretations of the data; paleoethobotany refers to a more specificlly defined inquiry about the data: what do the data tell us about human-plant interactions? Where this distinction leaves quantitative analysis is unclear. Sometimes quantitative methods are used with specific cultural questions in mind. As a simple (and somewhat artificial) example, the ratio of collected plants to cultivated plants might be used to assess the importance of agriculture in an economy. The researcher has imbued this ratio with a cultural meaning and therefore may want to characterize this method as paleoethnobotany. At other times a researcher uses quantitative methods to organize and describe data without assuming any cultural meaning for the resulting patterns. This would fall under archaeobotany.

1. Uses of the term ethnobotany as part of ethnoscience are discussed in Conklin 1954 and Ellen 1982:206-11.

Paleoethnobotany in America grew out of ethnobotany, "the study of the direct interrelations between human and plants" (Ford 1978:44). The great potential of paleoethnobotany was recognized by Melvin Gilmore and Volney Jones at the University of Michigan in the 1930s when they expanded the scope of study beyond taxonomic determinations and uses of plants (Jones 1941; Ford 1978, 1979). Following from their lead, scholars realized that simple lists of the identified plants were not suitable for looking at questions such as the origins of plant domestication, dietary change, how a group produced surpluses for trade or tribute, or the use of plants in rituals. These required recording quantitative information on the plant remains, understanding the ecological characteristics of plants, and looking at material and nonmaterial aspects of cultures.

The expanding scope of paleoethnobotany challenges us to develop collection methods, analytical procedures, and interpretive models that provide accurate information about human society from plant remains. This volume assesses the current state and future needs of paleoethnobotany by discussing the methods that paleoethnobotanists use to obtain the quality of archaeobotanical data needed to address research questions. These papers explore the assumptions underlying methods used to collect and analyze archaeobotanical data and assess how these methods and assumptions color paleoethnobotanical interpretations. By making our methods and interpretations more explicit, we invite all scholars to apply, discuss, and improve them.

As we develop new methods and models, we should be sure that they are appropriate for our research goals. Unfortunately, little integration of research goals and procedures has been provided in paleoethnobotanical publications. Although many papers have discussed the techniques of flotation, soil collection, seed identification, counting procedures, and tabulation, these papers are scattered through the literature and frequently relegated to appendixes. (Exceptions include Ford [1978, 1979] and articles in the *Journal of Ethnobiology*.) Paleoethnobotanical reports often contain only cursory descriptions of the methods used in collection and analysis and almost never explain why the investigators selected particular methods. We need to integrate thinking about research goals and thinking about procedures to move beyond the techniques-oriented view of paleoethnobotany and to demonstrate its potential for illuminating past cultures and their relationships with the plant world.

Paleoethnobotany should be recognized as an important and integral part of archaeological research. This more active role for paleoethnobotanists depends on well-planned, systematic research. Paleoethnobotany, like much of archaeology, is labor intensive. Time and money constrain our analyses. Efficient research requires defining specific research questions and goals that direct the researcher to appropriate methods of data collection and analysis. Thinking through all collection, processing, and analytical methods at the beginning of a research project saves time and money and extracts more information from the botanical data. Paleoethnobotanists also must be flexible, changing their methods with unexpected field and laboratory conditions. At a minimum, we encourage archaeologists to consult a paleoethnobotanist about strategies for systematically collecting botanical remains before beginning their projects. Otherwise the data may be only minimally applicable to the archaeological problem.

The papers in this volume grew out of a symposium presented at the fiftieth annual meeting of the Society for American Archaeology in April 1985. Two papers (Minnis 1985a; Miksicek 1985) were presented at the symposium but are not included here. One additional paper (Kadane, chapter 11) was solicited after the symposium. The symposium's intent was to emphasize the assumptions underlying paleoethnobotanical methods and interpretations, not to present data. The expanded papers for publication tend toward one of two perspectives: methodological and interpretive. The methodological papers (except Toll, chapter 3) are more general and theoretical. They present the basic techniques of paleoethnobotany, providing background information to the nonspecialist. The interpretive papers are more specific and rich in data. It follows that these interpretive papers have a stronger regional orientation. Although some techniques and models are designed for use in particular regions, modifying and applying them to other regions bears consideration. Together the case studies and general discussions provide a broad view of paleoethnobotany and the tools we use to help reconstruct past cultures.

This volume is not an all-encompassing guide to the methods of archaeobotany and paleoethnobotany. Nor does it address all of the topics to which paleoethnobotanical research can contribute. Instead, this volume covers a series of key methodological steps and interpretive problems, examining how and why we use and tackle them. We hope this approach will be applied to other topics of paleoethnobotany not covered here.

We also hope this volume will prove useful to both specialists in paleoethnobotany and nonspecialists. We encourage other specialists to evaluate our methods and assumptions and theirs and to integrate research procedures with research objectives. In addition, we encourage archaeologists to draw on the expanding archaeobotanical data base to answer archaeological research questions.

Research Questions

All archaeological research, including paleoethnobotanical studies, begins with research questions. These questions direct field and laboratory work by prescribing the information we need to collect. The patterns of archaeobotanical data (i.e., types, quantities, and their distribution across time and space) reflect the interaction of humans with the plant world. Research questions about particular human-plant interactions direct us to the specific patterns of archaeobotanical data we need to answer the questions. Suitable collection and analytical methods better enable us to test our data for these patterns. As many authors in this volume point out, however, some patterning of archaeobotanical remains is noncultural. Noncultural sources of patterning have been dealt with extensively in the literature (Dimbleby 1967; Schiffer 1976; Butzer 1982), so we only summarize them here. Cultural and noncultural patterning do not imply order in archaeobotanical data (Pearsall, chapter 7; Asch and Sidell, chapter 6).

Patterns of Deposition and Preservation

Plant distributions on archaeological sites are affected by planned and unplanned cultural activities and by natural forces. Of these, differential preservation of plant remains presents the greatest challenge to paleoethnobotanical analyses. Whether a plant or part of a plant is preserved depends only partially on its physical properties, such as density, surface characteristics, or size. Plant preservation is affected also by the cause of charring, the frequency and method of use and disposal by the site inhabitants (Dennell 1976; Hubbard 1976; Pearsall, chapter 7), and the site-formation process (soil type, depth of deposit, moisture regime). Experiments on the biological element of plant taphonomy will help us evaluate the extent of these biases (Ford, chapter 12). Paleoethnobotanical methods and models attempt to reduce the effects of these intrinsic biases in archaeobotanical data on our interpretations. Many of the papers in this volume (in particular see Johannessen, chapter 9) illustrate how we account for noncultural sources of patterning, because this issue must be addressed before we can unravel the cultural sources of patterning in our data.

Collecting and Processing Plant Remains

During excavation, methods of collecting and processing plant remains can bias our sample of the plant distribution on a site (Wagner 1982, chapter 2; Toll, chapter 3; Smart and Hoffman, chapter 10). Aside from the need for systematic sampling, which is discussed below, the papers in this volume stress several imperatives for excavation. Almost every paper (particularly Pearsall, chapter 7, and Hastorf, chapter 8) places crucial importance on defining the cultural contexts of excavated archaeobotanical samples. Asch and Sidell (chapter 6), Miller (chapter 5), and Popper (chapter 4) stress the need for on-site evaluation of the preservation potential of deposits and possible disturbance of deposits. Butzer (1982) suggests how geoarchaeological studies help evaluate these geobiochemical modifications. Appropriate excavation and recording procedures minimize additional bias in the patterning of archaeobotanical data and assist the paleoethnobotanist in the interpretation of patterning in the data.

The research problem and a site's characteristics determine the appropriate sampling strategy for plant remains. No one sampling scheme is appropriate in every case. The more carefully defined the research question and the more familiar one is with the probable distribution of remains at a site, the more specific a sampling scheme one can design. If, as in many cases, the extent of the cultural contexts is not determined until after the excavation is finished (Harris 1979), a broader standardized collection procedure is required. If we collect too many samples, we need not process them all. However, if we collect too few, we usually cannot return to the site to collect more.

Archaeologists use several strategies for collecting flotation samples. In theory, different strategies are appropriate for particular contexts and research questions. The three most common strategies are pinch (grab) samples, column samples, and bulk samples (Bohrer and Adams 1977:15-20; see Pearsall [in press] for a more complete discussion of sampling strategies). Archaeologists frequently use the pinch method to sample ephemeral occupation surfaces and stratified trash. Small "pinches" of soil are collected throughout one excavation level or locus to total a set volume of soil. This sample should provide an average representation of the provenience contents (Adams and Gasser 1980). Archaeologists often collect column samples when they look for chronological changes in large undifferentiated deposits. For this method, one collects a standard amount of soil from each cultural or arbitrary level, for example every 10 cm, in a vertical column to provide a chronological sequence. Gasser (1985) showed that a column sample may not be representative of an entire deposit. In his study, plant remains from four adjoining columns of a trash mound differed greatly, providing divergent evidence of chronological change. For locus-bulk sampling, the archaeologist collects a standard amount of soil from a specific location in every excavation level or locus. This provides botanical evidence from discrete locations and proves most useful with knowledge of the cultural context. To compare these sampling strategies, Hastorf is studying pinch and bulk samples from the same deposits.

Whatever the sampling strategy, one must sample less productive deposits to use as controls for evaluating the remains in features and richer deposits (Toll, chapter 3; Adams and Gasser 1980). In addition, plant remains from unclear contexts may, after analysis, help identify the contexts (Dennell 1978; Pearsall, chapter 7; Kadane and Hastorf 1988), or may provide stratigraphic information (Asch and Sidell, chapter 6).

Another sampling decision is determining an adequate flotation sample size for providing representative counts and ranges of taxa from different deposits. Sample size varies from whole sites (Jarman, Legge, and Charles 1972) to 1-liter samples (Miller pers. com.). The adequate soil volume for a sample is specific to the information sought from a deposit and its density of remains. For example, one needs more maize remains to analyze maize varieties than to document maize cultivation. Similarly, large soil samples may be required to examine the use of starvation foods during periods of food stress, because the remains of these foods are usually scarce (Wetterstrom 1986:144). In general, the better the organic preservation, the smaller the sample need be. A larger volume of soil per sample increases the number of remains per sample and the range of taxa. We must balance our need for representative taxa and sufficiently large counts of remains against the constraints of transportation of samples, processing time, and equipment costs. In cases where the density of remains at a site is unknown before excavation, the paleoethnobotanist may have to process a variety of deposits in different quantities before deciding on an appropriate soil sample size.

Soil flotation is only one method for collecting plant remains from archaeological sites. Wagner (chapter 2) demonstrates how flotation and two other methods, dry screening and water screening, recover disparate types and quantities of remains. Because these three methods alter our sample of the plant assemblage in different ways, data recovered by different methods are not directly comparable. Comparability is a problem with different flotation techniques as well. Paleoethnobotanists tailor flotation systems to process efficiently a soil volume and soil type with an appropriate rate of retrieval. Because systems will differ according to these conditions, we need more complete descriptions of our techniques in our reports suitably to compare data collected from different sites.

Classification

Once the plant remains are extracted from the soil, the most labor-intensive, yet often unreported, stage in paleoethnobotanical research begins: sorting, identifying, and tabulating the remains. Paleoethnobotanists use a variety of techniques, but all have a systematic procedure designed to minimize bias in the selection of remains for processing and identification, to minimize the breakage of fragile remains, and to maximize the information recorded about the plant assemblage. When collections are too large to be analyzed completely, chemical and mechanical separation techniques offer subsampling strategies (Bohrer and Adams 1977; Bodner and Rowlett 1980; van der Veen and Fieller 1982). Toll (chapter 3) provides a useful two-level sampling procedure for large collections. The first level involves scanning samples to record the presence or absence of taxa, which shows the broad patterning in the data. The second level is the complete tabulation of samples for detailed analysis. The first-level analysis can help in the selection of samples for the second level. This two-level procedure proves particularly useful when analyzing samples from many sites in a region. The ability to analyze large bodies of data in a relatively short time encourages more complete sampling of archaeological sites and the regional analysis of human-plant interaction.

Toll's method has the advantage of reducing the time devoted to counting remains, while maintaining the importance of taxa identification. The specificity with which we identify plant remains—whether seeds, wood, or other anatomical parts—bears greatly on our interpretations. Smart and Hoffman (chapter 10) point out the importance of specific identifications to reconstruct the environment from charcoal. Paleoethnobotanists identify plant remains by comparing them to modern reference collections, to well-preserved and securely identified archaeological specimens, and, less preferably, to pictures and descriptions of seeds, wood, fibers, and so forth. Identifying a remain as to species (not just genus or family) requires caution and explanation so that other researchers can evaluate the validity of the identification. Two principal criteria allow for species identification (Johannessen, chapter 9; Smart and Hoffman, chapter 10). In some cases, the area vegetation contains only one species of a genus and the plant remains match its morphology. In other cases, the area vegetation contains several species, but the remains clearly match the morphology of only one. These criteria are not without problems. As Smart and Hoffman (chapter 10) illustrate, modern distributions and associations of plants may differ from prehistoric ones. In addition, comparing modern and archaeological seeds may be misleading, for example, when human manipulation of plants, such as domesticates and field weeds, has changed their morphology. Moreover, carbonization itself can alter the morphology of plants (e.g., size of seeds). Experiments with carbonizing modern plants help, but do not always succeed in identifying these changes (Smart and Hoffman, chapter 10; Walker 1973). Nonetheless, paleoethnobotanists should continue working together to improve their understanding of plant anatomy, to adopt the use of high-powered scientific instruments (e.g., petrographic microscopes, scanning electron microscopes, high-quality binocular microscopes, and electronic balances), and to build comparative plant collections to increase the specificity of their identifications (Bohrer 1986).

Quantification

The next step in the analysis of plant remains is quantification: how we use types and counts of remains to explore our research interests. No one method of quantifying data is appropriate for all analyses, because each technique has its own biases and conditions. As Popper (chapter 4) and Miller (chapter 5) stress, we must chose our quantitative techniques on the basis of our understanding of these biases and conditions, the quality of our data, and the patterns we seek as defined by our research questions.

Popper (chapter 4) compares the strengths and weaknesses of four quantitative methods: absolute counts, ubiquity (presence-absence or percentage presence), ranking (ordinal sequence), and taxa diversity. Each method has its own assumptions and possible sources of error. The measurements also provide different information about the data and use the data with different degrees of specificity. Popper suggests the conditions under which each method is useful and appropriate. Popper and Miller both note that in most cases the absolute-counts (raw counts) method is not an adequate quantitative method, because it does not take into account patterning in the data introduced by differential preservation and deposition. Raw counts should be standardized at least by the size of the sample matrix or by a measure of sample richness (Scarry 1986:214). (Wagner [chapter 2] describes standardization in detail.) Consequently, researchers must justify their use of absolute counts.

Miller (chapter 5) discusses the many forms of a powerful and commonly used quantitative measurement, the ratio. The forms include density measures, percentages, proportions, and comparison ratios. She illustrates that both the type of ratio and the variables chosen must be relevant to the question asked. In addition, she cautions that grouping of taxa and of samples can lead to errors if use and preservation potential are not equivalent. Under the appropriate conditions, the potential of using multiple data sets with ratios is great. The comparisons may be between two parts of the same taxon (*Zea mays* kernels and cobs), two taxa, two groups of taxa (nuts and seeds), or botanical data and nonbotanical data (crop seeds and stone hoes). More comparison of data sets will strengthen our paleoethnobotanical interpretations (Minnis 1978, 1985a; Hastorf, chapter 8).

An initial analysis to describe the data may reveal that our assumptions about the data are inaccurate and the use of a particular method invalid.

Therefore we must be ready to modify our analysis to account for this new information. Comparing two or more quantitative measurements on the same data set may reveal additional information (Pearsall 1983; Pearsall, chapter 7).

Statistics and Presentation

The description and analysis of botanical remains should not end with quantitative measurements. Statistical techniques, such as multivariate and nonparametric techniques, organize the data and reveal patterns. However, Miksicek (1985) and Marquardt (pers. com.) caution that principal components analysis, factor analysis, and cluster analysis are inappropriate for confirming hypotheses, because the use of these techniques relies on assumptions and constraints that often are not met with the archaeobotanical data. Simpler statistics may be appropriate for testing the significance of patterns and trends revealed in the analysis. These help us evaluate the validity of inferences from our data.

Kadane (chapter 11) comments on the papers in this volume from a statistician's viewpoint. He recommends applying the Poisson count model to the distribution of archaeobotanical data and suggests other areas of statistical research which can help paleoethnobotanists overcome problems with plant data.

Data presentation provides another valuable tool for describing data structure and interpreting plant assemblages. Most presentation is tabular, although computers can produce more easily comprehended graphs and plots. Recent literature on the graphic presentation of data (see in particular Kosslyn 1985; Chambers, Cleveland, Kleiner, and Tukey 1983; Tufte 1983; and Tukey 1977) discusses the types of data most suitable for different graphic presentations.

Scarry (1986) provides an excellent example of using simple statistics and graphic presentation to investigate the structure and variability of archaeobotanical data. She applies exploratory data analysis to plant remains from the Moundville system of west central Alabama to study changes in subsistence strategies. Her analysis shows that medians and measures of dispersion around the median are better than means and standard deviations for measuring the central tendency of data that are not normally distributed. Scatter plots, probability plots, stem-and-leaf plots, and boxplots illustrate the distribution of taxa and the relationships between taxa. These methods also provide information on the significance of observed relationships and identify samples which depart from the norm. Scarry uses these methods, for example, to examine changes in the distribution of taxa over time, among contexts, and by site location.

Interpretation

Assigning a valid paleoethnobotanical meaning to the values and patterns revealed by quantitative and statistical analysis of archaeobotanical data is difficult. Nonetheless, Miller (chapter 5) and Popper (chapter 4) stress that we must be more explicit in linking the resulting values from quantitative analyses with the information we are trying to obtain. We must thoughtfully evaluate human-plant interactions and the patterns of plant remains they produce at an archaeological site. Ford (chapter 12) cautions that paleoethnobotanists must consider and reject alternative interpretations of their data before accepting the seemingly most logical interpretation. Pearsall (chapter 7), Hastorf (chapter 8), Johannessen (chapter 9), and Smart and Hoffman (chapter 10) discuss some problems of interpreting archaeobotanical data and their solutions.

Pearsall (chapter 7) develops a theoretical model of the source and deposition of plants at Panaulauca Cave to interpret the frequencies of plant remains from the site. She investigates how plants were brought into the site, how they were charred, and the proposed function of depositional contexts to sort out the specific activities that created the plant assemblage at Panaulauca. The frequency and persistence of these activities is reflected in the relative and changing frequencies of taxa through time and among contexts. Thus, source and context must be carefully understood before abundance of taxa can be interpreted.

Hastorf (chapter 8) discusses models and procedures related to identifying plant production, processing, and consumption using archaeobotanical data. Her discussion of these three types of economic activities shows where we can find specific information about them in the archaeological record. In some deposits botanical evidence of these activities is not preserved. In other deposits the evidence is ambiguous, possibly representing a number of activities. In many deposits, however, plant remains that relate to production and processing have been incorrectly interpreted as evidence of consumption. To identify these activities we must improve our models. Hypothetical models of plant deposition should, when possible, be replaced by models based on ethnographic examples of plant deposition, providing botanical correlates to production and consumption activities (Hillman 1984). Unraveling the production data from the scarcer consumption data hinges on the context from which the botanical data were collected. In addition, multiple data sets, such as coprolites, chemical analysis of human bones, and ceramics help us address questions of consumption.

Smart and Hoffman (chapter 10) investigate the complex relationship between the charcoal excavated from a site and the environment from which it came. Like Pearsall, they stress the importance of understanding how and why wood was brought to the site and charred. Smart and Hoffman caution against an uncritical use of modern vegetation patterns for the interpretation of charcoal remains and an uncritical use of quantitative data for specific reconstructions of vegetation abundance. Accurate environmental reconstruction requires multiple data sets (charcoal, pollen, tree rings) and regional data.

Johannessen (chapter 9) examines the role of human-plant interaction in culture change. She collected data on changes in food production and the gathering of food and fuel in the central Mississippi River valley by systematically sampling many sites. She translates changes in the quantities of these plant remains into behavioral correlates to suggest how human-plant interaction changed with the development of agricultural systems.

Turning away from cultural interpretations, Asch and Sidell (chapter 6) show how archaeobotanical data can assist in the stratigraphic interpretations of a site. They discuss the depositional and postdepositional processes that favor the accumulation of plant remains in vertical sequences that can be correlated across a site. Using plant remains to unravel site stratigraphy is particularly useful when there are few diagnostic artifacts for dating strata or when the diagnostic artifacts are too general to assist in fine-scale stratigraphic analysis. Asch and Sidell conclude that archaeobotanists and paleoethnobotanists must take a more active role in the interpretation of site stratigraphy and site formation processes.

Conclusion

This volume addresses only a few of the major areas of paleoethnobotanical research: environmental reconstruction, economic models, and culture change. Other important topics not addressed here include nutrition and food stress (Wing and Brown 1979; Minnis 1985b; Wetterstrom 1986) and processes of food production and domestication (Crawford 1983; Rindos 1984; Van Zeist and Casparie 1984; Ford 1985). Ford (chapter 12) encourages new research on plant domestication and human modification of the environment, with greater emphasis on their biological components. The papers in this volume illustrate how to evaluate and use models of the environment, human behavior, and human-plant interactions to interpret the patterning of plant remains.

Paleoethnobotanists also study a broader range of data than the macroremains mentioned in this volume. Pollen provides information on local and regional environments, crops, and use of plants (such as flowers) which do not normally survive in archaeological sites (Holloway and Bryant 1986). Phytoliths (silica structures deposited in the cells of plants) can be difficult to identify, but provide evidence of plants which have not been preserved (Rovner 1971). Stable isotope analysis can identify plant remains that lack defining morphological characteristics (Hastorf 1983) and provides dietary information from bones (van de Merwe and Vogel 1978; DeNiro 1987). Each data base has its own methods of collection and quantification, but interpreting the data requires the same careful consideration as the interpretation of macroremains.

Several themes are repeated throughout this volume, evidencing their extreme importance in paleoethnobotanical studies. First is the long-recognized problem of preservation and deposition. Although many of our methods attempt to control for these constraints on our data, we must discuss in full how these constraints affect our analyses. Second, a number of improvements have been suggested for paleoethnobotanical and archaeobotanical research. Systematic sampling is essential. More attention must be paid to the contexts of archaeobotanical data. Regional data sets and the use of multiple data sets can strengthen our interpretations. Paleoethnobotanical reports should include complete descriptions of methods and raw data, which allow others to evaluate research and use data for comparative purposes. And finally, paleoethnobotanists must work closely with archaeologists before, during, and after excavation to achieve the full potential of their research. By tackling these issues, archaeologists will address research questions more successfully.

Acknowledgments

We thank Greg Morgan and our anonymous reviewers for editorial assistance with this Introduction, as well as with the entire volume. Our first reviewer was especially thoughtful and helpful in broadening and compiling these symposium papers into a publishable book. The Center for Advanced Studies in the Behavioral Sciences provided clerical support under the grant BNS8411738.

References Cited

Adams, Karen R., and Robert E. Gasser. 1980. Plant microfossils from archaeological sites: Research considerations and sampling techniques and approaches. *The Kiva* 45(4):293-300.

Bodner, Connie C., and Ralph M. Rowlett. 1980. Separation of bone, charcoal, and seeds by chemical flotation. *American Antiquity* 45(1):110-16.

Bohrer, Vorsila L. 1986. Guideposts in ethnobotany. *Journal of Ethnobiology* 6(1):27-43.

Bohrer, Vorsila, and Karen Adams. 1977. Ethnobotanical techniques and approaches at Salmon Ruin, New Mexico. *Contributions in Anthropology* 8(1). Eastern New Mexico University.

Butzer, Karl W. 1982. *Archaeology as human ecology: Method and theory for a contextual approach.* Cambridge: University Press.

Chambers, J. M., W. S. Cleveland, B. Kleiner and P. A. Tukey. 1983. *Graphical methods for data analysis.* Belmont, California: Wadsworth.

Conklin, H. C. 1954. An ethnoecological approach to shifting agriculture. *Transactions of the New York Academy of Sciences* 17:133-42.

Crawford, Gary W. 1983. *Paleoethnobotany of the Kameda Peninsula, Jomon.* Anthropological Papers no. 73. University of Michigan, Museum of Anthropology.

DeNiro, Michael J. 1987. Stable isotopy and archaeology. *American Scientist* 57(2):182-91.

Dennell, Robin W. 1976. The economic importance of plant resources represented on archaeological sites. *Journal of archaeological science* 3:229-47.

_____. 1978. *Early farming in South Bulgaria from the sixth to the third millenia B.C.* British Archaeological Reports International Series 45. Oxford: British Archaeological Reports.

Dimbleby, G. W. 1967. Plants and archaeology. London: John Baker.

Ellen, Roy. 1982. *Environment, subsistence and system.* Cambridge: University Press.

Ford, Richard I., M Brown, M. Hodge, and W. L. Merrill, ed. 1978. *The nature and status of ethnobotany.* Anthropological Papers no. 67. University of Michigan, Museum of Anthropology.

Ford, Richard I., 1979. Paleoethnobotany in American archaeology. In *Advances in archaeological method and theory* 2, ed. M. Schiffer, pp. 285-336, New York: Academic Press.

_____. 1985. *Prehistoric food production in North America.* Anthropological Papers no. 75. University of Michigan, Museum of Anthropology.

Gasser, Robert E. 1985. Archaeological trash mounds and floor features: Don't believe everything. Paper presented at the fiftieth annual meeting of the Society for American Archaeology, Denver.

Harris, Edward C. 1979. *Principles of archaeological stratigraphy.* New York: Academic Press.

Hastorf, Christine A. 1983. Prehistoric agricultural intensification and political development in the Jauja region of Central Peru. Ph.D. diss. Department of Anthropology, University of California, Los Angeles; Ann Arbor: University Microfilms.

2

Comparability among Recovery Techniques

Gail E. Wagner

Introduction

Dry screening, water screening, and flotation are three commonly used recovery techniques that result in different kinds and amounts of artifacts. The use of any one of these techniques biases not only *for* the recovery of particular artifacts, but also *against* certain artifacts, and can create a data base that is inadequate or misleading for answering the researcher's questions. As a result, comparability of data among and within sites has become a major interpretive problem. In this chapter, I present an overview of differences among recovery techniques and suggest methodological, analytic, and interpretive approaches to handling comparability of materials recovered by different recovery techniques.

This chapter deals unequally with two related issues: comparability among recovery techniques and methods and comparability in the analysis and interpretation of the resulting data. I outline no standard recovery technique and provide no solution to the problem of analytic comparability. Instead I offer quite basic observations, with the thought that perhaps even those who are closely involved in recovery and analytic procedures are not always aware of problems that may arise under different excavation and laboratory situations. For instance, someone who has always worked with dry, sandy sediments that yield up their plant remains rather readily may wonder why researchers with other types of sediments are so concerned with reprocessing the flotation heavy fractions. My hope is that by pulling together these diverse sets of observations, I can illustrate how bias is introduced into the data set by our choice of recovery technique.

Many of the chapters in this book are concerned with quantification and mathematical manipulation of data sets recovered by a variety of techniques. The data that we so painstakingly analyze are only as good as our biased recovery permits. It is crucial to understand what biases have been introduced by our sampling and recovery techniques. Only then may we confidently apply analytical and interpretive manipulations to the materials recovered.

By necessity, this chapter is an overview rather than a detailed analysis and solution to the problem of comparability among recovery techniques. The emphasis here is on flotation and the recovery of plant remains, as these are revealed through the North American literature. Nevertheless, the following comments bear also upon the recovery of other classes of artifacts. It is hoped that researchers in other parts of the world and analysts of other types of artifacts will be able to draw upon parallel observations within their own fields of study and thus may arrive at a suitable understanding of the problem.

Recovery Techniques

Archaeologists use three basic techniques to separate small-scale lithic, ceramic, faunal, and floral artifacts from the dirt matrix at a site: dry screening, water screening, and flotation. The quantities and types of artifacts recovered by any one of these three techniques will differ from those produced by the other two. Variations in method within each technique also produce different results. The following discussion summarizes the basic differences among the three techniques.

Dry Screening

Dry screening is the most common small-scale artifact recovery technique (for descriptive examples, see Diamant 1979; Payne 1972). The size of mesh screen most often used is 0.25 in (6.35 mm), but sometimes 0.5 in (12.7 mm) or 0.125 in (3.2 mm) is used. The type of sediment and its moisture content are important factors in determining how the screening will be accomplished and what kinds of artifacts will be recovered in an undamaged condition. Dry sand sifts easily through a screen, leaving the artifacts behind with a minimum of abrasion and damage. Moist clay lies at the other extreme and must be pushed through the screen. Only those artifacts larger than the openings in the mesh and stronger than the abrading action will be recoverable. The artifacts most commonly recovered by dry screening include lithics, ceramics, and well-preserved bone and shell.

Charred plant remains may be lost or damaged, especially when the dirt—and therefore the charcoal—are moist. Clayey sediments in particular may best be processed by a combination of water screening and flotation rather than by dry screening.

Water Screening

Most water screening (Broyles 1969; Dye and Moore 1978) is done on a series of nested screens with progressively smaller mesh sizes down to 0.0625 in (1.6 mm). The dirt is spread in the uppermost or largest mesh screen and sprayed with a fine mist of water. If the water pressure is too high and direct, it destroys fragile remains and may damage some of the harder artifacts, such as pottery. With water screening, one may expect to recover lithics, nonfragile bone, and sturdy ceramics down to the size of the smallest screen mesh opening. Shell and botanical remains, however, are damaged and often lost by this process (e.g., Chapman and Shea 1981:65).

Water sieving, as described by Payne (1972), is a type of water screening. Dirt placed in a basket made of screen mesh is lowered into a body of water and shaken. Dirt and artifacts smaller than the mesh openings (3.2 mm) are washed away; artifacts larger than the mesh openings are cleaned and retained. This technique has been used to recover ceramics, lithics, and bone at a number of Old World sites.

Water screening and water sieving are *not* the same as flotation, nor do they produce similar results. With flotation, fragile and nondense artifacts such as seeds and gastropods are suspended in a liquid and can be removed without abrasion. During water screening and water sieving, small artifacts such as seeds are lost through the screen (which is larger than that used in flotation) along with the dirt; only larger and harder artifacts will be retained.

Flotation

Flotation has been called a recovery revolution (Watson 1976:79), and indeed it is a revolution that most of us now take for granted. In the simplest kind of flotation, dirt from an archaeological context is added to a body of liquid, usually water. Objects with a specific gravity less than that of the liquid remain suspended and can be scooped, siphoned, or poured off: these comprise the "light fraction." The dirt matrix passes through a screen in the bottom of the container. Objects heavier than the liquid but larger than the screen mesh in the bottom of the container are caught by the screen: these comprise the "heavy fraction."

A wide variety of flotation systems has been designed, each with different equipment and methods. The simplest are hand-flotation systems, where dirt is added to a screen-bottomed container that is agitated by hand in a body of water, or even more simply added to a bucket of water where the dirt is allowed to settle to the bottom (Bohrer and Adams 1977; Lange and Carty 1975; Matson 1955; Minnis and LeBlanc 1976; Schock 1971; Spector 1970; Stewart and Robertson 1973; Struever 1965, 1968; Wagner 1976, 1979, 1982a). The more complex systems are mechanically assisted so that a spray of water can be directed up against the bottom of the screen-bottomed container (Cobb and Faulkner 1978; Davis and Wesolowsky 1975; Dye and Moore 1978; French 1971; Jarman, Legge, and Charles 1972; Limp 1974; Pendleton 1979a; Wagner 1983, 1984; Watson 1976; Weaver 1971; Williams 1973). Either type of system may use seawater or chemical solutions to enhance the buoyancy of small but dense objects or to disperse unwanted matrix (Bodner and Rowlett 1980; Diamant 1979; Jarman, Legge, and Charles 1972; Lange and Carty 1975; Stenholm 1976; Struever 1968; Wiant 1983). In froth flotation, bubbles of air combine with chemicals to float dense remains that otherwise would remain in the heavy fraction.

Two critical differences distinguish the machine-assisted systems from hand-flotation systems: (1) the presence of a constant spray of liquid up against the bottom of the screen-bottomed container in the machine system, thus lessening the loss of small but dense artifacts through that screen; and (2) the capture of the light fraction as a result of overflow of liquid from the surface of the machine, as opposed to capture by scooping. This latter point is not a critical factor in hand systems that decant rather than scoop the light fraction. In hand-flotation systems that use a scoop, the effectiveness and gentleness of capture of the light fraction is in large part dependent upon the operator's dexterity and skill in wielding a scoop. Because of this, damage, loss, and inconsistent recovery are much more likely to occur with hand systems that use scoops than with systems that do not.

An often-unreported but important feature of all flotation systems is the mesh size of the screens used to capture the light and heavy fractions (see Mead 1981:27-30). It should go without saying that the mesh used to capture the light fraction must be small enough to retain the smallest seeds possible. Unmodified kitchen strainers are not adequate (Munson 1981). The best scoops I have used were made with a 15-cm circle of brass mesh screen (0.4 mm openings) sewn to a slightly smaller wire rim and attached to a wooden handle. The result is a slightly concave circular screen that can be popped out to completely expel the scooped remains. Some systems use material (such as women's stockings or diapers) wrapped around a strainer; subsequently, the light fraction is hung to dry in the same material (e.g., Minnis and LeBlanc 1976). Machine and hand flotation systems that decant the light fraction into a screen or a series of nested screens that must be immediately reused undoubtedly result in more damage and loss than do systems that decant directly into a fine-mesh cloth used to dry the sample. Loss and damage are likely to occur during the transfer of the wet plant remains from the screen(s) to a suitable drying container.

The mesh size of the screen used to capture the heavy fraction is critical for good recovery of plant remains, especially with hand flotation systems. Observation and experimentation have established that many plant remains sink all or most of the time in water, although fragments of some of these may float (Jarman, Legge, and Charles 1972:41; Pendleton 1983; Schock 1971). Even very small seeds that normally float, such as tobacco (*Nicotiana*, ca. 0.9 mm) and purslane (*Portulaca*, ca. 0.6 mm), will sink when they are caught up in matrix or are waterlogged (Wagner, 1987). The heavy-fraction mesh should be only as large as is necessary to allow the dirt particles to pass through, yet many researchers continue to use window screen. With clay and loess, the mesh openings may be as small as 0.4 mm; with sand and gravel, they may need to be as large as 0.6 to 1.0 mm. The indiscriminant use of window screen, which ranges from at least 1.0 to 1.8 mm in size, has resulted in the loss of much valuable information (see Mead 1981; Schaaf 1981). When window screen is used, the actual size of the mesh opening (which varies widely) should be measured and reported.

The flotation heavy fraction must be processed further. I recommend hand sorting down to 4 mm or 2 mm, then refloating the remainder in either water or a chemical solution such as zinc chloride ($ZnCl_2$). I do not recommend total hand sorting—even when the sample is small—because of the inordinately long amount of time this may take (see Diamant 1979; Lopinot [1982:684] figures chemical flotation "is nearly three times more efficient" than hand sorting) and because surprisingly tiny seeds may still be present (and would be missed by hand sorting). The use of a seed blower (Ramenofsky et al. 1986) would be an acceptable alternative to refloating that part of the heavy fraction that passes through the 2-mm sieve. Both refloating and seed blowing must be followed by a minimal amount of hand sorting. Some froth flotation systems are able to float nearly all plant remains into the light fraction (see Jarman, Legge, and Charles 1972:41). When the siphon technique is used (Gumerman and Unemoto 1987), heavy-fraction plant remains may be removed at the end of regular flotation, before the recovered remains are dried. Recovery after one wetting is preferable to recovery by multiple wettings, as will be discussed in a later section.

FORD SAYS THIS MAY NOT BE TRUE—HE SORTS BY MICROSCOPE

Differences Between Techniques

Whichever recovery system we use, whether it be dry screening, water screening, or flotation, we would like ideally to recover a statistically representative sample of each artifact class from each collecting situation. At the very least, we hope our data are adequately representative for answering whatever level of questions we are asking (see Popper, chapter 4, Toll, chapter 3, Payne 1972). The type of recovery technique chosen and the method used for that technique result in a sample bias that all too often is unacknowledged by the excavator (Watson 1972). That differences do exist is logical when we consider the single factor of screen mesh openings (ranging from 12.7 mm to 0.4 mm or less) normally used with each technique. In general, the smaller the artifacts saved, the more accurate our picture of the complete assemblage from the ground. There is, of course, a point of diminishing returns in striving to recover smaller and smaller fragments, and this point differs for each class of artifact and each set of research goals (Watson 1972).

In tests of the differences in recovery between dry screening and water sieving at three Old World sites, Payne (1972) found that the smaller sherds and animal bones were underrepresented when only dry screening was used. Less expected was his discovery that when the dry-screened residue was put through a smaller mesh (3.2 mm) by water sieving, even the large bone percentages changed significantly: water sieving produced twice as many cow bones, ten times as many pig bones, and over twenty times as many sheep/goat bones. The greater recovery with water sieving was attributed to the smaller mesh size and to the fact that the artifacts were cleaned by the water; therefore they were much easier to see and pick out than when coated with dirt.

The differences in recovery are greater still between screened and floated assemblages. Morse and Morse (1983) note that most of the lithic debitage indicative of point manufacture was recovered only with flotation using 0.0625-in mesh. Eighty to one hundred percent of the fish remains from FAI-270 project sites in the American Bottoms were recovered by flotation (Kelly and Cross 1984). The greatest impact of the flotation revolution on our concept of past lifeways has been in the recovery of plant remains. In their report on excavations at Ali Kosh, Hole, Flannery, and Neely (1969:24) say:

> The reader will note that our preliminary report on the 1961 season states confidently that "plant remains were scarce at Ali Kosh" (Hole and Flannery, 1962:125). Nothing could be farther from the truth. The mound is filled with seeds from top to bottom: all that was "scarce" in 1961 was our ability to find them, and when we had added the "flotation" technique (Struever 1965) in 1963 we recovered a stratified series of samples totaling over 40,000 seeds.

Munson, Parmalee, and Yarnell (1971:421) estimate flotation to be "on the order of 50 times as effective as quarter-inch field-screening in the recovery of plant remains in quantity."

Biases Within Flotation

The mere use of flotation does not ensure the recovery of all possible artifacts and in fact may result in differential breakage among the charred plant remains. Some dry carbonized plant remains fragment when they come into contact with water or other liquids. Thus, one should carefully consider the extent to which dirt should or should not be dried prior to flotation. Some paleoethnobotanists prefer not to dry the dirt at all (Lopinot 1982:676). Others consider the greater ease of flotation and more complete separation of plant remains from the matrix that result from partial drying to more than offset the moderate amount of fragmentation caused by a first wetting (e.g., Lange and Carty 1975:120). The greater dangers are seen in totally drying the dirt before flotation and in drying and then refloating the heavy fraction. New techniques such as siphoning at the conclusion of regular flotation (Gumerman and Unemoto 1987) or seed blowing the heavy fractions (Ramenofsky et al. 1986) undoubtedly will help to alleviate this problem.

Some experimental data have accumulated, yet more work must be done before we can fully understand the effects of drying and then wetting charred plant remains. Jarman, Legge, and Charles (1972) ran tests on a sample of 500 archaeological charred grains: 4% of the seeds broke after five minutes immersion and gentle agitation in a froth solution; two subsequent wettings after drying resulted in the near-total destruction of the sample. Lopinot (1984:108-10) has documented differential fragmentation and reduction caused by rewetting of the charred plant remains during reprocessing of the heavy fraction.

Informal observations from other investigators confirm that multiple or even single wettings and dryings can be quite destructive to some or all of the charred archaeological plant remains. Charred wood in particular is liable to fragment; other charred plant remains that have been noted to fragment upon contact with water include walnut shell, butternut shell, plum pits, and honey locust seeds (Munson, Parmalee, and Yarnell 1971; Wiant 1983; Yarnell 1982). Helbaek (1969:407) found that gypsum and calcium coats on the extremely charred plant remains from Tepe Sabz caused the majority of the grains to explode when they touched water, hydrochloric acid, or acetic acid, yet other types of plant remains were not destroyed. The point here is that analyses of plant remains which have undergone differential fragmentation during recovery should account for the skewed proportions of identified remains.

Recovery tests run on flotation sytems indicate that different flotation equipment and methods not only produce quite different amounts of damage, contamination, and loss of plant remains, but also vary in the consistency of their results (Kaplan and Maina 1977; Pendleton 1979b, 1983; Wagner 1982b). Figure 2.1 summarizes the test results for recovery of floating seeds by different systems and illustrates the variety of results that may occur with changes in equipment (compare tests B, C, and D) or method (compare tests E and F). The overall low scores for the Illinois Department of Transportation (I.D.O.T.) samples reflect the multiple wettings and soaking that were necessary to process dirt with an extremely high clay content. Tests run on froth flotation document a higher recovery in the light fraction of seeds that normally would sink. Such recovery is critical when the seeds are small and the heavy fraction screen mesh openings are large. Tests by Pendleton (1979b) on small seeds that sink show 80% recovery by froth flotation, but only 15% recovery by hand

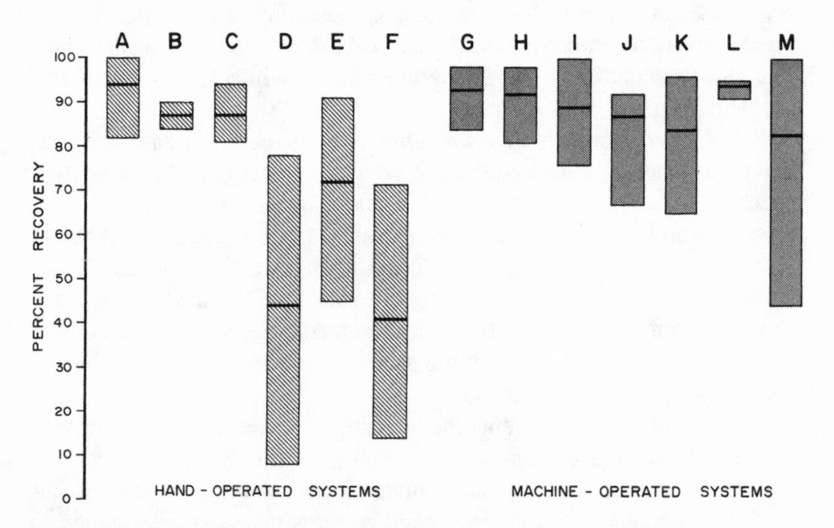

Figure 2.1. Flotation recovery rates for floating seeds.

Bars mark the high, mean, and low test results. All tests except A and K were run with carbonized poppy seeds (*Papaver somniferum*). (A) Tub flotation (Pendleton 1979b). (B) Incinerator boxes, 0.4-mm sides, 0.6-mm bottom; N = 6 tests (Wagner 1979, 1982b). (C) Incinerator boxes, 0.6-mm sides and bottom; N = 3 tests (Wagner 1979, 1982b). (D) Incinerator boxes, 0.4-mm sides and 1.0-mm bottom; N = 7 tests (Wagner 1979, 1982b). (E) I.D.O.T. (Illinois Deparment of Transportation) boxes, 0.4-mm sides and bottom; river; N = 9 tests (Wagner 1976, 1982b). (F) I.D.O.T. boxes, 0.4-mm sides and bottom; tank; N = 5 tests (Wagner 1976, 1982b). (G) S.M.A.P. (Shellmound Archaeological Project) machine, 1/16-in bottom; N = 11 tests (Wagner 1982b). (H) Piyush One machine, 1.5-mm bottom; N = 5 tests (Wagner 1983, 1984). (I) B.M.A.P. (Black Mesa Archaeological Project) machine, 1/16-in bottom; N = 7 tests. (J) S.M.A.P.-type machine; N = 6 tests (Wymer 1984:4-5). (K) Froth flotation (Pendleton 1979a, 1979b). (L) D.A.P. (Dolores Archaeological Project) Izum-type machine; N = 4 tests (Matthews 1985:54-57). (M) D.A.P. air-bubble machine; N = 29 tests (Matthews 1985:54-57).

flotation. Jarman, Legge, and Charles (1972:41) found that 62% of the barley, 58% of the oats and emmer, and 28% of the vetches recovered in their froth flotation light fractions from the Udal site would have sunk during water flotation. Adjustments in the amounts of chemicals added during froth flotation also result in different recovery rates (Pendleton 1983).

The logical question at this point is whether we should adopt standardized flotation recovery techniques. Admittedly a degree of standardization would help, but without flexibility in method and design, many researchers would be unable to incorporate flotation into their recovery strategies.

Choosing a Technique

A number of factors combine to determine the suitability of the technique for the recovery of particular artifact types. For example, although a smaller mesh can be used with water screening than with dry screening and will result in good recovery of lithics, all sizes of plant remains will not be recovered systematically with either technique. On the other hand, sheer practicality demands that we dry or water screen the bulk of the matrix from a site and choose a smaller, representative sample for flotation. Thus, two or more recovery techniques are commonly used at a single site. Under such conditions, all excavators are faced with the problem of comparability among results, not only among sites, but also within a single site. The only effective way to deal with the problem of comparability is to understand the biases that may result from using one technique rather than another.

In order to decide which recovery technique(s) to use—dry screening, water screening, or flotation, the researcher must consider a number of questions. These same questions must be answered in order to construct an effective flotation system:

1. Are the samples chosen for processing representative of the site, time period, or features of interest?
2. What constraints are implicit in the sediment type, project budget,available equipment, personnel, and project schedule (e.g., Keeley 1978)?
3. What damage, contamination, or loss of artifacts occurs with the use of a particular technique and method?

Considerations of this sort will affect the recovery not only of plant remains but also of most other classes of artifacts, such as pottery, bone, lithics, and shell.

Sampling for plant remains has been discussed in detail by a number of researchers (Adams and Gasser 1980; Bohrer and Adams 1977; Jarman, Legge, and Charles 1972; Limp 1974; Lopinot 1982:675; Schaaf 1981;

Spector 1970; van der Veen and Fieller 1982) and is covered in this book by Toll. Ultimately, the sampling design chosen hinges upon the specifics of the site, the soil, the project limitations, and the research goals. The quantity of dirt taken for each flotation sample should be whatever size is necessary to yield adequate data: one or two liters suffice at many sites in the Southwest, whereas four to eight or more liters per sample often are necessary at sites in the eastern United States. Samples above eight to ten liters in size are too large and heavy for ease of handling during flotation.

The remaining two sets of questions about project constraints and recovery rates are of more immediate concern to this section on techniques and method. Two examples may serve to illustrate how these questions were handled in setting up flotation systems for different projects. In 1977 I devised a flotation recovery system for a museum in southwestern Ohio (Wagner 1979). Most of the samples to be processed were to come from a single site characterized by a sandy loam grading into gravel. The problem I faced was to construct a low-budget operation that could be run by one person. I considered using a machine-assisted system, but at that time the one with which I was acquainted (the S.M.A.P. [Shell Mound Archaeological Project] machine [Watson 1976] was designed for use by no less than two people. Additional drawbacks were that it was moderately expensive and troublesome to build, it required a continuous and large supply of pressurized water, and by necessity one had to dispose of an equally large supply of water. The advantages of constructing a hand-operated system were that I could build it cheaply and quickly by myself, it required and therefore disposed of less water, and it could be run by one or several people.

In order to keep costs to a minimum, we tried to use resources that already were on hand (see Davis and Wesolowsky 1975 for another example of scavenging resources). Several available items included a fire hydrant and hose for the supply of water, a sewer drain for disposal of the water, and a large metal horse trough for the flotation tank. All other items had to be built. Light fraction scoops made of 0.4-mm brass wire mesh were used to capture suspended charred and uncharred seeds, wood charcoal, gastropods, fish scales and other light bone, modern insects, and modern rootlets. Wooden boxes with screen mesh in two sides and on the bottom were used to hold the sample during flotation and to capture the heavy fractions. The heavy fractions from this site often included pottery sherds, bone, fish scales, chert, gravel, sand, charred nutshell, and other dense plant remains.

The construction and subsequent trial of the wooden boxes provided a valuable lesson that in retrospect seems obvious: the heavy fraction mesh must be larger than the grain size of the sediment to be floated. After experimentation and testing with poppy seed recovery tests (fig. 2.1: tests B, C, D), it was found that boxes with 0.6 mm mesh in the bottom and 0.4mm mesh in the sides produced consistently high rates of recovery, yet allowed adequate amounts of the sandy matrix to pass through. Boxes with window screen (1.0 mm) in the bottom did not produce acceptable recovery rates. Boxes with 0.4 mm mesh in the bottom did not allow the dirt to escape.

Light fractions were placed on polyester cloth squares (ca. 80 x 100 threads per inch); these were tied into bags and hung on a clothesline to dry. Dried light fractions were stored in glass baby food jars prior to microscopic separation and analysis.

Heavy fractions were dried and stored in newspaper. Separation of the plant remains was accomplished by putting the dried fraction through 4-mm and 2-mm sieves and handsorting to 2-mm; the remaining smaller particles were refloated in either zinc chloride or warm water. A final hand sort of the new light and heavy fractions was necessary to isolate the last of the plant remains from all other types of artifacts.

In retrospect, I can list several disadvantages of this hand system compared to a machine system: (1) it is physically demanding and requires constant attention to manual dexterity in order to maintain acceptably high standards of recovery; (2) after several months of use in water, the wooden boxes (chosen over metal because of their buoyancy) require constant repair; and (3) because archaeological plant remains are so abundant from this particular site, the wooden boxes are too small for effective recovery.

In 1981 I designed a flotation system for a project in northwestern India (Wagner 1982a). I needed a hand-flotation system that used very little water (all carried in by hand), that used no electricity, and that was simple and quick to construct and yet could be converted to a machine-assisted system as the project expanded. With the exception of two pieces of brass screen with 0.4-mm and 0.6-mm mesh openings, all materials were bought in India. We used a screen-bottomed metal bucket and two 55-gallon metal drums. A metal stand placed inside a drum provided support for the bucket. All metal items were constructed at a local metalworking shop. I made a screen mesh scoop (0.4-mm) and bought cotton-polyester cloth to hold the light flotation fraction during drying. Each barrel was used on alternate days to allow the fine dirt particles to settle out and clear the water in the other barrel. Whenever one barrel was being refilled with fresh water (a process that took several hours), flotation could continue in the other.

The dirt at the site did not easily lend itself to flotation: upper levels and features were impregnated with fine root hairs that clogged the screens; lower levels required secondary processing of the heavy fractions because of high clay content. None of the dirt would pass through a mesh screen with 0.6-mm openings; therefore the next available size mesh (window screen, 1.75 mm) was used in the base of the bucket. Heavy fractions with numerous dirt lumps were dried and then soaked in a bucket of hot water to which several tablespoons of sodium bicarbonate had been added. This mixture was stirred with a stick, left to soak for 30-45 minutes, and the resultant sludge refloated to produce a second light and heavy fraction. Because I did not at that time know what seeds were likely to be recovered locally, no recovery tests (Wagner 1982b) were run.

In subsequent years, the project has been located near larger towns, and electricity and water have been more readily available. We converted our original barrel to a modified S. M. A. P.-type machine (called Piyush One) that can be operated by a single person (Wagner 1983, 1984). Water is supplied by a buried four-inch PVC pipe connected to a local irrigation system powered by a single-stroke diesel engine. An insert similar in appearance to a washtub was made of galvanized tin and fitted with a down-sloping sleeve that fits into a rectangular hole cut in the lip of the barrel. The bottom of the insert consists of window screen (1.5-mm) supported by 0.25-in wire cloth. Light flotation fractions are caught in polyester cloth squares (min. 80 x 100 threads per inch) tacked to a wooden screen-bottomed (0.4 mm) box. Recovery tests run with charred poppy seeds (figure 2.1) indicate that 81-98% of floating seeds are recovered, despite problems with mineral skins on most pottery, bone, and plant remains.

Methodological Review

Before moving on to discuss the analytic and interpretive problems of dealing with comparability among recovery techniques, I review briefly several pragmatic aspects of method as they relate to the recovery of plant remains. The three basic techniques used to recover small artifacts are dry screening, water screening, and flotation. Flotation supplies us with the bulk of our information about archaeological plant remains, even though dry screening and water screening remain more widely used. Although flotation itself is not particularly time-consuming, the analysis of the resultant botanical material is. Therefore sheer practicality demands that we dry or water screen the bulk of the matrix from a site and float only a representative sample. Recovery tests indicate that different flotation equipment and methods produce differing amounts of damage, contamination, and loss of plant remains. Despite these differences, flexibility is necessary in order to accomodate each unique set of sediments, budget, and equipment. Any flotation system will be adequate so long as full consideration has been given to the three sets of questions recently outlined. One rule of thumb that should be adopted is to use the smallest possible mesh screen in the bottom of the float box to capture the heavy fraction. Another is not to screen the dirt prior to flotation, or at least to screen with extreme caution, recognizing that screening is likely to damage those plant remains one is hoping to recover. Finally, in order to ascertain the effectiveness and consistency of any particular system, recovery tests should be run at each site on every change of equipment, personnel, dirt, and method.

Comparability of Data

Given this broad set of possible recovery techniques, each with slightly differing equipment and procedures, how may we compare the resulting sets of data? This is a problem not only between sites but also within sites. Often the analyst is faced with one set of data from features that have been screened and another set of data from features that have been floated. Even the specific method used to screen or float samples or to process heavy fractions from a site may differ from start to finish of a multiyear project (e.g. Diamant 1979).

Our first problem is to quantify the amounts of plant remains in a manner that lends itself to comparison. The simplest method is to count and/or weigh plant remains by size and amount of matrix examined. The result can be ratios such as 20 seeds per liter of fill or X fragments of wood greater than 2 mm in size per liter of midden (see Miller, chapter 5; Popper, chapter 4).

Obviously we will not be able to make direct comparisons between types of plant remains recovered by one of the techniques but unlikely to be recovered by the other. The two sets of data from screening and flotation are complementary rather than directly comparable to each other. Although flotation is particularly geared to recover small seeds and plant fragments otherwise unnoticeable to the excavator, it is not well suited for recovering larger plant remains such as corn cobs or chunks of wood. The plant remains picked out of the dirt by hand or caught by screening are often also those that are exceptional in some manner. Collections such as these are valuable for the unusual or less common types recovered and for the specimens (such as corn cobs) that can be measured. Comparison between the two would have to overcome differences not only in the size of the artifacts recovered but also in differential breakage (abrasion vs. fragmentation due to wetting) and quantity of dirt processed (large, unmeasured amounts screened vs. smaller, measured amounts floated; see Munson, Parmalee, and Yarnell 1971:421). We can combine the two sets of data to formulate a summary that is both quantified and descriptive.

The same approach used for comparisons within a site may, with caution, be applied between sites. Direct comparisons even with the same recovery technique are really not possible, given different sediments, a multitude of ancient behavior patterns leading to differential deposition, and the unique postdepositional histories of the deposits studied. Therefore I suggest that comparisons be made, not directly by quantities (except in a gross fashion), but rather by indirect methods such as ubiquity, amounts per volume of matrix, or percentages (see Miller, chapter 5; Popper, chapter 4). One way to compare data sets derived from totally dissimilar recovery methods is to prepare a simple presence-absence list (Hubbard 1980).

Comparisons are difficult, if not impossible, to make when details are not given for the recovery technique(s) used. The analyst who wishes to compare data must know the sampling procedure, the method used to quantify the matrix, and what screen mesh sizes and procedures were used. It is not enough to say that plant remains were recovered by "the Apple Creek method" or by using "a modified S.M.A.P. machine". As tests and observations have shown, quite different recovery results are obtained by slight changes in equipment or method. Particularly critical are the size of mesh screens (given in mm) used to capture heavy and light flotation fractions. Also of interest are the manner of treatment of flotation heavy fractions and the results of recovery tests.

When first choosing which flotation samples to identify and quantify, the analyst may be guided by the results of the recovery tests. Should any particular method, personnel, or change in equipment result in unsatisfactory recovery, the samples so affected may be excluded from analysis. Although recovery tests can indicate the quality and consistency of flotation recovery, they cannot provide quantifiable adjustments or corrections to the numbers and types of plant remains recovered.

Comparisons are hindered when the raw, untransformed, uncorrected data are not presented. Just as there are a multitude of "correction factors" for ^{14}C dates, there are a number of ways to manipulate the botanical data derived from flotation. Unless the raw data are presented, as all too often they are not, other analysts are unable to interpret them in any way other than as they were originally presented. One prime example of this is the practice of presenting estimated rather than actually counted and quantified results (e.g., estimating the amounts of various types of plant remains of one size range on the basis of the actual amounts quantified in another, often larger, size range).

Will it be possible to develop correction factors for comparison of data recovered by different techniques (e.g., Watson 1972)? I would say that too heavy a reliance on the absolute numbers generated by recovery and analysis (rather than on the resultant ratios, percentages, or other relative measurements) imparts to our data more accuracy than the situation warrants. However, in order to ensure that our relative measurements reflect as closely as possible the actual preserved data set, we need to account for as many as possible of the transformations caused by our recovery techniques (Hastorf, chapter 8). In addition to more frequent tests on recovery rates, we need further experimentation and formalized observation on the effects of our recovery techniques upon the data we wish to recover.

Summary

In conclusion, dry screening, water screening, and flotation are three commonly used recovery techniques that result in different kinds and quantities of artifacts. The use of any one of these techniques biases not only *for* the recovery of particular artifacts, but also *against* that of certain others, and can create a data base that is inadequate or misleading for answering the researcher's questions. Because total standardization of recovery techniques is impractical, the solution to the problem of comparability lies in understanding what biases have been introduced by our sampling and recovery techniques. Only then may we apply our analytical interpretations with confidence.

Acknowledgments

Thanks are due to Leonard W. Blake, Christine A. Hastorf, and Patrick M. Lubinski for comments on earlier versions of this chapter and to Valerie A. Haskins for initial help with the computer. Special appreciation goes to Naomi F. Miller and Patty Jo Watson for ideas and discussions, as well as comments on earlier versions of this chapter.

References Cited

Adams, Karen R., and Robert E. Gasser. 1980. Plant microfossils from archaeological sites: Research considerations, and sampling techniques and approaches. *The Kiva* 45(4):293-300.

Bodner, Connie Cox, and Ralph M. Rowlett. 1980. Separation of bone, charcoal, and seeds by chemical flotation. *American Antiquity* 45:110-16.

Bohrer, Vorsila L., and Karen R. Adams. 1977. Ethnobotanical techniques and approaches at Salmon Ruin, New Mexico. *Eastern New Mexico University, Contributions to Anthropology* 8(1).

Broyles, Betty. 1969. The sluicing system used at the St. Albans site. *Southeastern Archaeological Conference Bulletin* 9:45-52.

Chapman, Jefferson, and Andrea Brewer Shea. 1981. The archaeobotanical record: Early Archaic period to Contact in the lower Little Tennessee River Valley. *Tennessee Anthropologist* 6(1):61-84.

Cobb, James E., and Charles H. Faulkner. 1978. The Owl Hollow Project laboratory flotation device. *Southeastern Archaeological Conference*

Newsletter 20(1):4-11.

Davis, E. Mott, and Al B. Wesolowsky. 1975. The Izum: A simple water separation device. *Archaeology* 31(1):8-13.

Diamant, Steven. 1979. A short history of archaeological sieving at Franchti Cave, Greece. *Journal of Field Archaeology* 6(2):203-17.

Dye, David H., and Katherine M. Moore. 1978. Recovery systems for subsistence data: Water screening and water flotation. *Tennessee Anthropologist* 3:59-69.

French, D. H. 1971. An experiment in water-sieving. *Anatolian Studies* 21:59-64.

Gumerman, George, IV, and Bruce S. Unemoto. 1987. The siphon technique: An addition to the flotation process. *American Antiquity*, 52(2):330-36.

Helbaek, Hans. 1969. Plant collecting, dry-farming, and irrigation agriculture in prehistoric Deh Luran. Appendix I in *Prehistory and human ecology of the Deh Luran Plain*, by Frank Hole, Kent V. Flannery, and James A. Neely, pp. 383-426. University of Michigan, Memoirs of the Museum of Anthropology, no. 1.

Hole, Frank, Kent V. Flannery, and James A. Neely. 1969. *Prehistory and human ecology of the Deh Luran Plain*. University of Michigan, Memoirs of the Museum of Anthropology, no. 1.

Hubbard, R. N. L. B. 1980. Development of agriculture in Europe and the Near East: Evidence from quantitative studies. *Economic Botany* 34:51-67.

Jarman, H. N., A. J. Legge, and J. A. Charles. 1972. Retrieval of plant remains from archaeological sites by froth flotation. In *Papers in economic prehistory*, ed. E. S. Higgs, pp. 39-48. Cambridge: University Press.

Kaplan, Lawrence, and Shirley L. Maina. 1977. Archaeological botany of the Apple Creek site, Illinois. *Journal of Seed Technology* 2(2):40-53.

Keeley, H. C. M. 1978. The cost-effectiveness of certain methods of recovering macroscopic organic remains from archaeological deposits. *Journal of Archaeological Science* 5:179-83.

Kelly, Lucretia S., and Paula G. Cross. 1984. Zooarchaeology. In *American Bottom archaeology: A summary of the FAI-270 Project contribution to the culture history of the Mississippi River Valley*, ed. Charles J. Bareis and James W. Porter, pp. 215-32. Urbana: University of Illinois Press.

Lange, Frederick W., and Frederick M. Carty. 1975. Salt water application of the flotation technique. *Journal of Field Archaeology* 2:119-23.

Limp, W. Frederick. 1974. Water separation and flotation processes. *Journal of Field Archaeology* 1:337-42.

Lopinot, Neal H. 1982. Plant macroremains and paleoethnobotanical implications. In *The Carrier Mills Archaeological Project: Human adaptations in the Saline Valley, Illinois*, vol. 2, ed. Richard W. Jeffries and Brian M. Butler, pp. 671-860. Carbondale: Southern Illinois University, Center for Archaeological Investigations Research Paper no. 33.

_____. 1984. Archaeobotanical formation processes and late Middle Archaic human-plant interrelationships in the mid-continental U.S.A. Ph.D. diss., Department of Anthropology, Southern Illinois University at Carbondale. Ann Arbor: University Microfilms.

Matson, Frederick R. 1955. Charcoal concentration from early sites for radiocarbon dating. *American Antiquity* 21(2):162-69.

Matthews, Meredith H. 1985. Botanical studies: Nature and status of the data base. In *Dolores archaeological program: Studies in environmental*, comp. K.L. Peterson, V.L. Clay, M.H. Matthews, and S.W. Neusius, pp. 41-60. Denver: U.S.D.A. Bureau of Reclamation Engineering and Research Center.

Mead, Barbara. 1981. Seed analysis of the Meehan-Schell site (13BN110), a Great Oasis site in central Iowa. *Journal of the Iowa Archeological Society* 28:15-90.

Minnis, Paul, and Steven LeBlanc. 1976. An efficient, inexpensive arid lands flotation system. *American Antiquity* 41:491-93.

Morse, Dan F., and Phyllis A. Morse. 1983. *Archaeology of the central Mississippi Valley*. New York: Academic Press.

Munson, Patrick J. 1981. Note on the use and misuse of water-separation ("flotation") for the recovery of small-scale botanical remains. *Midcontinental Journal of Archaeology* 6(1):123-26.

Munson, Patrick J., Paul W. Parmalee, and Richard A. Yarnell. 1971. Subsistence ecology of Scovill, a terminal Middle Woodland village. *American Antiquity* 36:410-31.

Payne, Sebastian. 1972. Partial recovery and sample bias: The results of some sieving experiments. In *Papers in economic prehistory*, ed. E. S. Higgs, pp. 49-64. Cambridge: University Press.

Pendleton, Michael W. 1979a. A flotation apparatus for archaeological sites. *The Kiva* 44(2-3):89-93.

_____. 1979b. Flotation methodology. Paper presented at the American Anthropological Association seventy eighth annual meeting, Cincinnati.

_____. 1983. A comment concerning "Testing flotation recovery rates." *American Antiquity* 48(3):615-16.

Ramenofsky, Ann F., Leon C. Standifer, Ann M. Whitmer, and Marie S. Standifer. 1986. A new technique for separating flotation samples.

American Antiquity 51(1):66-72.

Schaaf, Jeanne M. 1981. A method for reliable and quantifiable subsampling of archaeological features for flotation. *Midcontinental Journal of Archaeology* 6(2):219-48.

Schock, Jack M. 1971. Indoor water flotation—a technique for the recovery of archaeological materials. Plains Anthropologist 16:228-31.

Spector, Janet Doris. 1970. Seed analysis in archeology. *The Wisconsin Archeologist* 51:163-90.

Stenholm, Nancy A. 1976. Botanical flotation: A deflocculation schedule for archeological clay soils. Paper presented at the Society for American Archaeology forty first annual meeting, St. Louis.

Stewart, Robert B., and William Robertson IV. 1973. Application of the flotation technique in arid areas. *Economic Botany* 27:114-16.

Struever, Stuart. 1965. The "flotation" process for recovery of plant remains. *Southeastern Archaeological Conference Bulletin* 3:32-35.

_____. 1968. Flotation techniques for the recovery of small-scale archaeological remains. *American Antiquity* 33:353-62.

van der Veen, Marijke, and Nick Fieller. 1982. Sampling seeds. *Journal of Archaeological Science* 9:287-98.

Wagner, Gail E. 1976. I.D.O.T. Flotation Procedure Manual. Illinois Department of Transportation, District 8, and the University of Illinois-Urbana FAI-270 Project.

_____. 1979. The Dayton Museum of Natural History Flotation Procedure Manual Rev. ed. Dayton, Ohio: Dayton Museum of Natural History.

_____. 1982a. Flotation for small-artifact recovery at Oriyo Timbo. Philadelphia: University Museum, University of Pennsylvania.

_____. 1982b. Testing flotation recovery rates. *American Antiquity* 47(1):127-32.

_____. 1983. The 1982-83 Ethnobotany Laboratory at Rojdi. Philadelphia: University Museum, University of Pennsylvania.

_____. 1984. The 1983-84 Ethnobotany Laboratory at Rojdi. Philadelphia: University Museum, University of Pennsylvania.

_____. 1987. Uses of Plants by the Fort Ancient Indians. Ph.D. diss., Department of Anthropology, Washington University, St. Louis.

Watson, J. P. N. 1972. Fragmentation analysis of animal bone samples from archaeological sites. *Archaeometry* 14(2):221-28.

Watson, Patty Jo. 1976. In pursuit of prehistoric subsistence: A comparative account of some contemporary flotation techniques. *Midcontinental Journal of Archaeology* 1:77-100.

Weaver, Martin E. 1971. A new water separation process for soil from archaeological excavations. *Anatolian Studies* 21:65-68.

Wiant, Michael D. 1983. Deflocculants and flotation: Considerations leading to a low-cost technique to process high clay content samples. *American Archaeology* 3:206-9.

Williams, David. 1973. Flotation at Siraf. *Antiquity* 47:288-92.

Wymer, Dee Anne. 1984. A preliminary analysis of the Zencor/Scioto Trails site (33FR8) archaeobotanical assemblage. Columbus: Prehistory Laboratory, Department of Anthropology, Ohio State University.

Yarnell, Richard A. 1982. Problems of interpretation of archaeological plant remains of the eastern woodlands. *Southeastern Archaeology* 1(1):1-7.

3

Flotation Sampling: Problems and Some Solutions, with Examples from the American Southwest

Mollie S. Toll

There is patterning to the preservation of archaeobotanical data; the more we know about that patterning, the greater is the temptation to emphasize in sampling those units (site types or such provenience categories as hearths and trash middens) known to be more productive of cultural plant debris and to avoid others. However reasonable may be the goal of maximizing cultural information gained for the considerable per sample investment of time at the microscope, therein lies a serious risk of prejudicing or skewing data. Significantly, those factors affecting botanical preservation often operate systematically, such that certain classes of plant debris are consistently lacking at all but the best-preserved sites, and sites that are structurally more ephemeral consistently produce fewer, less-diverse plant remains, whether or not subsistence activities were reduced or less varied. A sampling plan favoring sites or proveniences likely to be productive of plant remains only compounds these perceptions, whether or not they are based on any real differences in plant utilization. This chapter offers by example some pragmatic suggestions for providing a broad overview of all site and provenience types, while still taking advantage of the full potential of locations rich in floral remains.

Archaeological sites vary tremendously in botanical productivity, and each situation must be dealt with as an individual sampling problem. As an aid to working out sensible, balanced procedures elsewhere, I will discuss two very simple methodological tools that have proven useful in sampling sites with poor-to-very-good preservation in the arid American Southwest.

The examples illustrate problems of broad-scale and intensive, detailed description of subsistence remains. The Southwest offers wide expanses of federal land that have been little used in the historical period and are now slated for mineral exploitation in large chunks, resulting in a series of large survey and mitigation projects. The Southwest also harbors a number of truly spectacular, large pueblos from the relatively recent prehistoric past (from ca. A.D. 900, merging with historical and contemporary Pueblo occupations). Masonry walls and in some cases intact roofs or cliff overhangs protect deposits, so that perishable remains are often present in considerable quantity and in a larger number and variety of provenience contexts. By example, the procedures discussed here may help others to solve their own problems.

When all samples are in from the field and the time comes to sit down with a sample inventory and choose which to look at, both archaeologists and botanists commonly come up against a budgetary squeeze. Flotation analysts have variously attempted to cut microscopic sorting time by examining a fraction of their bigger samples (splitting by weight or by volume or using a riffle box; van der Veen and Fieller 1982) and calculating an estimate of total sample seed content, hoping it is comparable with full sample counts. Such a procedure is nearly essential in dealing with sites with good-to-excellent preservation, to keep laboratory analysis time from reaching unmanageable proportions. Sample splitting, however, does not make any real dent in the problem of getting an adequate grip on patterning in a large and highly variable body of floral data when time and money are limited. Some crude numbers might be helpful in visualizing the situation. While splitting a very large sample might reduce sorting time from perhaps ten hours to a more reasonable one or two hours, the analyst is still left with a sizable unit of time at the microscope and at calculating and tabulating seed frequencies.

A simple two-level sampling procedure has proven useful in this respect, in more ways than originally anticipated. Scanning a larger number of samples in the first phase allows assessment of overall archaeobotanical productivity, preservation, and contamination, while traditional full sorting of flotation samples in the second phase allows more detailed data collection from sites or site areas of greatest interest. Since scanning involves a per sample investment of approximately 20 minutes, while full sorting may involve an average of 90 or more minutes, scanning greatly increases the numbers of samples that can be accommodated within a given budget.

In scanning, all flotation samples are first separated by screening into major particle-size categories that correspond generally with taxonomic divisions. The analyst can reduce sorting time tremendously by not collecting and labeling all seeds and by cutting out much of the time invested in examining the smaller particle sizes. Screen sizes must be selected with some information in hand of the likely distribution of botanical materials by size. Archaeobotanists will need to experiment and establish screen sizes appropriate to the categories of data they wish to recover. Since the scanning method used involves a full sorting of material larger than 2.0 mm and most material larger than 1.0 mm, in the Southwest, it provides a reliable review of the presence or absence of cultivated taxa (table 3.1). Experience has shown that corn kernels and cob fragments (relatively common in flotation samples) and bean and squash remains (rare in flotation samples) are almost entirely restricted to the larger screen sizes. In these screens, recovered wild taxa of the northern Southwest include juniper (*Juniperus* spp.) twigs and berries; pinyon (*Pinus edulis*) nutshells and cone fragments; yucca (*Yucca* spp.), squawberry (*Rhus trilobata),* and prickly pear (*Opuntia* spp.) seeds, and grass and weed taxa with particularly large seeds, such as rice grass (*Oryzopsis*) and beeweed (*Cleome).* Most annual weed seeds are caught in the 1.0- or 0.5-mm mesh screens. Scanning accurately picks up the presence of higher-frequency weed taxa (the cheno-ams, purslane, mustard, and several others on the Colorado Plateau). Among particles smaller than 0.5 mm, botanical remains are often completely absent or else consist of fragments of seed types encountered in larger screens. Rarely, low frequencies of small seed types, such as tansy mustard or drop seed, will occur in the smallest screens without also occurring in the larger screens. For the time invested, then, scanning seems to provide relatively reliable presence/absence flotation data, as well as general information about relative quantities of specific taxa and about

Table 3.1. Scan recovery of botanical remains by screen size in the northern Southwest

	Scan Procedure	Materials Recovered
Screen 10 (2.0 mm)	All	Cultivars, most perennials, and a few large grass and weed seeds
Screen 18 (1.0 mm)	All, or up to 5 minutes for large samples	Fragmentary cultivars, some perennials, some grass and weed seeds
Screen 35 (0.5 mm)	Up to 5 minutes	Most grass and weed seeds
Bottom pan (< 0.5 mm)	None	Very few remains: mostly fragments of weed-size and larger seed types, and a very few whole specimens of small grass and weed seeds

whether carbonized specimens are present. The chief limitation lies in the omission of low-frequency, small-dimension seed types. Again, others will need to examine their own data base to determine a reasonable lower size limit for useful information return.

In projects of all sizes, when time and money do not allow full analysis of all the existing samples, scanning provides a liberating option. Scanning makes it possible to take a brief look at all members of every site or provenience class the analyst needs to know about, without the problems of influencing results by the selection process itself. Even the most conscientious archaeologist balks at allocating a sizable portion of his sample budget to blocks of samples from shallow, eroded Archaic sites likely to produce very few botanical remains. In a regional study, scanning allows including such sites on an equal footing without incurring major expense, and at isolated sites the scan procedure is a way of dealing responsibly with the obligation to look for potential botanical information. If floral remains are lacking, scan data provide reasonable documentation of that fact, and if they are present, scan data provide a rationale for moving on to more detailed analysis. Because scan data are collected and tabulated in very compact form (figure 3.1), and because the focus is on broad patterns, this phase of analysis can be quick.

Scanning played a particularly satisfying role at a large and complex site in Chaco Canyon, New Mexico (Toll 1985a; figure 3.2). As a means of dealing with sample size limitations at Pueblo Alto, analysis was stratified with respect to provenience category. Full sorting was used for a representative sample of each feature type and of each major time period present in the large, formal trash mound. The scan procedure was used to make it possible to look at alternate meter grids of occupation surfaces in all excavated rooms. In several habitation rooms, happily not confused by overlying postoccupational trash, we see remarkable evidence of the patterning of plant-use activities within individual rooms. In each case, a constellation of several economic taxa occurred carbonized in numerous heating features and then uncarbonized in decreasing frequency with increasing distance from the concentration of food-processing features (multiple heating pits, as well as formal fire pits and mealing bins; table 3.2). Scan data also provided a basis for reliable differentiation of room function. Use of the scan procedure at Pueblo Alto allowed the inclusion of blocks of floor samples from several empty rooms that would otherwise have been left out of the sampling scheme as an economy measure. The repeated low density and diversity of economic seeds in these rooms are critical components in the argument that habitation rooms at Alto by contrast were the locus of numerous and varied food-processing activities resulting in a recognizable distribution of seed remains (table 3.3.).

Project U11: L119549 Scanned by MST Date 8-5-82

Sample	Comments	Wt.	Charcoal	Disturbance	WEEDS				GRASSES			OTHER ECON.				CULTIVARS			# TAXA	# TAXA B
					C	A	P	Others	Or	Sp	Others	Pin	Jun	Op	Others	K	Corn Cup	Others		
BS 1	Sarcobatus fruit Coal Salsola bracts Atriplex lvs.	B	(✓)	R F (mouse) MV	+ ++			++ Lappula + Cleome + Phacelia + Monolepis	+		(Gramineae stem-grain)								10	0
2	Coal Sarcobatus fruits Atriplex lvs.	B	✓ some conif.	R F MV	+			+ Cleome + Lappula + Polygonaceae	++										7	0
3	Coal	B	(✓)	R MV														+ Cucurbita	1	0
4	little bit of coal	B	no	MV	+ ++		+	+ Cleome	+										4	0
5	Coal Atriplex lvs Salsola bracts Borag. bracts	B	no	F rabbit I ant MV	++			+++ Lappula + Cleome + Monolepis + Mentzelia albic.						+					7	0
loaded w/ seeds. 6	Salsola bracts Sarcobatus fruits Borag. bracts coal Atriplex lvs.	B	no	F rabbit mouse I MV	++		Mentz. albic.	++ Lappula ++ Phacelia ++ Cleome ++ Monolepis + Sphaeralcea	+										11	0
little bit of coal 7	Sarcobatus fruits Atriplex lvs.	M	(✓)	R F rabbit I MV	++		++	+ Descurainia ++ Lappula + Cleome + Phacelia + Monolepis											9	0
8	Coal	B	no	R MV I ants	++		+	++ Lappula + Monolepis + Solanum + Cleome + Descurainia											7	0
9	Coal Atriplex lvs Salsola bracts, fruit	M	✓ conif	R F mouse MV I	+			+ Cleome ++ Lappula ++ Monolepis + Phacelia + Mentz. albis.											8	0
10	coal; unb. decayed wood Atriplex lvs.	B	no	R, I	+++		+	+ Lappula + Monolepis + Euphorbia											8	0
loads of seeds in sample 11	Atriplex lvs. Salsola bracts, fruits Sarcobatus fruits	L	no	R	++			++ Monolepis + Lappula ++ Phacelia + Mentzelia albic											8	0
12	Coal Salsola capsule,	B	✓ conif	F (large) R				+ Cleome				+* twig							3	1

Figure 3.1. Example of scan data collection format.

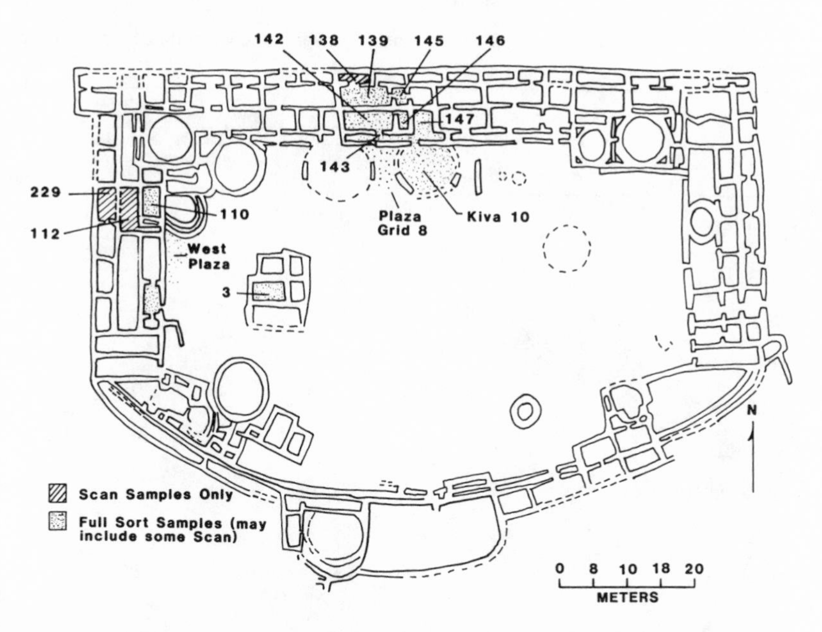

Figure 3.2. Proveniences excavated and sampled at Pueblo Alto, Chaco Canyon, New Mexico.

The patterning observed at Pueblo Alto bears both on interpretation of function and on notions of suitable sampling schemes. Though we can isolate provenience categories that reliably produce paleoplant materials both more abundant and more clearly cultural, Pueblo Alto provides an excellent case in point for why flotation analysis should routinely include less productive cultural proveniences, such as floors. Alto's floor and features, viewed in concert, provide internally corroborative evidence for the use of certain economic plant taxa and the spatial disposition of food-processing activities within rooms and throughout the pueblo. Repetition of the results—in multiple features and floor grids within each room and then in successive rooms—is vital to our confidence in their validity.

In addition to standing on its own as a record of broad scale patterning, scan information can provide guidelines for the selection of samples for full analysis. As a case in point, scanning of all 212 samples collected for the Navajo Mine project in the Four Corners area of northwestern New Mexico (Toll 1984a) revealed that the flotation record ran counter to expectations based on extensive data collection in nearby areas. In samples from the Navajo Nation Irrigation blocks (Ford 1980; Struever and Knight 1979; Toll and Donaldson 1981; Donaldson and Toll 1982a), the Gallo Wash coal lease

Table 3.2. Flotation data from Pueblo Alto, Chaco Canyon: occupation floors with specific economic taxa

	West Room Block		North Room Block		
Taxa	Rm 103 Fl 3[a]	Rm 110 Fl 1[a]	Rm 139 Fl 2[b]	Rm 143 Fl 2 Rm 236 Fl 4[a]	Rm 147 Fl 1[c]
Pinus edulis	x	x	x	x	
Opuntia			x		
Yucca	x				
Sporobolus			x		x
Oryzopsis			x	x	x
Amaranthus	x	x	x	x	
Chenopodium	x	x	x	x	
Cycloloma	x	x	x		x
Descurainia	x	x	x		
Mentzelia					x
Physalis		x	x		
Portulaca	x	x	x		
Solanum			x		
Sphaeralcea				x	x

Note: These taxa occur burned in heating features and unburned on floors.

[a]Gallup ceramic period.
[b]Red Mesa ceramic period.
[c]Late Mix ceramic period.

(Donaldson and Toll 1982b), the McKinley Mine area (Toll and Donaldson 1982), and elsewhere in the San Juan Basin (Toll 1983a, 1983b), Archaic sites have produced very little—presumably because of shallow, unprotected deposits. In the same projects, many sites from the historic Navajo period have contained abundant material, helping to document the interplay between traditionally gathered food products and the wide variety of modern cultivars in the changing Navajo diet. Yet several Navajo Mine Archaic sites consistently produced significant quantities of prehistoric floral debris, while in the Navajo period samples, plant remains were numerous, but uniformly attributable to modern contamination (tables 3.4

Table 3.3. Taxonomic diversity and presence of key economic species by room type at Pueblo Alto, Chaco Canyon

		Average Sample Diversity[b]		Percentage of Samples With	
	Samples[a]	All Taxa	Burned Taxa Only	Corn	Pinyon
Living room floors					
Room 103 fl. 3	9FS	8.4	3.8	67	56
Room 110 fl. 1	23FS	5.1	2.8	65	30
Room 143 fl. 2					
Room 236 fl. 4	5FS,3S	7.3	2.0	50	100
Total	37FS,3S				
Storage room floors					
Room 112 fl. 1	8S	1.8	0.8	25	0
Room 229 fl. 1	9S	1.2	0.1	0	0
Room 103 fl. 4,5	8FS	3.1	0.3	25	13
Room 110 fl. 3	6FS	2.8	0.3	17	0
Room 138 fl. 1	6S	3.0	0	0	0
Room 145 fl. 1	8FS	3.1	0	0	25
Room 139 fl. 1	9FS	5.1	2.1	33	11
Total	31FS,33S				
Ceremonial room floors					
Kiva 15 fl. 1	5FS	7.0	2.6	100	20
Mixed or uncertain function					
Room 103 fl. 1	4FS	5.0	0.8	25	0
Room 110 fl. 2	7FS	1.3	0.1	14	0
Room 139 fl. 2	17FS	12.1	2.8	59	71
Room 142 fl. 3,8	4FS	12.8	6.0	75	75
Room 146 fl. 3	1FS	2.0	2.0	100	100
Room 147 fl.1	2FS, 7S	7.1	3.6	44	0
Plaza feature 1	2FS, 6S	6.1	2.9	38	13
Total	37FS,13S				

Source: Toll 1985, table 55.

[a]FS indicates full sort samples: S indicates scan samples.
[b]Diversity in each sample is measured simply as the number of taxa present.

and 3.5). Knowledge of the general patterning of the botanical record allowed deemphasis of the Navajo period in favor of the Archaic in the full-sort phase of analysis. Scan data stood as the principal documentation of the poor floral record at historical sites. Full-sort seed counts provided quantitative information, which is particularly valuable in view of recent interest in regional economic patterns of the Archaic. While clearly throwing any semblance of randomized sampling out the window, the two-phase analysis

Table 3.4. Taxa in archaic site flotation assemblages, Navajo Mines Archaeological Program

Taxa	Full Sort % Samples (N=32)	Full Sort % Seeds[a] (N=593.5)	Scan % Samples (N=54)	Full Sort & Scan % Sites (N=4) Total	Full Sort & Scan % Sites (N=4) Burned only
SHRUBS AND TREES					
Atriplex (saltbush)	3	< 1	2	25	25
Sarcobatus (greasewood)	0	0	4	50	0
Juniperus (juniper)	9	0	11	75	0
GRASSES					
Oryzopsis (ricegrass)	34	24	38	100	25
Sporobolus (dropseed)	25	2	11	50	50
POSSIBLE ECONOMIC ANNUALS					
Amaranthus (pigweed)	3	2	0	25	25
Chenopodium (goosefoot)	31	64	24	75	75
Corispermum (tickseed)	3	< 1	4	50	25
Descurainia (tansymustard)	3	< 1	2	25	25
Mentzelia (stickleaf)	9	< 1	4	50	0
PROBABLE CONTAMINANTS					
Cryptantha (hiddenflower)	6	< 1	7	75	0
Eriogonum (buckwheat)	3	< 1	4	25	0
Euphorbia (spurge)	9	< 1	9	75	0
Salsola (Russian thistle)	13	< 1	9	75	0
Sphaeralcea (globemallow)	6	< 1	2	25	25

Source: Toll 1984a
[a]Standardized to number of seeds per liter of soil.

procedure has served to maximize some critical information otherwise in short supply.

A second, simple but effective methodological tool is nothing new to archeologists: I wish to advocate the pleasures and rewards of the regional perspective. Viewing individual site assemblages in the context of the much larger regional sample is exceedingly satisfying as a means of focusing on broad-scale subsistence adaptations and evening out small-scale sampling and recovery problems that abound in flotation and macrobotanical analyses. A recent comparison of more than a thousand Archaic, Anasazi, and

Table 3.5. Taxa in Navajo site flotation assemblages, Navajo Mines Archaeological Program

Taxa	Full Sort % Samples (N=5)	Full Sort % Seeds[a] (N=1022.3)	Scan % Samples (N=57)	Full Sort and Scan % Sites (N=14) Total	Full Sort and Scan % Sites (N=14) Burned Only
SHRUBS AND TREES					
Juniperus (juniper)	40		5	21	7
Pinus edulis (pinyon)	20	< 1	5	21	7
GRASSES					
Oryzopsis (ricegrass)	40	< 1	49	79	0
Sporobolus (dropseed)	20	74	11	21	0
POSSIBLE ECONOMIC ANNUALS					
Amaranthus (pigweed)	60	1	5	14	0
Chenopodium (goosefoot)	80	4	67	93	0
Cleome (beeweed)	20	< 1	30	36	0
Descurainia (tansymustard)	80	6	18	50	0
Mentzelia (stickleaf)	60	1	44	79	0
Portulaca (purslane)	60	5	18	36	0
PROBABLE CONTAMINANTS					
Cryptantha (hiddenflower)	60	< 1	19	29	0
Euphorbia (spurge)	80	1	23	64	0
Lappula (stickseed)	0	0	35	57	0
Phacelia (scorpionweed)	40	< 1	56	79	0
Salsola (Russian thistle)	60	1	54	71	7

Source: Toll 1984a

[a]Standardized to number of seeds per liter of soil.

historical flotation samples from dozens of projects throughout the San Juan Basin (Toll 1984a:343-46) illuminated some previously elusive patterning. Results from individual sites of poor-to-moderate preservation, which I had come to think of as minimally informative, became strikingly reiterative when viewed in concert. It is indeed possible to distinguish changes in general subsistence adaptations through time, modified by localized variability in the resource base. In the Archaic period, the pattern observed throughout is one of dependence on a few economic taxa, with singular

Table 3.6. Presence of specific taxa in flotation assemblages from archaic sites, northwestern New Mexico

	NMAP	UII	NIIP II	NIIP III	NIIP VI-VII	NIIP VIII-IX	NIIP VIII-XI	Cortez CO_2
N of sites	3	1	2	5	4	8	7	5
N of samples	32	3	5	38	9	21	41	28
SHRUBS/TREES								
Atriplex (saltbush)	+[a]			+	+[a]			
Juniperus (juniper)	+		+	+[a]	+		+	+[a]
GRASSES								
Oryzopsis (ricegrass)	+[a]		+	+[a]	+	+		
Sporobolus (dropseed)	+[a]	+			+	+		
other grasses	+[a]			+[a]		+[a]		
ECONOMIC WEEDS								
Amaranthus (pigweed)	+[a]			+[a]	+			
Chenopodium (goosefoot)	+[a]			+[a]	+[a]	+	+[a]	+
Corispermum (bugseed)	+[a]			+[a]				+
Descurainia (tansymustard)	+[a]			+[a]	+			
Mentzelia (stickleaf)	+			+	+			
Portulaca (purslane)						+		+
Physalis/Solanum				+[a]				
Sphaeralcea (globemallow)	+[a]			+	+	+		
ECONOMIC PERENNIALS								
Opuntia (pricklypear)				+				
Echinocereus (hedgehog cactus)								+
PROBABLE CONTAMINANTS								
Cryptantha/Lappula	+			+		+		
Dicoria				+				
Eriogonum (buckwheat)	+							
Euphorbia (spurge)	+			+	+	+		+
Oenothera (evening primrose)						+		
Salsola (Russian thistle)	+			+				
Suaeda (seepweed)						+		
Total taxa	15	1	2	16	10	11	2	8
Total burned taxa	8	0	0	8	2	1	1	2

Sources: Columns from left to right:
Toll 1984a; Knight 1980; Ford 1980; Struever and Knight 1979; Toll and Donaldson 1981; Donaldson and Toll 1981; Donaldson and Toll 1982a; Toll 1985b.

[a]Some or all items charred.

predominance of rice grass among grasses and of goosefoot (*Chenopodium*) among annual weeds (table 3.6). The most complete Archaic data sets for this area provide documentation of individual site occupations as loci of single-season exploitation, consistent with opportunistic camp shifting during the growing cycle. A pattern of short-term occupation during the Archaic is also reinforced by fuel use, which is almost entirely saltbush (*Atriplex*), available in abundance within the immediate vicinity of sites for which such data are available. Anasazi samples, on the other hand,

Table 3.7. Presence of specific taxa in flotation assemblages from Navajo sites, northwestern New Mexico

	NMAP	UII	NIIP II	NIIP III	NIIP VI-VII	NIIP VIII-XI	Pitt-Mid	Cortez CO_2
N of sites	14	3	13	15	7	5	9	4
N of samples	57	12	78	34	15	9	18	16
SHRUBS/TREES								
Atriplex (saltbush)	+	+		+			+	
Juniperus (juniper)	+[a]	+[a]	+[a]	+[a]	+[a]	+[a]	+[a]	+[a]
Pinus edulis (pinyon)	+		+	+	+		+[a]	
GRASSES								
Oryzopsis (ricegrass)	+	+	+	+[a]	+	+[a]		
Sporobolus (dropseed)	+				+	+	+	+[a]
other grasses	+[a]	+	+	+[a]	+	+		
ECONOMIC WEEDS								
Amaranthus (pigweed)	+		+	+	+[a]	+	+[a]	+[a]
Chenopodium (goosefoot)	+[a]	+		+[a]	+[a]	+[a]	+[a]	+[a]
Corispermum (bugseed)					+	+[a]		+
Descurainia (tansymustard)	+	+		+		+	+	+[a]
Mentzelia (stickleaf)	+	+		+	+		+	
Portulaca (purslane)	+			+	+		+[a]	+[a]
Physalis/Solanum	+	+[a]		+		+[a]	+	
Sphaeralcea (globemallow)	+	+		+	+	+		
ECONOMIC PERENNIALS								
Opuntia (pricklypear)	+[a]			+		+[a]	+	
PROBABLE CONTAMINANTS								
Cryptantha/Lappula	+	+		+[a]	+	+[a]	+	
Dicoria	+	+		+				
Euphorbia (spurge)	+	+		+	+		+	+
Oenothera (evening primrose)	+			+	+	+		+
Phacelia (scorpionweed)	+	+		+[a]	+		+	
Salsola (Russian thistle)	+[a]	+		+[a]	+[a]		+[a]	
CULTIVARS								
Arachis hypogea (peanut)		+	+	+	+			
Anacardium (cashew)		+						
Citrullis (watermelon)			+	+	+		+	
Cucumis melo (melon)			+	+[a]			+	
Cucurbita (squash)	+	+	+	+	+	+	+	
Juglans (walnut)				+				
Lagenaria (bottlegourd)		+		+				
Malus (apple)			+					
Phaseolus (bean)			+	+			+[a]	
Pistacia (pistachio)					+			
Prunus armeniaca (apricot)			+	+	+			
Prunus domestica (plum)			+					
Prunus persica (peach)	+		+[a]?	+	+[a]?	+		
Rubus (raspberry)					+			
Triticum (wheat)	+[a]							
Vitis (grape)					+			
Zea mays (corn)	+[a]	+[a]	+	+[a]		+[a]	+[a]	+[a]
Total taxa	29	23	18	30	27	18	24	13
Total burned taxa	7	3	3	9	6	8	8	8

Sources: Columns from left to right:
Toll 1984a; Knight 1980; Ford 1980; Struever and Knight 1979; Toll and Donaldson 1981; Donaldson and Toll 1982a; Toll and Donaldson 1982; Toll 1985b.

[a]Some or all items charred.

Table 3.8. Presence of specific taxa in flotation assemblages from Anasazi sites, Northwestern New Mexico

	NMAP	NIIP II	NIIP III	NIIP VI-VII	NIIP VIII-IX	NIIP VIII-XI	Cortez CO_2	Little Water
N of sites	7	5	10	1	6	5	2	3
N of samples	37	12	44	6	14	62	10	45
SHRUBS/TREES								
Atriplex (saltbush)	+[a]		+[a]	+[a]				+[a]
Juniperus (juniper)	+[a]	+				+[a]	+[a]	+[a]
Pinus edulis (pinyon)		+						+[a]
Sarcobatus (greasewood)	+						+	
GRASSES								
Oryzopsis (ricegrass)	+[a]	+	+[a]		+	+	+	+[a]
Sporobolus (dropseed)	+[a]			+	+	+[a]		+[a]
other grasses	+[a]		+		+[a]			+[a]
ECONOMIC WEEDS								
Amaranthus (pigweed)	+[a]		+[a]		+	+		+[a]
Chenopodium (goosefoot)	+[a]		+[a]	+	+	+[a]	+[a]	+[a]
Cleome (beeweed)	+[a]		+					+[a]
Corispermum (bugseed)	+[a]					+		
Cycloloma (winged pigweed)	+[a]		+[a]			+[a]	+[a]	+[a]
Descurainia (tansymustard)	+[a]		+[a]	+	+		+	+[a]
Helianthus (sunflower)	+		+		+	+		+[a]
Mentzelia (stickleaf)	+[a]		+	+			+	
Monolepis (patata)	+		+					+
Portulaca (purslane)	+[a]		+[a]		+		+	+[a]
Physalis/Solanum	+		+[a]		+	+		
Sphaeralcea (globemallow)	+[a]		+		+	+	+[a]	+[a]
ECONOMIC PERENNIALS								
Opuntia (pricklypear)			+		+	+	+[a]	
Echinocereus (hedgehog cactus)			+[a]			+		+
Scirpus (sedge)			+					
PROBABLE CONTAMINANTS								
Cryptantha/Lappula	+		+		+			+
Euphorbia (spurge)	+[a]		+	+	+			+
Phacelia (scorpionweed)	+		+[a]					+
Salsola (Russian thistle)	+		+		+		+	+
Suaeda (seepweed)	+[a]		+		+			
CULTIVARS								
Cucurbita (squash)	+	+						+
Zea mays (corn)	+[a]	+	+[a]	+[a]		+[a]	+[a]	+[a]
Total taxa	27	9	26	7	15	15	13	23
Total burned taxa	18	0	11	2	1	5	8	17

Table 3.8, cont. Presence of Specific Taxa in Flotation Assemblages from Anasazi Sites, Northwestern New Mexico

	Tsaya	Pitt-Mid	Elena Gallegos Farmington	Elena Gallegos Atrisco
N of sites	2	12	1	6
N of samples	29	76	35	19
SHRUBS/TREES				
Atriplex (saltbush)				+
Juniperus (juniper)		+[a]	+[a]	+[a]
Pinus edulis (pinyon)	+[a]	+[a]	+	
Sarcobatus (greasewood)				+
GRASSES				
Oryzopsis (ricegrass)	+[a]	+[a]		+
Sporobolus (dropseed)	+[a]	+[a]		+
other grasses	+[a]			
ECONOMIC WEEDS				
Amaranthus (pigweed)	+[a]	+[a]		+[a]
Chenopodium (goosefoot)	+[a]	+[a]	+	+[a]
Cleome (beeweed)	+[a]	+[a]		
Corispermum (bugseed)	+[a]	+[a]		
Cycloloma (winged pigweed)		+[a]		
Descurainia (tansymustard)	+[a]	+[a]	+	+
Helianthus (sunflower)	+[a]	+		
Mentzelia (stickleaf)		+		+
Monolepis (patata)				+
Portulaca (purslane)	+[a]	+[a]		+
Physalis/Solanum		+[a]		+
Sphaeralcea (globemallow)	+[a]	+		+
ECONOMIC PERENNIALS				
Opuntia (pricklypear)		+[a]		+[a]
Echinocereus (hedgehog cactus)			+	
Scirpus (sedge)		+		
PROBABLE CONTAMINANTS				
Cryptantha/Lappula		+	+	+
Euphorbia (spurge)		+		+
Phacelia (scorpionweed)				+
Salsola (Russian thistle)				+
Suaeda (seepweed)				
CULTIVARS				
Cucurbita (squash)	+			
Zea mays (corn)	+[a]	+[a]		+[a]
Total taxa	14	22	8	30
Total burned taxa	13	14	1	9

Sources: Columns, from left to right:

Toll 1984a; Ford 1980; Struever and Knight 1979; Toll and Donaldson 1981; Donaldson and Toll 1981; Donaldson and Toll 1982a; Toll 1985b; Struever 1980; Minnis 1982; Toll and Donaldson 1982; Donaldson 1984; Toll 1984b.

[a]Some or all items charred.

consistently reveal tapping of a wide resource base, spanning the entire growing season (table 3.8). Wild plant foods and fuels utilized reflect foraging efforts in both upland and lowland zones. During the historical era, diversity of edible weed species recovered remains high, but most specimens are unburned and very new looking, and they probably are contaminants rather than by-products of intentional use (table 3.7). Cultivars (including a wide array of modern introductions) are the principal class of plant foods that can be linked with site habitation.

Summary

In the effort to maximize information gained for research effort expended, there is a real temptation to concentrate sampling on site types and provenience categories known to produce cultural plant material. Two essential points should be kept in mind, however: low-frequency or negative data are frequently essential parts of the whole picture, and there are cost-efficient methods of accumulating and evaluating balanced data sets. One way of including a broad cross section of samples without eating up a large part of the budget is to allocate some samples to a shorter scanning procedure. Further, the perspective we can gain from the cumulation of small data sets on a regional level encourages us to persevere with data collection even from eroded, structureless sites with notoriously poor preservation.

A programmatic attitude towards flotation analysis of less-productive proveniences is required. With the knowledge that such locations can and do provide critical information, and that such data can be procured using sampling and laboratory techniques appropriate to the amount of information gained, archaeologists should not write these situations off: once the archaeologist is out of the field the opportunity to collect these data will be lost.

References Cited

Donaldson, Marcia L. 1984. Botanical remains from eight archaeological sites near Farmington, New Mexico. Castetter Laboratory for Ethnobotanical Studies, technical series 110. Albuquerque: U.S. Forest Service.

Donaldson, Marcia L., and Mollie S. Toll. 1981. A flotation study with implications for the planning of archaeological testing programs: Navajo Indian irrigation project blocks VII and IX. Cultural resources management program, Navajo nation. Castetter Laboratory for Ethnobotanical Studies, technical series 35. Farmington, New Mexico.

_____. 1982a. Analysis of flotation samples and macro-botanical remains: NIIP Blocks VIII and IX mitigation and X and XI testing. Window Rock, Arizona: Cultural Resources Management Program, Navajo Nation. Castetter Laboratory for Ethnobotanical Studies, technical series 58. Albuquerque: University of New Mexico.

_____. 1982b. Flotation analysis of samples from six sites in the Gallo Wash Mine area. In *Prehistoric adaptive strategies in the Chaco Canyon region, northwestern New Mexico*, vol. 1, assembled by Alan H. Simmons. Window Rock, Arizona: Navajo Nation Papers in Anthropology 9.

Ford, Richard I. 1980. *Plant Remains. In Prehistory and history of the Ojo Amarillo*, vol. 4, ed. D. Kirkpatrick. Las Cruces: Cultural Resources Management Division, New Mexico State, University, Report 276.

Knight, Paul J. 1980. Flotation and macrobotanical analysis. In *Human adaptations in a marginal environment: The UII mitigation project*, ed. J. L. Moore and J. C. Winter. Albuquerque: Office of Contract Archaeology, University of New Mexico.

Minnis, Paul E. 1982. Early prehistoric ethnobotany in Chaco wash: Plant remains from the Tsaya project, New Mexico. In *The Tsaya project: Archaeological excavations near Lake Valley, San Juan county, New Mexico.*, ed. R. N. Wiseman. Santa Fe: Museum of New Mexico, Laboratory of Anthropology note 308.

Struever, Mollie S., and Paul J. Knight. 1979. Analysis of flotation samples and macro-botanical remains: Block III mitigation, Navajo Indian Irrigation Project. Window Rock, Arizona: Cultural Resources Management Program, Navajo Nation. Castetter Laboratory for Ethnobotanical Studies, technical series 39. Albuquerque: University of New Mexico.

Toll, Mollie S. 1980. Flotation and macrobotanical indicators of prehistoric environment and economy: The Little Water project. Santa Fe: Museum of New Mexico, Laboratory of Anthropology, Research Section (Project 41-67.21). Castetter Laboratory for Ethnobotanical Studies, technical series 17.

_____. 1982a. Further testing of LA 18091: Flotation and macrobotanical studies. In *Prehistoric adaptive strategies in the Chaco Canyon region, northwestern New Mexico,* vol. 3, assembled by Alan H. Simmons. Window Rock, Arizona: Navajo Nation Papers in Anthropology 9.

_____. 1982b. Flotation analysis of outlying structures of Nuestra Señora de Dolores Pueblo (LA 677). In *Excavations at Nuestra Señora de Dolores Pueblo (LA 677), a prehistoric settlement in the Tiguex province*. ed. Michael P. Marshall. Albuquerque: Office of Contract Archaeology, University of New Mexico.

_____. 1983a. Food and fuel use at a late Archaic/Basketmaker II base camp (site LA 2-13) near Farmington, New Mexico: Flotation, macro-botanical, and charcoal analyses. Albuquerque: USDA Forest Service, Southwest Region.

_____. 1983b. Flotation, macro-botanical, and charcoal analyses at Archaic, Basketmaker, and Navajo sites along the Shell CO_2 pipeline, northwestern New Mexico. Albuquerque: Office of Contract Archaeology, University of New Mexico. Castetter Laboratory for Ethnobotanical Studies, technical series 93.

_____. 1984a. Changing patterns of plant utilization for food and fuel: Evidence from flotation and macrobotanical remains. In *Economy and interaction along the lower Chaco River: The Navajo Mine archaeological program,* ed. Patrick Hogan and Joseph C. Winter. Albuquerque: Office of Contract Archaeology and Maxwell Museum of Anthropology, University of New Mexico.

_____. 1984b. Floral remains from late Basketmaker/early Pueblo sites in the Rio Puerco Valley, New Mexico. Albuquerque: U.S. Forest Service. Castetter Laboratory for Ethnobotanical Studies, technical series 123.

_____. 1985a. Plant utilization at Pueblo Alto, a Chacoan town site: Flotation and macrobotanical analyses. Santa Fe: Division of Cultural Research, National Park Service.

_____. 1985b. Flotation, macrobotanical, and charcoal analyses. Appendix 2 in the excavation of the Cortez CO_2 pipeline project sites, 1982-83, by Michael P. Marshall. Albuquerque: Office of Contract Archaeology, University of New Mexico.

Toll, Mollie S., and Marcia Donaldson. 1981. Analysis of flotation samples and macro-botanical material: Blocks VI and VII mitigation, Navajo Indian Irrigation Project. Window Rock, Arizona: Cultural Resources Management Program, Navajo Nation. Albuquerque: University of New Mexico. Castetter Laboratory for Ethnobotanical Studies, technical series 29.

_____. 1982. Flotation and macrobotanical analyses of archaeological sites on the McKinley Mine lease: A regional study of plant manipulation and natural seed dispersal over time. In *Anasazi and Navajo Land Use in the McKinley Mine area near Gallup, New Mexico,* vol. I, part 2, ed. Christina G. Allen and Ben A. Nelson, pp. 712-86. Albuquerque: Office of Contract Archaeology, University of New Mexico.

van der Veen, Marijke, and Nick Fieller. 1982. Sampling seeds. *Journal of Archaeological Science* 9:287-98.

4

Selecting Quantitative Measurements in Paleoethnobotany

Virginia S. Popper

Introduction

Paleoethnobotanists learn little about human interaction with the plant world from raw plant-remains data. Cultural and noncultural factors bias the types and numbers of remains we recover from archaeological sites. Consequently, taxa frequencies alone do not directly reflect the human-plant interaction, and paleoethobotanists have developed methods of interpreting the frequencies. Ideally, paleoethnobotanists first define how taxa frequencies can answer research questions. We posit meanings to taxa frequencies through models, hypotheses, and assumptions (nonnumerical criteria). Then we derive from these nonnumerical criteria the types, numbers, distributions, and associations of taxa (i.e., the patterning) that we expect to find in the archaeobotanical data. In general, we use quantitative measurements to describe the patterning found in the data and to distinguish the patterning defined by our research questions from other sources of patterning.

This paper presents the determinants for selecting quantitative measurements. It discusses the sources of patterning in archaeobotanical data and four methods of quantifying these data: absolute counts, ubiquity, ranking, and diversity. Miller (chapter 5) discusses a fifth method, ratios, and Pearsall (chapter 8) provides examples of the ubiquity (presence) and ratio (frequency) methods. These three papers show that no one method of quantifying archaeobotanical remains is appropriate or even useful for every paleoethnobotanical analysis. Quantitative measurements differ in their assumptions about archaeobotanical data and in the information that they provide about such data. The measurements we select will depend on our research questions and the quality of our data. To select the appropriate measurement, we must understand the possible sources of patterning in our data and the patterning we want to measure with our data. The more carefully and systematically we collect, process, and identify archaeobotanical samples, the more choices we have in selecting an appropriate quantitative measurement.

Sources of Patterning in Archaeobotanical Remains

Paleoethnobotanists must identify the many sources of patterning in a collection of plant remains to interpret the collection accurately. The sources of patterning are cumulative, beginning with human exploitation of plants and continuing through the paleoethnobotanist's recording of taxon frequencies. Figure 4.1 depicts the sequence of factors that may affect the types and frequencies of plant remains in a collection.

Patterning in the collection begins with people's beliefs about plants. Beliefs determine people's behavior toward the plant world (Ford 1979:290, 320-23). For example, beliefs prescribe how a plant is used or where it is planted. Plant remains vary depending on how people used, processed, stored, and prepared the plants and disposed of their by-products (Dennell 1976, 1978; Hillman 1984; Jones 1984). The remains form the underlying patterning from which we try to reconstruct the role of the plants. Two examples follow which illustrate how the same taxon can leave differently patterned remains. In the first example, one taxon is put to two uses; in the second example, the same crop is deposited at different stages of processing.

First, making chicha beer from maize will leave remains different from those resulting from toasting maize popcorn. To make chicha, kernels are soaked until they sprout and then are added to water, along with some chewed kernels, to ferment. To make popcorn, maize kernels are toasted whole in a pot or griddle over a fire. The broken-down chicha maize kernels are unlikely to be burned or dropped in a fire and therefore will probably leave no remains. In contrast, some popcorn kernels will probably burn, be discarded, and survive as remains.

The second example comes from Hillman's (1984:1-13) detailed description of traditional cereal processing in Turkey. Table 4.1 summarizes his data on two of the many stages in the processing of glume wheats (emmer, spelt, and einkorn) in areas with wet summers. Processing begins with harvesting and ends with cooking the prime grains. The wheat is stored

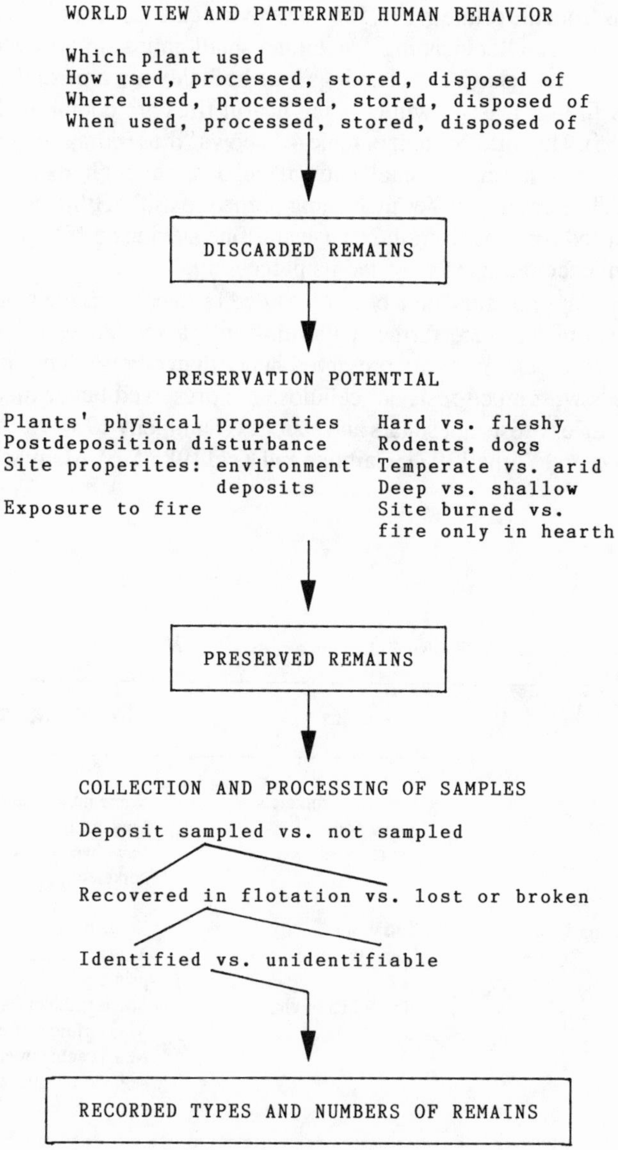

WORLD VIEW AND PATTERNED HUMAN BEHAVIOR

Which plant used
How used, processed, stored, disposed of
Where used, processed, stored, disposed of
When used, processed, stored, disposed of

DISCARDED REMAINS

PRESERVATION POTENTIAL

Plants' physical properties	Hard vs. fleshy
Postdeposition disturbance	Rodents, dogs
Site properites: environment	Temperate vs. arid
deposits	Deep vs. shallow
Exposure to fire	Site burned vs. fire only in hearth

PRESERVED REMAINS

COLLECTION AND PROCESSING OF SAMPLES

Deposit sampled vs. not sampled

Recovered in flotation vs. lost or broken

Identified vs. unidentifiable

RECORDED TYPES AND NUMBERS OF REMAINS

Figure 4.1. Cumulative stages of patterning of archaeobotanical data.

as spikelets before the second (coarse) and third (fine) sievings, which occur daily as grain is used. The coarse sieving removes some of the larger by-products from the prime grain. The fine sieving catches the prime grain and removes the smaller cleanings, including small grains, small weed seeds, and heavy bits of chaff. The cleanings from both sievings are usually thrown into the fire, at least in winter when hearth fires are common (Hillman 1981:155). The third column of table 4.1 shows "those components which, when exposed to fire, are small enough and dense enough to drop into the ashes and be charred rather than being burned to ash" (Hillman 1984:11). The charred remains from the coarse and fine sievings differ greatly, but both evidence the same crop and its processing.

After plant remains have been discarded or deposited, the vagaries of preservation introduce further patterning into assemblages of plant remains. Some plant parts are preserved better than others. Dense nutshells and seeds with much-resistant cellulose are preserved better than fleshy fruits with less-resistant sugars and starches (Dimbleby 1967:95; Munson, Parmalee, and Yarnell 1971; Carbone and Keel 1985:5-6). Many softer and

Table 4.1. Second and third sieving of glume wheats

Activity	By-Product	Likely Charred Remains
Coarse Sieving [a]	Unbroken spikelets Straw nodes Large weed seeds	Some intact spikelets Few culm nodes Few "weeds smaller than spikelets"
Fine Sieving [b]	Tail grain Small weed seeds Heavy bits of chaff	Some tail grain Many "weeds smaller than prime grain" Some spikelet forks Many glume bases Many rachis internode segments

[a] Prime grain passes through
[b] Prime grain retained
Source: Hillman 1984: fig. 5, table 1.

some harder plant parts may be eaten or chewed by insects, rodents, and dogs (Gasser and Adams 1981). Plants favored by these scavengers will be underrepresented in the assemblage. Environmental conditions at a site (soil type, temperature, moisture) affect preservation by allowing or inhibiting the activity of microorganisms (Carbone and Keel 1985:11-15). Remains from waterlogged sites and arid sites resist decay because many microorganisms cannot tolerate the lack of oxygen and water, respectively. Although extremely high or low temperatures, acidic soils, and toxic metal and salt compounds also inhibit microbial activity, in most sites environmental conditions allow decay, and only carbonized plant remains are likely to be preserved (Butzer 1982:114-17, fig. 7-16). The elemental carbon of carbonized remains does not support microbial activity. But erosion, root growth, and plowing can destroy carbonized remains. Sites with deep deposits or structures best protect carbonized remains from erosion and decay.

The cause of carbonization also influences frequencies and distributions of taxa. As Hillman (1981:139) notes: "On most well-drained sites . . . plant materials are preserved only by the chance of exposure to fire, and, even then, only when heating is relatively gentle (200-400 degrees C) or, if temperatures are higher, when they are smothered in the ashes (i.e., deprived of oxygen while heated) such that they are preserved intact by charring rather than being burned away altogether to mineral ash." A house that burns down, burying plant remains in situ, will provide a more complete record of its plant contents at the time of the burning than an abandoned, unburned house in which only plants exposed to a hearth fire are preserved. Hally (1981) shows that frequencies of plant remains in three houses at the Little Egypt site differed in part because two of the houses burned down before abandonment. Only the burned houses contained abundant remains of pokeweed, squash, persimmon, and honey locust (i.e., taxa not usually exposed to fire during processing or at disposal). About the different interpretive value of plant remains from burned and unburned structures, Hally (1981:738) states:

> The most important advantage inherent in carbonized botanical material from unburned structures is that its accumulation will generally be the result of accidents that are repeated with some degree of frequency and regularity through time. Such samples, therefore, will be little affected by short-term fluctuations in the availability of plant species or the frequency of particular processing activities.

Hally's data provide two views of plant use at the Little Egypt site. Differences in the cause of carbonization explain some of the patterning in the remains.

Further patterning can result from strategies for collecting, processing, and analyzing archaeobotanical remains. As discussed in the Introduction, archaeologists use a variety of sampling strategies to select deposits of plant remains for analysis. Too small or too few collected samples can misrepresent the types, frequencies, and distribution of plant remains at a site. Wagner (chapter 2) explains how different flotation and screening procedures for processing soil samples can influence the patterning of remains. For example, screening deposits with 0.25-in. mesh loses the many seeds and plant remains smaller than 0.25 inch. In analyzing plant remains, our proficiency at identification affects plant frequencies. Identifying remains only to family or genus may obscure patterning of the constituent species. If we cannot distinguish one species used commonly as a food from another used infrequently as a medicine, we lose information about the latter. We also chose in our analysis to measure remains by count, weight, or volume. Which units of measurement most accurately reflect the quantities of tiny seeds, nutshell fragments, and charcoal? As Miller (chapter 5) explains, the best measurement depends on the type of plant remains. Finally, by grouping samples for analysis (discussed in more detail below) we change patterning if we combine samples from different populations.

The sources of patterning in archaeobotanical data are many. Uncritically applying quantitative measurements to interpret patterning can lead to erroneous conclusions. Paleoethnobotanists must consider the cumulative sources of patterning in their data to isolate the underlying patterning that supports or refutes the hypotheses developed from their research questions.

Research Questions

The complexity of the patterns we seek in our data will vary according to our research questions. For example, a basic question in the interpretation of plant remains is how the plants were used. To distinguish possible uses, we draw predictions (from ethnographic models and other data about plant use and processing) about how use affects, among other things, the part of the plant that would be deposited. Two different uses may lead to disposition in different contexts or with different sets of plants. In the first case we look for patterns relating one taxon to its context (fig. 4.2a), and in the second case patterns relating one taxon to the assemblage of taxa in a sample (Fig. 4.2b).

Another question is the relative importance of plants in the economy. To evaluate relative importance, we begin again with nonnumerical criteria. We make an assumption about what we mean by importance. Do we

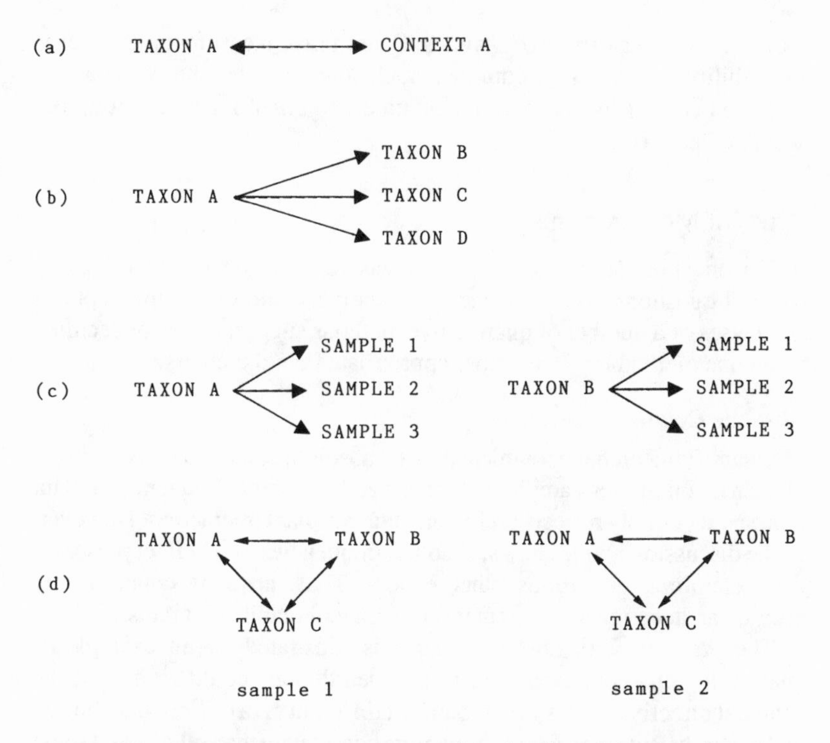

Figure 4.2. The complexity of the patterns sought in archaeological data depends on the complexity of research questions.

evaluate the importance of food sources by the quantity of particular food sources, by their nutritional contribution to the diet, or by the time and labor required to procure them? Can we compare food and nonfood resources? Whatever the criterion we use to define importance, we translate it into an expected numerical relationship between taxa. Depending on the criterion, we may look for patterns which compare the significance of different taxa in a group of samples (fig. 4.2c), or for patterns which compare the relationships among taxa in a group of samples (fig. 4.2d).

Different research questions lead us to look for different patterns of data and to look at different scales of patterns. As research questions become more complex, spanning different time periods or sites, our analysis includes a greater variety of samples. Quantitative measurements differ in their ability to handle such complexity. Of course no quantitative measurement can correct for inaccurate nonnumerical criteria used to set up our predicted patterns.

Types of Measurements

No one method of quantitative measurement is suitable for every research question or every analysis. The summary below of the assumptions and biases of a number of quantitative methods suggests ways of deciding when one method might be more appropriate than the others.

Absolute Counts

Quantifying archaeobotanical data by absolute counts (the raw number of each taxon in each sample) assumes that the absolute frequency of plant remains accurately reflects prehistoric human-plant interaction. However, as the discussion above shows, absolute frequencies may reflect preservation, sampling, or various other factors. Thus, absolute counts rarely provide an adequate measurement for archaeobotanical remains.

The problem with absolute counts is illustrated by an example of quantifying charcoal excavated from a hearth. One could argue that the charcoal directly reflects the amounts of different taxa of firewood burned in the hearth. But some woods burn more completely than others, and some fracture more easily than others (Smart and Hoffman, chapter 10). In addition, clearly the significance of oak is different in one sample, where it comprises 100 fragments out of 1,000, from in another, where it comprises 100 fragments out of 150. Moreover, if the first group of charcoal was extracted from a 5-liter soil sample and the second from a 1-liter soil sample, the difference is even greater. A 5-liter soil sample must have 500 pieces of oak charcoal to be equivalent to the 100 pieces from the 1-liter sample. At the very least, the absolute counts must be standardized (converting them into ratios) to account for differences in sample size (see Miller, chapter 5) or differences in sample abundance (Scarry 1986:214). Paleoethnobotanists frequently use these standardized counts in further quantitative and statistical analyses.

Ubiquity

A common method for quantifying archaeobotanical data is ubiquity or presence analysis (Godwin 1956; Willcox 1974; Hubbard 1975, 1976, 1980). This method disregards the absolute count of a taxon (it assumes that the absolute counts of any particular taxon are too influenced by the degree of preservation to be meaningful) and instead looks at the number of samples in which the taxon appears within a group of samples. Each taxon is scored present or absent in each sample. The taxon is considered present whether the sample contains 1 remain of the taxon or 100, thereby giving the same weight to 1 or 100. The frequency score of a taxon is the number of samples in which the taxon is present expressed as a percentage of the total number of samples in the group. For example, maize recovered in 8 of 10 samples receives a score of 80%. Chili pepper in 6 of those 10 samples receives a score of 60%.

An important characteristic of ubiquity is that the score of one taxon does not affect the score of another, and thus the scores of different taxa can be evaluated independently. Hubbard (1980:53) cautions that a single frequency score has significance only in comparison with other scores of the same taxon, and that ubiquity analysis "is intrinsically comparative and not absolute so that, while presence values can be compared within taxa, they probably cannot be used to compare the absolute importance of different taxa directly (e.g., emmer (wheat) at 70% P might be five times as important as hulled barley at 70% P)." But ubiquity scores of different taxa can provide information on the relative importance of taxa.

The primary methodological assumption in ubiquity analysis is that all samples in a group are independent. In addition, each sample must have two or more taxa. Two examples show that where sampling and recording are inadequate for assessing the homogeneity of deposits or the differences of context, it may be difficult to fulfill the assumption of independent samples and to insure that the data are appropriate for answering the research question. Table 4.2 shows how ubiquity scores will change if one sample (sample 1 in table 4.2) is mistakenly treated as two independent samples or analytical units (samples 1a and 1b in table 4.2). Because the presence of a taxon in each analytical unit receives equal weight, mistakenly splitting one sample into two analytical units inflates the frequency scores of the taxa in those analytical units. This could happen if one inadvertently takes two samples from one archaeological deposit and treats them as independent analytical units; or one might intentionally take two samples but then inadvertently score them as independent samples instead of averaging or combining them in an appropriate fashion. Clearly, mistakes alter the frequency scores less significantly when a group contains many samples.

Hubbard (1980:64) provides a second example from Çayönü, showing that similar problems arise if independent samples are mistakenly grouped. Hubbard's (1975: fig.3) initial ubiquity analysis grouped samples chronologically and showed a shift in high scores from cereals to pulses (lentils, peas, and *Vicia ervilia*). Hubbard (1975:203) concluded that plant use at the site changed over time. However, when Hubbard (1980:64) reanalyzed the data, grouping samples by location at the site, other patterns appeared. The

Table 4.2. Ubiquity and independent samples

Taxon	Sample No.[a]				Sample No.[a]				
	1	2	3	4	1a	1b	2	3	4
A	X				X	X			
B	X		X	X	X	X		X	X
C		X	X				X	X	
D		X		X			X		X
Frequency Score (%)									
A	25				40				
B	75				80				
C	50				40				
D	50				40				

Note: This table presents two versions of the same data to illustrate the two techniques.
[a] X indicates taxon present.

highest ubiquity of pulses came from a locality with no wheat. Wheat and pistachio ubiquity appeared correlated. (If the pistachios were used to flavor the grain this may represent a stage of food preparation.) The evidence suggests that the differences in ubiquity scores at Çayönü, more accurately reflect the differences in activities at different localities at the site. Hubbard's chronological grouping of the samples mistakenly assumed that each group represented the full range of plant use at Çayönü, at that time period. His regrouping by locality suggests that differences in plant processing in the different localities better account for the patterning in this small group of samples. The sample of plant remains was inadequate for answering questions about changing plant use over time.

Another methodological problem that can skew frequency scores is having too few samples, which inflates frequency scores. For example, in a group of four samples the minimum presence of a taxon is 25%, while in a group of twenty samples the minimum presence is 5%. Comparing scores from the two groups can be misleading. Similarly, "a taxon whose 'real' presence is 10% cannot be properly assessed with less than 10 samples" (Hubbard 1976:160). Having few samples more severely skews frequency scores of rare taxa, so with few samples rare taxa should be excluded from analyses or interpreted with caution.

In interpreting ubiquity scores, it is important to make explicit the relationship between the ubiquity scores and the information we seek. For instance, Minnis (1985:104,106) clearly explains his use of ubiquity:

> Making the assumption that charred remains are primarily the result of accidents, then ubiquity tends to measure the number of accidents, which is more closely related to the degree of utilization than is tabulation. Thus, I will assume that a change in the number of samples in which a taxon is present is an imprecise but useful measure of the relative change in the use of that resource.

Hubbard (1975:198; 1980) similarly uses ubiquity to examine crop introduction and use in Europe and the Near East over the past 10,000 years. Ubiquity analysis allows him to combine data from many sites, collected with different excavation and sampling strategies, to compare the use and spread of 11 crops within and between seven geographic areas. (Hubbard [1980] points out the possible sources of error with such data.) The broad view afforded by analyzing such a large data base suggests many interesting patterns and trends. For example, by correlating patterns of crop use with climate, Hubbard (1976:165; 1980) suggests that through time cultural preferences replaced ecological differences as the best explanation for many of these patterns.

In a second example of ubiquity analysis, Hastorf (1983) argues that ubiquity scores can measure crop production and land use of the prehistoric Wanka ethnic group. By using a smaller and more carefully controlled data base, she can draw more specific conclusions than Hubbard. Hastorf uses the standard error of the difference in proportions to test for the significance of trends across time and space and by context. For example, Hastorf (1983:256-59) tests for differences in use and processing of domesticated plants by examining the relationship between the frequencies of the domesticates and different contexts. Finding no significant patterns introduced by different processing, storage, or disposal methods, she concludes that all of the contexts represent the same group of activities. Consequently, she combines the frequencies of these remains from all contexts to test for trends in crop production and land use. Another method for testing the significance of trends is Spearman's coefficient of rank-order correlation (Minnis 1985:106).

In sum, ubiquity analysis is useful, within limitations, for showing general trends when one has little control over the sources of patterning in one's data. By measuring the frequency of occurrence instead of abundance, it reduces but does not eliminate the effects of differences in preservation and sampling. At the same time, however, ubiquity can obscure cultural patterns of plant use where the frequency of use remains the same, but abundance changes (Scarry 1986:193). The results of ubiquity analysis are highly dependent on the grouping of samples and to some extent on the number of samples.

Ranking

Ranking aims to measure plant frequencies more precisely than ubiquity analysis by estimating and adjusting for noncultural sources of patterning. Ranking translates the absolute counts of the data into an ordinal scale. We define a ranking scheme, and for each taxon we separately determine a scale of abundance which sets the frequency required to fall within each rank. To choose the criteria for determining a scale of abundance for each taxon, we select the most important noncultural sources of patterning in the data for which we want to control. We set the scale to neutralize the biases introduced by these sources of patterning.

In a simple hypothetical example, to confirm differences in status between households, we predict that high-status households in highland Peru predominantly ate maize, while low-status households ate quinoa (*Chenopodium quinoa*) and potatoes. We assume that differences in quantities of these taxa between household kitchen middens reflect differences in diet. To test this prediction, we assess differences in the relative quantities of these taxa while controlling for the patterning that variability in preservation and seed production introduce into the data. We establish the scale of abundance based on the expected preservation potential of each taxon under a particular set of conditions and the expected seed production under a particular set of environmental conditions. Using these two criteria, we can define three ranks for quinoa, maize, and potato (table 4.3). Quinoa plants produce a large number of small seeds, which are dense and are preserved well. Therefore, in this example, 501 and 1,000 quinoa seeds per sample have equal significance. Maize plants produce many kernels. The kernels are starchy and are preserved moderately well. Potato plants produce a few large starchy tubers, which are rarely preserved in archaeological sites.

Table 4.3. Scales of abundance [a] for quinoa, maize, and potato

	Rank		
	1	2	3
Quinoa	1-50	51-500	501+
Maize	1-10	11-25	26+
Potato	1-2	3-5	6+

[a] Counts are the number of quinoa seeds, maize kernels, or potato tubers per 5-liter flotation sample.

Using these ranks, we look for differences in the abundance of these taxa in kitchen middens of three households. Independent criteria identify household 3 as high status. The plant remains confirm the predicted association between status and diet. Households 1 and 2 have more quinoa and potato and Household 3 has more maize (table 4.4). These differences are clearer when we look at the ranks instead of the absolute counts.

Table 4.4. Quinoa, maize, and potato counts

	Households		
	1	2	3
		Counts	
Quinoa	700(3)	70(2)	40(1)
Maize	24(2)	9(1)	30(3)
Potato	6(3)	3(2)	1(1)

Note: Counts show number of quinoa seeds, maize kernels, or potato tubers per 5-liter flotation sample. Numbers in parentheses are ranks.

The assumptions we must satisfy to apply ranking depend on the criteria used to create each taxon's scale of abundance. In this example, we assume first that the preservation conditions are the same for every sample. We cannot apply the same scale of abundance to maize from a dry rock shelter, where uncarbonized kernels are preserved, as to maize from a shallow open-air site with poor preservation. Because preservation conditions differ between contexts at the same site, the ranking method increases in accuracy if we only compare samples from the same context.

Second, we assume a relative weighting of seed production to establish the scales of abundance. This assumption is worthwhile only with a large number of remains in each sample and high counts of individual taxa. In this example (table 4.3), 100 and 400 quinoa seeds per sample are of equal significance, while 600 seeds are of greater significance. If no sample contains more than 10 quinoa seeds, this scale is useless. In addition, because of quinoa's high seed production, we should not divide 0 to 10 seeds into several ranks. Ranking this small range of data will probably introduce errors into our results rather than control for variation in seed production. Consequently ranking is not suitable.

In sum, ranking might be useful for evaluating the abundance of plant remains at a site that has consistently excellent preservation of plant remains and high counts of taxa in each sample. If these criteria limit us to applying ranking only to samples from one context at one site, we are limited in the types of questions we can answer with ranking. Ranking is advantageous because it allows taxa to be evaluated independently. But the subjective weighting of taxa frequencies to determine their scales of abundance increases the potential for introducing errors into the results. In many cases the complication and potential for error with ranking will exceed ranking's potential for measuring plant frequencies more precisely.

Diversity

A diversity measurement summarizes data to describe the composition of a plant assemblage. Of the several methods for measuring diversity, this paper uses the Shannon-Weaver information index as an example. This measurement incorporates the total number of taxa in an assemblage and the relative abundance of each taxon to express the certainty of predicting the identity of a randomly selected plant remain (Yellen 1977:107-8; Pearsall 1983:130). If there are many taxa evenly distributed in the assemblage, the certainty of predicting the identity of the selected plant is low and the index indicates high diversity. If the taxa are few and unevenly distributed, the index indicates low diversity. Pielou (1977:292) cautions that "since diversity depends on two independent properties of a collection ambiguity is inevitable; thus a collection with few species and high evenness could have the same diversity as another collection with many species and low evenness."

Pearsall (1983:130-31) introduced the use of the Shannon-Weaver index to paleoethnobotany. She analyzed an assemblage of plant remains from Pachamachay, a multioccupation site in Peru, to distinguish remains of a specialized or temporary occupation from those of a base camp of sedentary hunter-gatherers. Pearsall's results showed partial agreement between the diversity index and independent measurements of intensity of occupation. Six of the eight phases showed constant, increasing, or decreasing diversity that corresponded to similar trends in intensity of occupation. Two phases with predicted low intensity of occupation (a sporadic hunting camp and a ceramic workshop) produced moderately high diversity indices. Pearsall (1983:134) suggests that low abundance of plant remains in these two phases probably skewed the results. Caddell (1983) and Scarry (1986) use the Shannon-Weaver index to examine variability in maize populations based on cob row number.

Pearsall (1983:137) used the following formula to calculate the Shannon-Weaver index. (Although her formula calls for natural logarithms, her example results are based on common logarithms. One converts to the other using a constant. Pearsall's [pers. com.] recalculation of her example using natural logarithms shows that the natural log curve parallels the common log curve in its shifts and supports the same conclusions.)

$$H = - \mathrm{Sum}(N_j/N) \log (N_j/N)$$

where N = total number of seeds in the phase

N_j = total number of seeds of taxon j in the phase

A hypothetical example (table 4.5) points out some of the difficulties of the Shannon-Weaver index. The example looks at the diversity indices of plant remains from three excavated levels. Table 4.5 presents the counts (N_j) of five taxa in each level, totaling (N) 200 remains. The maximum possible diversity index in this example is .70, indicating even distribution ($N_j = 40$) of all five taxa.

The information derived from this analysis is necessarily general. The diversity index in level 1, close to the maximum, shows high diversity, while the lower index values in levels 2 and 3 show lower diversity. There is no simple statistic for measuring the significance of this difference in values. In addition, as Pearsall points out, the diversity index combines all frequency data from one period or level in one index, thus losing information on constituent data. Two samples with the same diversity measure may

Table 4.5. Example of diversity measurement

	Level 1	Level 2	Level 3
Lima beans	40	12	50
Avocado	37	10	0
Squash	29	140	70
Maize	50	15	0
Prickly pear	44	23	80
Total (N)	200	200	200
Diversity index (H)	.68	.44	.46

contain different taxa (Yellen 1977:108), and in this example, low diversity in level 2 comes from uneven distribution, while equally low diversity in level 3 comes from few taxa. Thus, this diversity measurement may be useful for looking for generalized (diverse) versus specialized (not diverse) plant assemblages, but gives only the broadest trends. We must look to the data themselves to understand the nature of the specialization. We may find that differences in seed production and preservation potential among taxa have influenced the measurement, thereby obscuring its cultural meaning. If prickly pear seeds, ranging from 0 to 1,000 per sample, are in the same index as avocado seeds, ranging from 0 to 20 seeds per sample, an automatic bias exists toward uneven distribution of the taxa and low diversity.

An advantage of the diversity measurement is that it is easy to calculate and provides a simple value. However, with more specific predictions about how, for instance, a permanent agricultural settlement's plant remains will differ from those of a temporary harvesting camp (e.g., differences in types, quantities, and contexts of remains) we could use other quantitative measurements which would provide more specific information. Finally, the Shannon-Weaver index requires high counts for each taxon, limiting its applicability to archaeobotanical data. Pearsall (1983:130) believes that counts under 10 could lead to inaccurate results. If, as occasionally happens, we must combine samples (possibly from different contexts) to reach counts over 10, we must be careful to group samples from the same population (a problem already discussed in terms of ubiquity measurement).

Conclusion

This paper shows that we cannot draw direct conclusions about human-plant interactions from the frequency of taxa alone. The patterns in the data derive from cultural and noncultural factors. Our research questions, models, and assumptions define the patterns we seek in our data and suggest meanings for these patterns of plant remains. But we must also account for other sources of patterning in the data. Quantitative measurements assist us in these tasks. With the increasing complexity of the research questions we address to archaeobotanical data, the importance of selecting an appropriate quantitative measurement also increases.

Examples of different quantitative measurements point out the strengths and weaknesses of each method. The different methods treat the data with different degrees of specificity, require different conditions, and provide different information. As the measurements move away from absolute frequencies, we lose information on abundance. But more specific measurements, such as absolute counts and ranking, require greater control over preservation and context than ubiquity. Ratios (see Miller, chapter 5) also treat the data with greater specificity than ubiquity analysis. When our patterns involve well-controlled data (e.g., comparing taxa between the same type of context at one site) we may want a more specific measurement. Even with the same collection, other research questions that involve comparing samples from diverse contexts may call for more general measurements.

When choosing between alternative measurements, we also consider the conditions they require. Ubiquity is less reliable (especially for measuring the frequency of rare taxa) when there are few samples in a group. Ranking requires high counts of taxa. All paleoethnobotanical analyses require careful grouping of samples for accurate results. This is particularly important in ubiquity analysis, because grouping samples is an integral part of the calculation. Miller (chapter 5) discusses the issues involved in averaging values.

In the information they give, ranking and ubiquity allow us to evaluate taxa independently. This does not hold true for ratios that standardize data by comparing the quantity of one taxon or category of remains to that of another taxon or category (see Miller, chapter 5). Diversity measurements are useful for summarizing groups of data but tell us nothing about individual taxa. The same cautionary note applies to the interpretation of all quantitative measurements. We must be explicit about how the values we receive from our measurements provide the information we need to answer our research questions.

This paper illustrates that one cannot generalize about the suitability of a particular quantitative method. Some methods may be better suited in general to some research questions, but the best method in any specific instance depends also on the condition of the archaeobotanical data. To choose a suitable method, we need to consider both the question and the data condition. Specific examples from this paper and this volume provide guidelines for the selection of quantitative measurements. Paleoethnobotanical analyses often include several methods of quantification and may benefit from comparing the results of different methods.

References Cited

Butzer, Karl W. 1982. *Archaeology as human ecology: Method and theory for a contextual approach.* Cambridge: University Press.

Caddell, Gloria M. 1983. Floral remains from the Lubbub Creek archaeological locality. In *Studies of material remains from the Lubbub Creek archaeological locality*, ed. C. S. Peebles, pp. 274-381. Prehistoric Agricultural Communities in West Central Alabama, Vol.2. Report submitted to the U. S. Army Corps of Engineers, Mobile District, by the University of Michigan, Museum of Anthropology, Ann Arbor.

Carbone, Victor A., and Bennie C. Keel. 1985. Preservation of plant and animal remains. In *The analysis of prehistoric diets*, ed. R. I. Gilbert, Jr., and J. H. Mielke, pp. 1-19. Orlando: Academic Press.

Dennell, Robin W. 1976. The economic importance of plant resources represented on archaeological sites. *Journal of Archaeological Science* 3:229-47.

_____. 1978. *Early farming in south Bulgaria from the sixth to the third millenia B.C.* Oxford: British Archaeological Reports International Series 45.

Dimbleby, G. W. 1967. *Plants and archaeology.* London: John Baker.

Ford, Richard I. 1979. Paleoethnobotany in American Archaeology. In *Advances in archaeological method and theory* ed. M. Schiffer, New York: Academic Press 2:285-336.

Gasser, Robert E., and E. Charles Adams. 1981. Aspects of deterioration of plant remains in archaeological sites: The Walpi Archaeological Project.

Journal of Ethnobiology 1(1):182-92.

Godwin, H. 1956. *The History of the British Flora*. Cambridge: University Press.

Hally, David J. 1981. Plant preservation and the content of paleobotanical samples: A case study. *American Antiquity* 46(4):723-42.

Hastorf, Christine A. 1983. Prehistoric agricultural intensification and political development in the Jauja region of Central Peru. Ph.D. diss., Department of Anthropology, University of California, Los Angeles; AnnArbor: Universtiy Microfilms.

Hillman, Gordon C. 1981. Reconstructing crop husbandry practices from charred remains of crops. In *Farming practice in British prehistory*, ed. R. Mercer, pp. 123-62. Edinburgh: University Press.

_____. 1984. Interpretation of archaeological plant remains: The application of ethnographic models from Turkey. In *Plants and ancient man: Studies in palaeoethnobotany*, ed. W. Van Zeist and W. A. Casparie, pp. 1-41. Rotterdam: A. A. Balkema.

Hubbard, R. N. L. B. 1975. Assessing the botanical component of human paleoeconomies. Bulletin of the Institute of Archaeology 12:197-205.

_____. 1976. Crops and climate in prehistoric Europe. *World Archaeology* 8(2):159-68.

_____. 1980. Development of agriculture in Europe and the Near East: Evidence from quantitative studies. *Economic Botany* 34(1):51-67.

Jones, G. E. M. 1984. Interpretation of archaeological plant remains: Ethnographic models from Greece. In *Plants and ancient man*, ed. W. van Zeist and W. A. Casparie, pp. 43-61. Rotterdam: A. A. Balkema.

Minnis, Paul E. 1985. *Social adaptation to food stress: A prehistoric southwestern example*. Chicago: University of Chicago Press.

Munson, P. J., P. W. Parmalee, and R. A. Yarnell. 1971. Subsistence ecology of Scovill, a terminal Middle Woodland village. *American Antiquity* 36:401-31.

Pearsall, Deborah M. 1983. Evaluating the stability of subsistence strategies by use of paleoethnobotanical data. *Journal of Ethnobiology* 3(2):121-37.

Pielou, E. C. 1977. *Mathematical Ecology*. New York: John Wiley & Sons.

Scarry, Clara Margaret. 1986. Change in plant procurement and production during the emergence of the Moundville chiefdom. Ph.D. diss., Department of Anthropology, University of Michigan, Ann Arbor: University Microfilms.

Willcox, G. H. 1974. A history of deforestation as indicated by charcoal analysis of four sites in Eastern Anatolia. *Anatolian Studies* 24:117-33.

Yellen, John E. 1977. *Archaeological approaches to the present: Models for reconstructing the past*. New York: Academic Press.

5

Ratios in Paleoethnobotanical Analysis

Naomi F. Miller

Ratios provide a simple means of standardizing data. If we understand the assumptions underlying their use, we can construct ratios that are appropriate for inter- and intrasite comparisons.

Archaeobotanists use standardizing ratios to compare (1) samples of unequal size, (2) samples differing in circumstances of deposition or preservation, and (3) quantities of different categories of material that are equivalent in some respect. Although it is easy enough to calculate a ratio, assigning a valid paleoethnobotanical meaning to it is quite another matter. We use our knowledge of archaeology and related fields to choose variables and units of measurement that are appropriate to the problem under consideration. Further discussion about choosing appropriate variables will appear in later sections with reference to particular examples.[1]

For clarity of presentation only, I divide the ratios commonly used by paleoethnobotanists into two general types. For the first type of ratio, the material represented by the numerator is included within the material represented by the denominator. Density measures, percentages, and proportions are in this group. For the second, which I call *comparison ratios*, the numerator and denominator are composed of mutually exclusive items, such as nutshell and charcoal, or wheat and barley. The only numerical restriction in constructing a ratio is that the denominator not be zero.

1. For example, if *Setaria* was not eaten, then its increase or decrease in the archaeobotanical record is not directly relevant to questions about diet.

Densitites, Percentages, and Proportions

One of the most basic ratios for paleoethnobotanists is density, where the denominator (sometimes called the *norming variable* [Mueller, Schuessler, and Costner 1974]) is the total volume of the sediment sample from which the plant remains were extracted. Typically, density is expressed as the number of charred items or the weight of the charred material in a given amount of sediment. It is largely a matter of convenience whether one uses count, weight, or some other unit of measurement. The basic assumption of density ratios is that all things being equal, larger sediment samples have more plant remains. By choosing volume of floated or processed sediment as the norming variable against which another variable can be measured, one can test the assumptions of uniform deposition, preservation, and recovery rates.

Asch and Asch use a density measure to compare rates of fuel consumption at simple village sites. They record similar densities of charred material from different *cultural features* and therefore suggest that wood use occurred at a fairly constant rate (1975:117).

Pearsall (1983:129) tests the proposition that density of charred remains is a measure of intensity of occupation. She finds that the density of charred botanical material corresponds fairly well with other archaeological measures of intensity of occupation through much of the 8,000-year history of the Pachamachay rock shelter high up on the Peruvian puna. However, a level characterized as a special purpose campsite had little archaeological material, yet had a high density of charred material. Pearsall therefore concludes that density of charred material measures intensity of activity involving fire rather than intensity of occupation.

Interpreting density measures is a little more complicated at Malyan, an ancient urban center in southern Iran (Miller 1982). First, Malyan's inhabitants burned fuel not only for cooking and heating but possibly for metallurgy and pottery firing as well. Second, some charred material was redeposited and dispersed during the thousand-year occupation of this multicomponent urban site. Much of the site consists of eroded mud brick. The density of charred material in these deposits is usually very low (less than 0.05 g/liter of sediment). Many hearths also have low densities of charred remains, which suggests they had been cleaned out in antiquity. By comparing the density of a hearth deposit with control samples from low-density mud brick collapse, I can assess how likely it is that a particular hearth contains in situ charred material. At Malyan, deposits with a relatively high density of charred material inform us about particular burning or ash-dumping episodes, but not about the overall intensity of burning activity on the site.

Another use for the measure *density of charred material* is as a test of seasonality in regions with a marked cold season. At Sharafabad, an ancient town in southwestern Iran, archaeological evidence and ethnographic analogy suggest that seasonal differences in garbage disposal practices account for the stratigraphy of a large pit (Wright, Miller, and Redding 1981). The seasonal interpretation is consistent with the seed evidence. A common seed source on Iranian sites is dung fuel (Miller and Smart 1984); at Sharafabad, "winter" strata average 28.72 to 30.55 seeds per liter of sediment, while "summer" strata average 6.35 to 9.00 seeds per liter of sediment.

Percentages and proportions are other forms of ratios in which the numerator is a subset of the denominator. A percentage is simply a proportion multiplied by 100. To compare the importance of one taxon relative to other taxa from sample to sample, paleoethnobotanists frequently use percentages to standardize the contents of each sample. In contrast to density measures, the numerator and denominator must be expressed in the same unit of measurement.

Paleoethnobotanists use percentages (or comparisons; see below) of functionally equivalent items to detect replacement of one category of material by another, through time or along a geographical cline. For example, Minnis (1978:359) identifies a period of agricultural expansion on the floodplain of the Mimbres valley, New Mexico, by comparing the charcoal percentages (based on counts) of *floodplain woods* : *total species of wood* in each time period. During times of relatively low population, a large percentage of the charcoal was from floodplain types; this suggests that trees grew in the floodplain then and were chopped down. In contrast, low percentages of floodplain wood during the later Classic Mimbres period indicate that the inhabitants had cleared the floodplain for agricultural land and obtained wood in other habitats.

Percentages are also used to assess variability between samples due to circumstances of preservation. For example, Green (1979:42-43) compares the percentages of plant taxa from dry and waterlogged contexts on medieval urban sites. He observes that cereal grains comprise less than 1% of the waterlogged seeds from floors but make up 31% of the charred seeds from floors. In contrast, there are no waterlogged cereals from aerobic pits, but cereals comprise 87% of the charred seeds from this context. Not only do "different types of features preserve different evidence" (1979:42), but different taxa are not equally likely to be preserved in different contexts.

Seed assemblages from different preservation contexts can be compared on other grounds, too. At Malyan, charred seeds are mostly from animal dung burned as fuel, and mineralized seeds are from latrine deposits; barley represents 92% of the identified charred cereal remains but only 33% of the mineralized grains (data available in Miller 1982). This suggests that animals ate more barley than wheat, and that humans ate more wheat than barley.

Comparisons

Comparisons, the second type of ratio I have designated, compare relative amounts of two different items. Comparisons focus attention on two mutually exclusive variables. They can be used to assess the effects of different preservation contexts or to identify different use contexts.

Seed : charcoal and *nutshell : charcoal* ratios are popular; they use charcoal or nutshell weight, count, or volume as the norming variable (Bohrer 1970; Asch and Asch 1975; Johannessen 1984; Pearsall 1983). On sites where it is reasonable to assume that charcoal represents ordinary, domestic fuel use (rather than, say, burning of structures), paleoethnobotanists put charcoal in the denominator to control for likelihood of preservation. As Bohrer (1970:423) notes, if seeds are preserved accidentally, "a greater concentration of burned seeds in a volume of charcoal should signify increased use."

The following example shows why, for investigating plant use, charcoal rather than sediment volume is the relevant norming variable (table 5.1). If nuts are as likely to fall into a domestic fire in one time period as another, a lower absolute density (*nutshell : sediment volume*) from one time period may just indicate that the charred remains from the fire were mixed with other material and dispersed. The quantity of nutshell relative to charcoal could indicate that nut use increased.

Hillman (1984:32-38) uses comparison ratios in his ethnographic model of grain processing. He observes that sieving removes only small weed seeds from a grain sample, and manual sorting is necessary to remove cereal-sized weed seeds. A simple comparison ratio-number of cereal-sized *weed seeds : number of prime grains* --can distinguish these two sorting

Table 5.1. Hypothetical example

Nut (g)	Charcoal (g)	Sediment Volume (liters)	Nut/ Sediment Volume	Nut/ Charcoal
1.0	2.0	1	1.0	0.5
1.0	0.5	2	0.5	2.0

practices; sieved grain has many large weed seeds and a ratio greater than 1 : 20, but hand-sorted grain generally has a ratio of less than 1 : 20 (Hillman 1984:34). These results can be applied to suitable archaeobotanical assemblages.

The numerator of a comparison ratio need not be expressed in the same unit of measurement as the denominator. Usually convenience dictates the choice of unit. For example, when seed weight is low, counts of whole seeds may provide a more accurate estimate of importance than weight. In contrast, since we cannot reconstruct the number of whole nuts from nutshell fragments, we may use the weight of the fragments. *Seed count : nutshell weight* will differ from *seed weight : nutshell weight*. However, assuming seed counts and weights are correlated, the comparisons are equivalent.

For some problems, comparison ratios and proportions are interchangeable. Because ratios cannot have zero in the denominator, we sometimes change a comparison ratio to a proportion. For example, wheat : barley (w : b) provides the same basic information as w : b + w. The latter differs only in not assuming all samples contain barley.

Constructing Ratios

Homogeneity

Let us say you want to estimate the fruit consumption of today. You can combine counts of apples and oranges eaten into one homogeneous variable, *fruit*. If, however, you add watermelon to your list of fruits, you will seriously skew your estimate, since one watermelon represents many portions of these other fruit types. To make the *fruit consumption* variable homogeneous, you could simply total the estimated number of watermelon portions that are equivalent to one apple or one orange and proceed. For paleoethnobotanists, who deal with more complex issues, it is a little harder to define homogeneous variables a priori.

Paleoethnobotanists use analytical categories that range from a single taxon to the sum of all botanical materials in a given sample. We frequently lump together taxa deemed similar in function, habitat, or other specified characteristics. To answer some questions, we combine species into ecological groups, as Minnis (1978) does with floodplain species in the charcoal and land use study mentioned earlier. Or following Hillman (1984), we combine taxa by seed size to identify the sieved by-products of crop processing.

Ideally, a composite variable combines equally durable and functionally equivalent taxa whose use remains constant through time. For ratios like *seed : charcoal*, where the numerator or denominator comprises more than one taxon, the composite variables must be homogeneous to accurately measure patterning in an archaeological assemblage. Even if the taxa are all members of one functional category, such as food, they may be represented by different plant parts. In this case, homogeneity cannot be assumed, and one may ask whether it is legitimate to use a conversion factor to create a theoretical comparability among disparate plant parts (see below).

Whatever the question, it may be difficult to decide which characteristics are valid when combining taxa. For example, will different breakage patterns of nut or charcoal remains mask important relationships between the numerator and the denominator (see below; cf. Lopinot 1984)? Will differential seed production of weedy species distort the numbers of weed seeds relative to grains? Because we may err in assuming that particular types of plant remains are similar on ecological or functional grounds, or that they are equally preservable, we should spell out the assumptions we have made. The reader will then be able to evaluate the argument presented.

Asch, Ford, and Asch (1972) use *seed : nutshell* to document increasing utilization of seeds relative to nuts in the Woodland period. They standardize against nutshell rather than charcoal, presumably because nuts are food items. They reasonably assume that the amount of nutshell, a regularly burned refuse product, is proportional to nut use. They use *seed count : nutshell weight* in order to compare relative quantities of seeds between sites: "At Koster, the seed/nut ratio is estimated as 230 seeds/1040 g. nuts = 0.22; at Macoupin the ratio is estimated as 2314 seeds/278 g. nuts = 8.32. The ratio of seeds to nuts is thus 38 times greater at the Middle Woodland Macoupin site than at Koster" (Asch, Ford, and Asch 1972). Asch, Ford, and Asch (1972) do not think that changes in preservation and burning conditions account for this increase. Although seeds and nuts may fall into a fire for different reasons, they assume that the circumstances of burning remained constant through time. Therefore, the increase in *seed : nutshell* reflects changing food preference.

Lopinot (1984:192) cautions against the uncritical use of *seed : nutshell* ratios in cultural interpretations. He points out that cooking practices affect seed preservation. A change from seed parching to boiling could lead one to "significantly underestimate the intensity of seed use relative to nuts" during the Woodland period, if preservation of seeds by burning depends on cooking accidents.

The homogeneity of a composite variable also depends on the physical properties of its constituents. For example, Lopinot (1984:134ff.) shows that acorn is more likely to fragment and turn to ash than a denser nutshell, such as hickory. Acorn would therefore be underrepresented in a mixed sample, because other nuts are preserved better. Since archaeobotanists are less likely to examine and identify nut fragments smaller than 2 mm, recording procedures biased against smaller fragments can also underestimate a taxon such as acorn. Thus, even if overall nut use was constant, an increase in acorn use relative to sturdier nuts could appear archaeologically as a decline in total nutshell density. In the Koster example cited above, acorn is a fairly minor component of both early and late assemblages, validating Asch, Ford, and Asch's (1972) original conclusion.

Conversion Factors

Conversion factors can improve the homogeneity of a composite variable. A valid conversion factor reduces the effects of ancient cultural practices or physical properties that make some plants or plant parts not comparable to one another.

Sometimes calculations are based on the analog of the archaeozoologists' "minimum number of individuals." The paleoethnobotanist estimates the actual percentage of different foods in a prehistoric diet by converting disparate plant parts to equivalent whole edible plants. MacNeish (1967) introduced this approach to diet reconstruction in the Tehuacan report (see recent revisions, Farnsworth, Brady, DeNiro, and MacNeish 1985; see also Pozorski 1983). The use of dietary equivalents has some serious flaws, however. It assumes that the archaeologist knows which plants were used as food and that there are no serious absences due to sheer unpreservability or localized absence of particular types of food remains not brought onto the excavated portion of the site (see Hastorf, chapter 8, for a discussion and critique of this method; also Begler and Keatinge 1979; Dennell 1979; Lopinot 1984:193). It also does not distinguish trash (e.g., a corn cob) from food (e.g. corn kernels).

A more acceptable use of conversion factors restricts comparisons to similar categories of remains. For example, to estimate the relative importance of different nuts in the diet, Lopinot (1984:150-52) recommends converting nutshell weights to an estimate of nutmeat weight. The nutmeat equivalent is based on the charred nutshell weight multiplied by two experimentally derived conversion ratios (table 5.2). Given the high fragmentation rate of acorn, the converted values might be very different from the unconverted ones. For example, Lopinot concludes that although hickory and acorn represent 87% and 13% by weight, respectively, of the charred nutshell from the early Archaic of the lower Little Tennessee Valley, the equivalent weights and presumed dietary importance of the uncharred nutmeats would be 11% and 89%, respectively. Used with caution, a conversion factor can bring out a significant pattern of plant remains in an assemblage. It is, however, important to report the conversion factor or the original data on which the estimated quanities are based.

Table 5.2. Equation for calculating nutmeat equivalent from charred nutshell

NUTMEAT = (X) (C) (M)

X: charred nutshell (g)

C: uncharred nutshell (g)/charred nutshell (g)

M: uncharred nutmeat (g)/uncharred nutshell (g)

Source: Lopinot 1984:151.

An Example

It is sometimes difficult to develop analytical categories appropriate to one's own research. For example, in search of patterning in the distribution of archaeobotanical materials from Malyan, I calculated a modified *seed : charcoal* ratio (Miller 1982; Miller and Smart 1984). The ratio I used is a proportion. The numerator is the weight of the seeds (S), and the denominator combines total charred material weight (seed and charcoal, S + C). I did not use charcoal alone because I could not assume all samples would contain charcoal. And because seed weight was negligible for most samples, I did not think adding seed weight to the denominator would significantly alter the value of the ratio.

Independent archaeological evidence suggested all burning took place in controlled fires of hearths, ovens, kilns, and perhaps a few trash deposits as well; no structures were burned. I therefore assumed all the charcoal was spent fuel. Prior to the analysis, however, I did not know the role of cultigen and weed seeds in the assemblage. The ratio therefore combined two disparate categories in the norming variable, fuel and possibly food remains.

Despite my weak justification for combining seeds and charcoal, the resulting ratio documented a major shift. The ratio S : S + C increased tenfold over the thousand-year occupation of the site. Through subsequent ethnoarchaeological research, I discovered that seeds from dung fuel could easily be preserved in contexts analogous to those found archaeologically. I concluded that the higher values of S : S + C could be explained by the increasing use of dung fuel relative to wood. This change in fuel was probably a result of tree clearance, an interpretation supported by the charcoal analysis (Miller 1985).

In retrospect, I uncovered this pattern of seed distribution because S + C was a homogeneous and appropriate variable—most seeds and all charcoal represented the same depositional context, that is, fuel use.

Recalculating the ratios without nutshell and grape pips—items which probably did not come from dung fuel—does not change the results.

Characterizing Archaeological Assemblages With Ratios

Archaeobotanists use ratios to describe and characterize plant remains, whether they are from a series of sediment samples, a group of excavated deposits, a whole site, or a series of sites. Frequently the analyst averages the results from several samples to simplify the discussion of the material.

Is Averaging Appropriate?

In combining samples to obtain an average value, one assumes that samples grouped together contain material from the same population. In the paleoethnobotanical context, this means that circumstances of deposition and preservation are not so wildly different as to make the samples incommensurable. For example, if charred material from a hearth and a pit represents fuel remains, the samples may be combined for analysis; if, on the other hand, the pit has a cache of charred seeds and the hearth contains charred firewood, it makes little sense to obtain an average of the two deposits. Similarly, combining the values of *nutshell : charcoal* from a hearth and a burnt structure may conflate a *food : fuel* ratio with a *food : building material* ratio. Thus it may be that a group of samples is so disparate in character that they should not be averaged together.

Calculating Average Ratios

Calculating average ratios is not always straightforward. First, the average of two ratios is not equal to the ratio of the sum of the denominator and the sum of the numerator. In addition, because of the vagaries of excavation and preservation, one may want to give unequal weight to the various deposits when constructing a combined or average ratio.

As table 5.3 shows, average ratios are based on the individual sample ratio (in this example, *seed : charcoal* expressed as S/C) multiplied by various weighting factors. Think of the two samples as coming from two different deposits. The weighting factor for each sample is a proportion, the sum of which is equal to 1.

Equation 1 in table 5.3, a simple numerical average, assumes that the two samples are equally important for providing a fair representation of the archaeological deposits. For example, one might have a series of pits or hearths thought to be filled with similar material, like burned trash.

Equation 2 takes a different tack. Conceptually, if one is not sampling archaeological deposits so much as sampling the botanical materials preserved in them, it makes sense to give more weight to the samples that

Table 5.3. Examples of calculating average ratios

	Sample 1	Sample 2
Seed weight	S_1	S_2
Charcoal weight	C_1	C_2
Sample volume	V_1	V_2
Volume of total deposit	D_1	D_2
Set the values of the variables:	$S_1 = 1$	$S_2 = 2$
	$C_1 = 2$	$C_2 = 3$
	$V_1 = 1$	$V_2 = 3$
	$D_1 = 2$	$D_2 = 1$

	Weighting Factor	Average	Value
Equation 1	none	$\frac{1}{2}\left(\frac{S_1}{C_1} + \frac{S_2}{C_2}\right)$	0.58
Equation 2	charcoal weight	$\frac{C_1}{C_1+C_2}\left(\frac{S_1}{C_1}\right) + \frac{C_2}{C_1+C_2}\left(\frac{S_2}{C_2}\right) = \frac{S_1+S_2}{C_1+C_2}$	0.60
Equation 3	sample volume	$\frac{V_1}{V_1+V_2}\left(\frac{S_1}{C_1}\right) + \frac{V_2}{V_1+V_2}\left(\frac{S_2}{C_2}\right)$	0.62
Equation 4	deposit volume	$\frac{D_1}{D_1+D_2}\left(\frac{S_1}{C_1}\right) + \frac{D_2}{D_1+D_2}\left(\frac{S_2}{C_2}\right)$	0.56

contain more material. In this example, I assume that the charcoal is the remains of fuel, so charcoal quantities reflect the amount of wood burning. The weighting factor is the proportion of charcoal contained in each sample. Sample 1 contains two-fifths of the charcoal, so its contribution to the average S/C value is weighted accordingly. The astute reader will recognize this commonly used ratio. It reduces to a simple summing of the numerators and denominators of a series of samples. Although one's first impulse may be to use this easily calculated ratio, equation 2 is not appropriate if there is no particular reason to weight by the denominator variable (charcoal, in this example).

Equation 3 is a weighted average that recognizes that some sediment samples are larger than others. It would be useful in the following situation: the excavator has provided you with two sediment samples of different size from one unstratified pit. In order to compare the first pit with others from which only one sample was obtained, the average of the first two samples weighted by the amount of sediment examined is appropriate. Equation 3 is particularly useful for evening out discrepancies in sample volume from various deposits prior to calculating a general average for the group as a whole.

Equation 4 weights the samples by the total volume of the deposits from which they come. It would be useful (in theory) for estimating ratios involving the total quantity of charred material on a site or excavated portions thereof. Ordinarily that is not an estimate paleoethnobotanists are particularly interested in, so weighting by deposit volume has relatively little utility.

The foregoing examples illustrate some of the choices involved in calculating an average ratio for a group of samples. Researchers have to decide whether their samples are uniform enough for comparison, and whether or not a particular weighted average will correct for sample variability.

Summary

Ratios allow us to compare archaeobotanical samples despite the inherent variability in the processes of deposition, preservation, recovery and analysis of plant remains. The choice of ratio used will depend on the question one is asking. In practice, numerically different ratios are sometimes used to answer similar questions. Initial quantification may point out unexpected peculiarities or consistencies in the data. Paleoethnobotanists should therefore be alert to the assumptions behind their use of ratios and be flexible enough to adopt new assumptions when the old ones prove inadequate. To allow others to evaluate our use of ratios, we should report the raw data on which they are based.

Although I cannot make a general statement about the utility of the various ratios discussed in this chapter, not all uses of ratios are equally valid. Density of botanical material is one of the most important and basic measures for interpreting depositional and preservational variability. Proportions and comparisons are particularly useful for identifying the replacement of one functional or ecological type by another. Combining disparate taxa in the numerator or denominator is problematic, because it is so difficult to control for all of the variables attendant upon the use of the necessary conversion factors.

Finally, one must ask the following questions every time one uses a ratio in a paleoethnobotanical analysis: (1) What will a particular density, proportion, or comparison measure in a given assemblage? (2) Are the variables chosen relevant to the question asked? (3) Are assumptions of the equivalence of use and preservability among taxa and among deposits warranted?

Although we may not always be able to answer these questions, ratios serve an important function in paleoethnobotanical analysis. In our search for spatial and temporal patterning, numerical methods which help to reduce the complexity of our data and isolate key changes in them are useful tools that allow us to move beyond simple comparisons and general overviews.

Acknowledgments

I am grateful to Donald Strickland of Southern Illinois University, Edwardsville, for sharpening my thinking about ratios, and for his incisive comments on earlier versions of this paper. He was the "astute reader" who pointed out that equation 2 is a variation of equation 1. I would also like to thank Deborah Pearsall, Virginia Popper, William Macdonald, Neal Lopinot, and an anonymous reviewer for their useful comments, and finally Christine Hastorf and Virginia Popper for suggesting a broader topic than I had originally envisioned.

References Cited

Asch, Nancy B., and David L. Asch. 1975. Plant remains from the Zimmerman Site—Grid A: A quantitative perspective. In *The Zimmerman site*, ed. M. K. Brown, pp. 116-20. Springfield: Illinois State Museum Reports of Investigations 32.

Asch, Nancy B., Richard I. Ford, and David L. Asch. 1972. *Paleoethnobotany of the Koster site: The Archaic horizons.* Springfield: Illinois State Museum Reports of Investigations 24.

Begler, Elsie B., and Richard W. Keatinge. 1979. Theoretical goals and methodological realities: Problems in the reconstruction of prehistoric subsistence economies. *World Archaeology* 11:208-26.

Bohrer, Vorsila. 1970. Ethnobotanical aspects of Snaketown, a Hohokam village in southern Arizona. *American Antiquity* 35:413-30.

Dennell, Robin W. 1979. Prehistoric diet and nutrition: Some food for thought. *World Archaeology* 11:121-35.

Farnsworth, Paul, James E. Brady, Michael J. DeNiro, and Richard S. MacNeish. 1985. A re-evaluation of the isotopic and archaeological reconstructions of diet in the Tehuacan Valley. *American Antiquity* 50:102-16.

Green, Francis. 1979. Collection and interpretation of botanical information from medieval urban excavations in southern England. In *Festschrift Maria Hopf,* ed. U. Körber-Grohne, pp. 39-55. Cologne: Rhienland-Verlag GMBH.

Hillman, Gordon C. 1984. Interpretation of archaeological plant remains: The application of ethnographic models from Turkey. In *Plants and ancient man,* ed. W. van Zeist and W. A. Casparie, pp. 1-41. Rotterdam: A. A. Balkema.

Johannessen, Sissel. 1984. Paleoethnobotany. In *American Bottom archaeology,* ed. Charles J. Bareis and James W. Porter, pp. 197-214. Urbana: University of Illinois Press.

Lopinot, Neal B. 1984. Archaeobotanical formation processes and Late Middle Archaic human-plant interrelationships in the midcontinental U.S.A. Ph.D. diss., Department of Anthropology, Southern Illinois University. Ann Arbor: University Microfilms.

MacNeish, Richard S. 1967. A summary of the subsistence. In *Environment and subsistence: Prehistory of the Tehuacan Valley,* vol. 1, ed. D. Byers, pp. 290-309. Austin: University of Texas.

Miller, Naomi F. 1982. Environment and economy of Malyan, a third millennium B.C. urban center in southern Iran. Ph.D. diss., Department of Anthropology, University of Michigan. Ann Arbor: University Microfilms.

_____. 1985. Paleoethnobotanical evidence for deforestation in ancient Iran: A case study of urban Malyan. *Journal of Ethnobiology* 5: 1-19.

Miller, Naomi F., and Tristine L. Smart. 1984. Intentional burning of dung as fuel: A mechanism for the incorporation of charred seeds into the archeological record. *Journal of Ethnobiology* 4:15-28.

Minnis, Paul E. 1978. Paleoethnobotanical indicators of prehistoric environmental disturbance: A case study. In *The nature and status of ethnobotany,* ed. Richard I. Ford, M. Brown, M. Hodge, and W. L. Merrill pp. 347-66. Anthropological Papers no. 60. University of Michigan, Museum of Anthropology.

Mueller, J. H., K. F. Schuessler, and H. L. Costner. 1974. *Statistical reasoning in sociology* 2d ed. Boston: Houghton Mifflin.

Pearsall, Deborah M. 1983. Evaluating the stability of subsistence strategies by use of paleoethnobotanical data. *Journal of Ethnobiology* 3:121-37.

Pozorski, Shelia. 1983. Changing subsistence priorities and early settlement patterns on the north coast of Peru. *Journal of Ethnobiology* 3: 15-38.

Wright, H. T., N. F. Miller, and R. W. Redding. 1981. Time and process in an Uruk rural center. In *L'archéologie de l'Iraq: perspectives et limites d'interpretation anthropologique des documents.* Paris: Colloques Internationaux du C.N.R.S. 580:265-82.

6

Archaeological Plant Remains: Applications to Stratigraphic Analysis

David L. Asch and Nancy Asch Sidell

Establishing the cultural affiliation of archaeological materials at sites having multiple occupations is one of the classical technical problems of archaeology. In the American Midwest, strategies and techniques of stratigraphic analysis have improved greatly since the days when deep sites were excavated in one-foot levels by geologically untutored investigators, with stratigraphic correlations tied largely to the distribution of a few artifact types that were thought to be temporally diagnostic. Still, stratified sites seldom conform very closely to a layer cake scheme of sealed and separated occupations, and there usually remain uncertainties in the archaeologist's segregation of assemblages from different components.

The thesis of this paper is that archaeological plant remains can contribute to stratigraphic interpretation. Upon reflection, the assertion seems obvious, yet plant remains rarely have been used for this purpose. In part, the neglect can be understood as a consequence of how research programs typically are organized. Plant remains usually are collected in bulk samples, and special processing is required to concentrate and clean them. Often, therefore, botanical collections only become available for study after the field work has been completed and most of the stratigraphic puzzle solving accomplished. Moreover, the botanical analyst commonly is a specialist who was not directly involved in recovering the remains. Because analysis is costly, the research director may choose to submit for identification only those remains that came from culturally unambiguous contexts. Thus the archaeological botanist becomes a consumer of stratigraphic interpretations derived from nonbotanical sources, rather than a collaborator in the development of the stratigraphy.

The usefulness of a botanical record for stratigraphic interpretation will depend on how plant remains have accumulated at a site. Let us consider two ideal models of accumulation. We will label them the "patchwork model" and the "homogenization model." They represent extremes in patterns of accumulation, and real-world data will fall somewhere in between. The patchwork model recognizes that human behavior is spatially organized and, accordingly, that at any moment of a site's occupation, the production of preservable remains such as charcoal will be spatially differentiated. If the remains do not subsequently become dispersed and intermingled, then—as sediments accumulate—the vertical sequence at a specific location will reflect a stacked sequence of activities. At a single locus, the stratigraphic potential of the record of plant remains will depend on how often activities varied there and on the extent of vertical mixing by postdepositional processes. If there was strongly expressed horizontal differentiation in the deposition of plant materials, then different loci may have very dissimilar botanical stratigraphies. If the patchwork model holds strictly, plant remains will not contribute efficiently to the establishment of stratigraphic intercorrelations across a site.

The homogenization model refers to the case in which plant remains from different locations within an occupation area show total spatial disorganization, so that archaeobotanical samples from the occupation are redundant in composition (though the overall charcoal concentrations may vary). The model is extreme, but it has been our experience, as well as that of other archaeobotanists, that to a first approximation, plant remains from midwestern sites often approach this distribution. Several factors can contribute to formation of a high-entropy record. For better or worse, archaeologists do tend to concentrate their investigations on sites within precincts that are richly productive of cultural debris. Such locations are likely to have served as multipurpose activity areas for a prehistoric community. For an intensive occupation, charcoal typically is a by-product of innumerable episodes of cooking and heating, with the remains of the various episodes becoming intermingled—partly because ashes were dispersed from the fires in which they were produced and partly because the locations of various activities have shifted during the occupation. Horizontal homogenization is perhaps most likely to result from intensive occupation by communities which lacked a well-organized system of refuse disposal and which had no permanent houses or facilities, that is, loci around which activities would recur over several years' time. The significance of horizontal homogenization for stratigraphic interpretation is that it increases the opportunity of finding correlated vertical sequences across the site.

Only to a limited degree do collections of plant remains contain temporally diagnostic indicators: indicators such as maize—a relatively late prehistoric introduction to the Midwest—or wheat, signifying Euroamerican disturbance. Instead, stratigraphy can be inferred from vertical changes in the relative frequencies of plant remains. Some attributes of the botanical record make it especially useful for this type of analysis:

1. Typically, plant charcoal is widely dispersed at prehistoric midwestern sites, occurring in virtually every context where material remains are preserved.

2. Because assemblages of plant remains have a diverse constitution, there are numerous potential indexes of systematic variation. For a midwestern site, for example, we can examine ratios of wood to nutshell, the composition of nutshell or wood charcoal spectra, the occurrence of tubers, or the composition of seeds and their abundance relative to other charcoal.

3. Empirically, we find that successive occupations at sites do frequently exhibit strong and consistent differences in archaeobotanical sample composition (cf. Asch and Asch 1985:393-98, Johannessen 1984).

4. Though archaeological plant materials are visually unimpressive in bulk, identifiable plant fragments are generally far more numerous in a midden than are temporally diagnostic markers, especially for preceramic occupations. For instance, in flotation samples from the Napoleon Hollow site, discussed below, 1 gram of charcoal from a > 2 mm sieve fraction contained about 100 fragments.

5. Given homogenization, flotation processing thus can readily provide statistically large samples of charcoal fragments. This minimizes meaningless between-sample fluctuations which stem from vagaries of small sample size.

6. Because charcoal fragments often are numerically abundant, it is possible to examine botanical variation within closely separated levels of intergrading occupational layers.

7. Where one lacks a finely resolved sequence of temporal diagnostics to partition successive occupations, conceivably debris classes such as plant remains can distinguish occupations, should there be activity variation from one occupation surface to the next.

8. Plant remains can aid in defining the cultural stratigraphy, which may not be a simple reflection of a site's natural sedimentary stratigraphy.

Uses of archaeobotanical stratigraphy can be illustrated from studies conducted at the Napoleon Hollow site in the lower Illinois River Valley. Napoleon Hollow is a stratified multicomponent habitation site that was excavated between 1979 and 1981 under the direction of Michael D. Wiant

(Wiant 1980; Wiant, Hajic, and Styles 1983; Wiant and McGimsey 1986; Styles 1985). The site is located at the western margin of the Illinois Valley where it extends from a colluvial slope onto the river's floodplain (figure 6.1). Three major Archaic occupations were identified on the colluvial

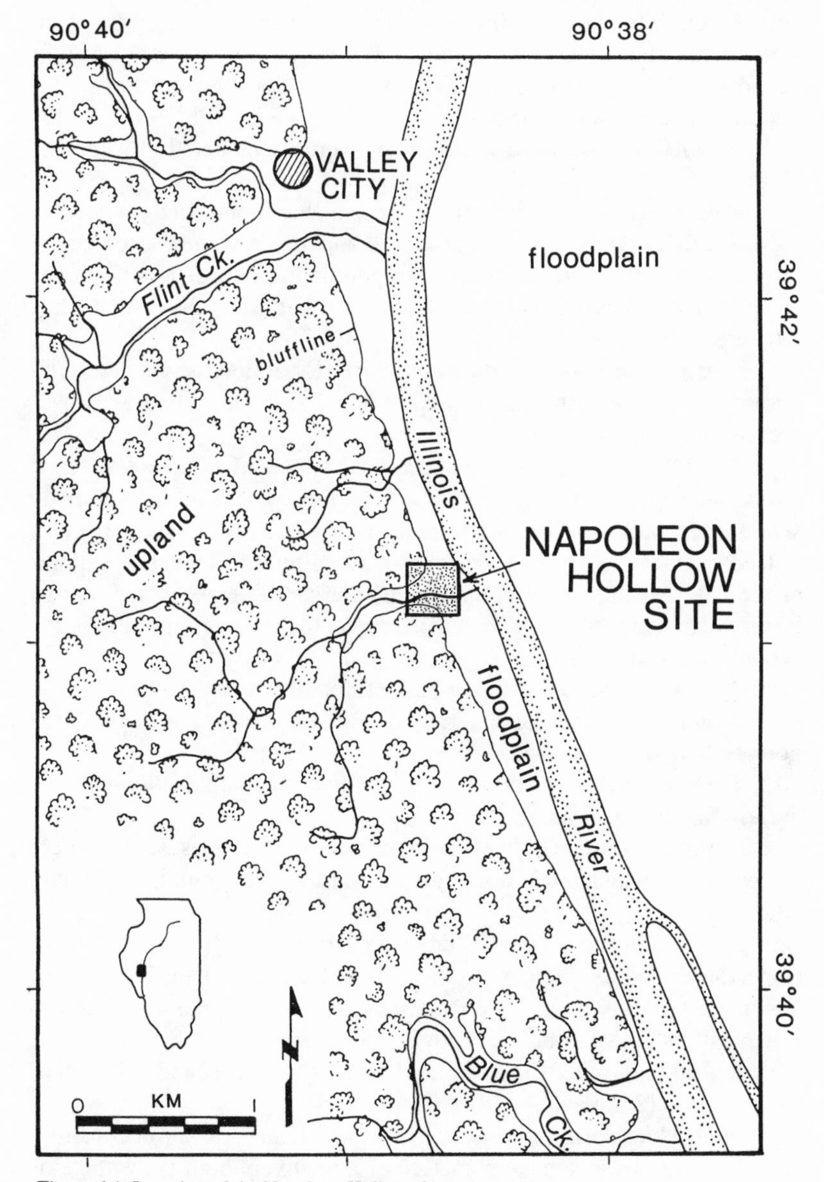

Figure 6.1. Location of the Napolean Hollow site.

slope. Each occupation was associated with, but not delimited by, one of the three dark soil horizons visible in the profile illustrated in figure 6.2. The earliest of these occupations has been dated between 7050 B.P. and 6630 B.P. on the Libby radiocarbon scale. The middle occupation was dated between 6080 B.P. and 5140 B.P., and a Late Archaic occupation of the Titterington phase occurred around 4000 B.P. A sparse scatter of Middle Woodland debris from about 2000 B.P. was found at the top of the uppermost buried soil horizon.

Some difficult stratigraphic problems were encountered at Napoleon Hollow:

1. It was necessary to construct and to correlate cultural stratigraphies for the colluvial slope and for the river floodplain. An episode of lateral migration by Napoleon Creek extensively eroded the base of the fan, erasing some of the evidence of occupation surfaces that originally spanned this juncture.

2. Successive occupations on the colluvial slope intergraded tratigraphically. For example, in the illustrated profile (figure 6.2), cultural debris was present from top to bottom of the sequence.

3. The Archaic components had a rather low density of time-diagnostic artifacts, chiefly projectile points, so that mixing could be difficult to recognize, especially if one relied solely on the evidence of such artifacts. Indeed, through the first field season, so few culturally diagnostic artifacts of the Late Archaic Titterington occupation had been recovered that its integrity could not be established with respect to the superimposed Middle Woodland occupation.

4. Stylistic differences among projectile points from the two Middle Archaic horizons were scarcely great enough to differentiate the occupations on that basis.

5. There was some reworking of the sediments on the colluvial slope during and after occupations.

6. During the initial field season, a series of scattered test squares were excavated, for which it was necessary to establish stratigraphic intercorrelations.

Figure 6.3 illustrates one of the botanical sequences from the colluvial slope, developed for charcoal from a 2.8-m-deep test square (square 36). The profile is based on a vertical sequence of 50 flotation samples. Botanical zones A through D were defined essentially independently of other information about the site and then were correlated with other stratigraphies (Asch and Asch 1980).

Zone D, which corresponds with the earlier Middle Archaic occupation, has the distinctive botanical signature of a relatively high percentage of pecan and black walnut nutshell. This contrasts with the near exclusive

Figure 6.2. Three buried soils on the colluvial fan. The lowermost soil is associated with the earlier Middle Archaic component, the middle soil with the later Middle Archaic component, and the uppermost soil with the Titterington Late Archaic component and later minor occupation. Reproduced from Styles (1985: fig. 24).

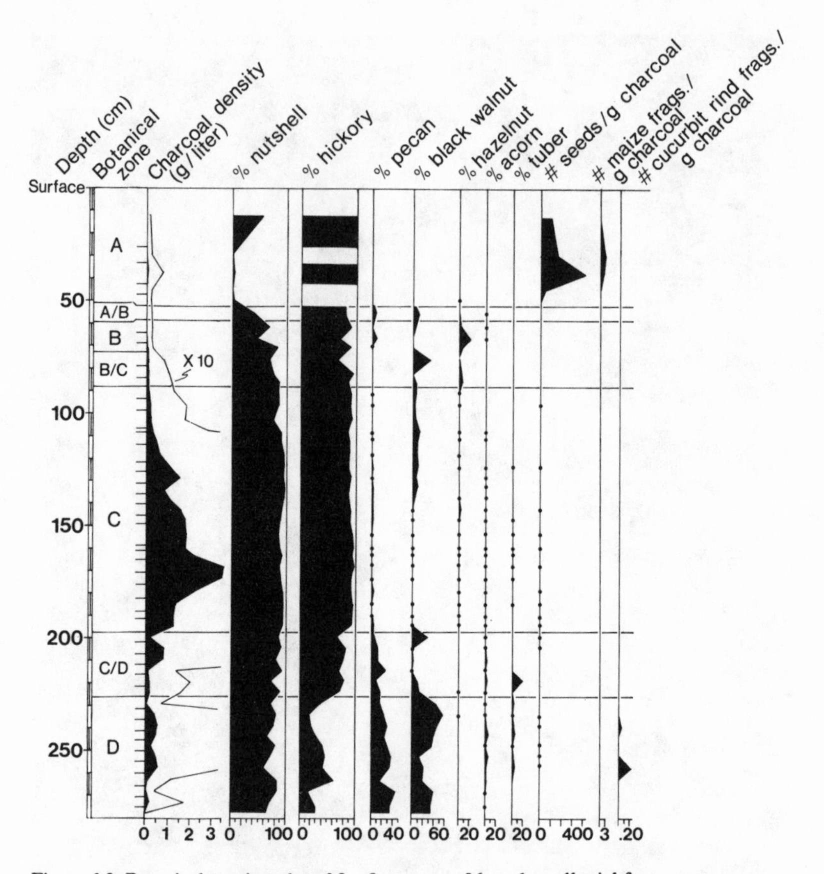

Figure 6.3. Botanical stratigraphy of 2 x 2 m square 36 on the colluvial fan.

occurrence of hickory nutshell in the overlying occupation of zone C. The percentage of nutshell relative to all charcoal types in zone D samples also was slightly, but consistently, less than for the zone C occupation. Another difference (not illustrated in figure 6.3) is that in the earlier Middle Archaic occupation of zone D, fragments of elm-family wood charcoal outnumbered oak-hickory wood charcoal by a margin of 4 to 1; the ratio was reversed for the subsequent zone C occupation.

There were small but distinct differences in the composition of zone C and zone B charcoal. In other test units than square 36 illustrated in figure 3, zone B stood out in its unusually high frequency of seeds. Elm-family wood also was better represented in zone B than in zone C. Though zone A contained some prehistoric debris, this uppermost botanical unit represents primarily a historic accumulation. The very high seed frequency in zone A is due to an abundance of *Polygonum pensylvanicum* (a smartweed), a species which was infrequent in the older deposits.

The botanical profile contributed interesting information about the vertical contacts of occupations. Zone C/D lies between the lower two dark A horizons seen in figure 6.2. It contained large mottles of darker sediment within the lighter matrix. Flotation samples revealed that the darker sediment had a composition like zone C, while the lighter sediment bodies had the characteristic charcoal signature of zone D. Thus, apparently this transition zone owed its intermediate character, not to gradual changes in plant use, but rather to physical mixing of the sediments from successive occupations.

Botanical zone C, it was found, incorporated not only the middle, somewhat eroded A-horizon soil but also the lighter sediment body above it. Either the substantial charaoal content of the overlying lighter unit was redeposited from sediments higher on the colluvial slope or else culturally similar occupations continued during and after the soil-forming episode.

Finally, the curve of charcoal density in zone B/C suggests that the Late Archaic Titterington midden unit was contaminated by a substantial fraction of charcoal from the earlier occupation. Had the density of Titterington charcoal not been much less than that of the intergrading earlier occupation, the Titterington botanical signature might have been sharper.

The point cannot be elaborated here, but we found that the vertical organization of charcoal seen in square 36 was similar across Napoleon Hollow's colluvial slope and that some of these botanical zones, as well as others, could be recognized in the adjacent floodplain. Though Napoleon Hollow was no botanical layer cake, plant-stratigraphic intercorrelations basically were no less evident and no less consistent than were intercorrelations of other cultural and natural data sets. Moreover, the stratigraphic implications of the Napoleon Hollow plant remains were generally conformable with those of a variety of artifact and debris classes and with the natural sedimentary record (M. D. Wiant, pers. com. 1987).

A second example of archaeobotanical stratigraphy comes from recent work at the Naples-Abbott site located a few kilometers upstream from Napoleon Hollow on the east bank of the Illinois River. There, in 1986, Barbara D. Stafford briefly investigated a buried 1-meter-thick midden/cumulic A-horizon that was exposed along a cutbank (Stafford 1987). The overlying sediments were culturally sterile, and pottery sherds recovered from the midden were exclusively of Middle Woodland origin (ca. 2,000 years old) except for two older Early Woodland sherds. No stratigraphy of Middle Woodland ceramic styles was noted, and indeed virtually the only field evidence of vertical organization within the buried midden was a consistent concentration of chunks of burnt limestone 20 cm to 30 cm above its base. Accordingly, at first it was believed that plant remains of the midden could be attributed to a single Middle Woodland occupation.

Three flotation columns were taken along the cutbank exposure, spaced at intervals of 10 m and 5 m. Each column sampled the midden in 7 or 8 arbitrary 10-cm levels. Botanical analysis (Asch and Asch 1987) disclosed a similar vertical organization of charcoal from each sample column: (A) two peaks of charcoal concentration—at the top of the midden and again near its base; (B) wood charcoal fragments outnumbering nutshell fragments at the top of the midden by a margin of 3 to 1 or more, reversal of the wood-to-nut ratio in middle levels, and a return at the bottom to wood dominance by about a 2 to 1 margin; and (C) concentration of carbonized seeds of probable noneconomic plants at the top of the midden, in contrast to predominance at lower levels of small starchy seeds belonging to the prehistoric Eastern Agricultural complex. The amount of charcoal collected was small, only 19 g in all, yet it included over 800 fragments in the >2mm size fraction and 636 seed specimens, mostly smaller than 2 mm. The numerical abundance of charcoal particles was great enough to establish that the vertical pattern—whatever its cause—was not simply a statistical fluke of sampling.

Radiocarbon dating was employed to test for a temporally meaningful stratigraphy at Naples-Abbott, using as samples the same charcoal upon which the botanical profiles were generated. In order to have enough carbon, it was necessary to combine flotation samples across the three columns. The resulting Libby radiocarbon ages—representing upper, middle, and lower midden levels, respectively—were 730±120 B.P. (ISGS-1644), 1810±70 B.P. (ISGS-1650), and 2100±130 B.P. (ISGS-1645). Since the ceramic types recovered from the Naples-Abbott midden are known to predate 1700 B.P., unquestionably most of the top-level charcoal was post-Middle Woodland in age (possibly noncultural in origin). The bottom-level sample dated 290 years older than the mid-level sample, and the difference in age estimates is enough to establish quite definitely that these samples contained charcoal produced over a long period.

Napoleon Hollow and Naples-Abbott, we believe, are not isolated, rarely-to-be-encountered examples of situations in which archaeobotanical materials could contribute to stratigraphic delineation. To the contrary, at multicomponent sites where we have taken the trouble to look, a stratigraphic organization of the archaeobotanical record had often been apparent. Furthermore, although this paper has emphasized applications of botanical stratigraphy in situation conforming to the horizontal homogenization model, one can readily think of interpretative uses for profiles of botanical remains at specific locations within a site which require no assumptions about the horizontal distribution of charcoal.

Speaking as archaeological botanists, we are committed to the development of botanical profiles since this technique provides an independent means of verifying stratigraphic conclusions with our own data sets. One reason to seek confirming evidence of stratigraphy is the possibility that vertical mixing of small objects like charcoal has resulted from processes (such as activities of soil microfauna) that are not identical to those that churn larger culturally diagnostic artifacts. Conceivably after years of bioturbation plant remains discarded on the same surface with projectile points may develop a different vertical distribution than the points.

As we asserted at the outset, the neglect of botanical stratigraphy in archaeology may be due partly to the organization of the research effort and to an isolation of specialist analyses from the mainstream of excavation strategy and evaluation of site structure. Field archaeologists should be urged to collect finely sampled botanical columns. Even if few are analyzed immediately, the samples can be held in reserve should stratigraphic questions arise for which a botanical analysis might prove illuminating. Also, since many excavations of stratified sites are multiseason operations, even if columns cannot be processed and analyzed with a short turnaround, the off-season gives time for analysis and feedback into the excavation program.

Acknowledgments

This chapter was Center for American Archeology, Archaeobotanical Laboratory, Report no. 71b. We thank Michael D. Wiant and Barbara D. Stafford for the opportunity to participate in the Napoleon Hollow and Naples-Abbott projects and for discussions that helped to shape this paper. We thank James Schoenwetter for comments on the original draft. Research reported in this paper was funded by the Illinois Department of Transportation and U.S. Army Corp of Engineers (St. Louis District). The Center for American Archeology funded preparation of the manuscript.

References Cited

Asch, David L., and Nancy B. Asch. 1985. Archeobotany. In *Smiling Dan: Structure and function at a Middle Woodland settlement in the lower Illinois Valley*, ed. B. D. Stafford and M. B. Sant, pp. 327-401. Research Series, vol. 2. Kampsville, Ill.: Center for American Archeology.

——. 1987. Middle Woodland and Historic Indian archeobotany of the Naples-Abbott site (Tabbycat and Smith areas), Scott County, Illinois.

In *Archeological Testing of the Naples-Abbott site: Smith and Tabbycat areas, Scott County, Illinois,* by B. D. Stafford, pp. 88-107. St. Louis District Historic properties Management Report no. 35. St. Louis: U.S. Army Corps of Engineers.

Asch, Nancy B., and David L. Asch. 1980. Archeobotany of Napoleon Hollow, a multicomponent site in Pike County, Illinois: Initial report. In *Napoleon Hollow interim report*, ed. M. D. Wiant, pp. 137-65. Report of Investigations no. 76a. Kampsville, Ill.: Center for American Archeology.

Johannessen, Sissel. 1984. In *American Bottom archaeology: A summary of the FAI-270 archaeological project*, ed. C. J. Bareis and J. W. Porter, pp. 197-214. Urbana: University of Illinois Press.

Stafford, Barbara D. 1987 *Archeological Testing of the Naples-Abbott site: Smith and Tabbycat areas, Scott County, Illinois.* St. Louis District Historic Properties Management Report no. 35 St. Louis: U.S. Army Corps of Engineers.

Styles, Thomas R. 1985. *Holocene and Late Pleistocene geology of the Napoleon Hollow site in the lower Illinois Valley.* Research Series vol. 5. Kampsville, Ill.: Center for American Archeology.

Wiant, Michael D., ed. 1980. *Napoleon Hollow interim report.* Report of Investigations no. 76a. Kampsville, Ill.: Center for American Archeology, Contract Archeology Program.

Wiant, Michael D., Edwin R. Hajic, and Thomas R. Styles. 1983. Napoleon and Koster site stratigraphy: Implications for Holocene landscape evolution and studies of Archaic period settlement patterns in the lower Illinois River Valley. In *Archaic hunters and gatherers in the American Midwest,* ed. J. L. Phillips and J. A. Brown, pp. 147-64. New York: Academic Press.

Wiant, Michael D., and Charles R. McGimsey, ed. 1986. *Woodland period occupations of the Napoleon Hollow site in the lower Illinois Valley.* Research Series vol. 6. Kampsville, Ill: Center for American Archeology.

7

Interpreting the Meaning of Macroremain Abundance: The Impact of Source and Context

Deborah M. Pearsall

Introduction

Several excellent articles written recently discuss sources of seeds in archaeological sites and the importance of considering what influence seed source and context of deposition of seeds have on how paleoethnobotanists interpret plant remains (Dennell 1976; Hubbard 1976; Miller and Smart 1984; Minnis 1981). These considerations also have important implications for quantitative analysis of seeds and other types of macroremains. However abundance may be measured, a basic question remains after calculations are done: what is the meaning of abundance? How does the source and context of deposition of a seed or other macroremain affect the meaning of abundance measures of that remain?

In this paper I address the quantitative issue of macroremains source and depositional context using paleoethnobotanical data from Panaulauca cave, Peru. I detail possible sources of macroremains recovered from Panaulauca and evaluate the impact of source on interpretation of two abundance measures. I then define depositional contexts present at the site and evaluate the impact of context on interpretation of small seed abundance. I hope to demonstrate that whatever quantitative approach one uses, a reliable interpretation of results depends on understanding the processes that led to deposition and preservation of remains. I define possible sources of macroremains to provide a clearer understanding of changing patterns of abundance through time. Detailed analysis of the variation of remains by

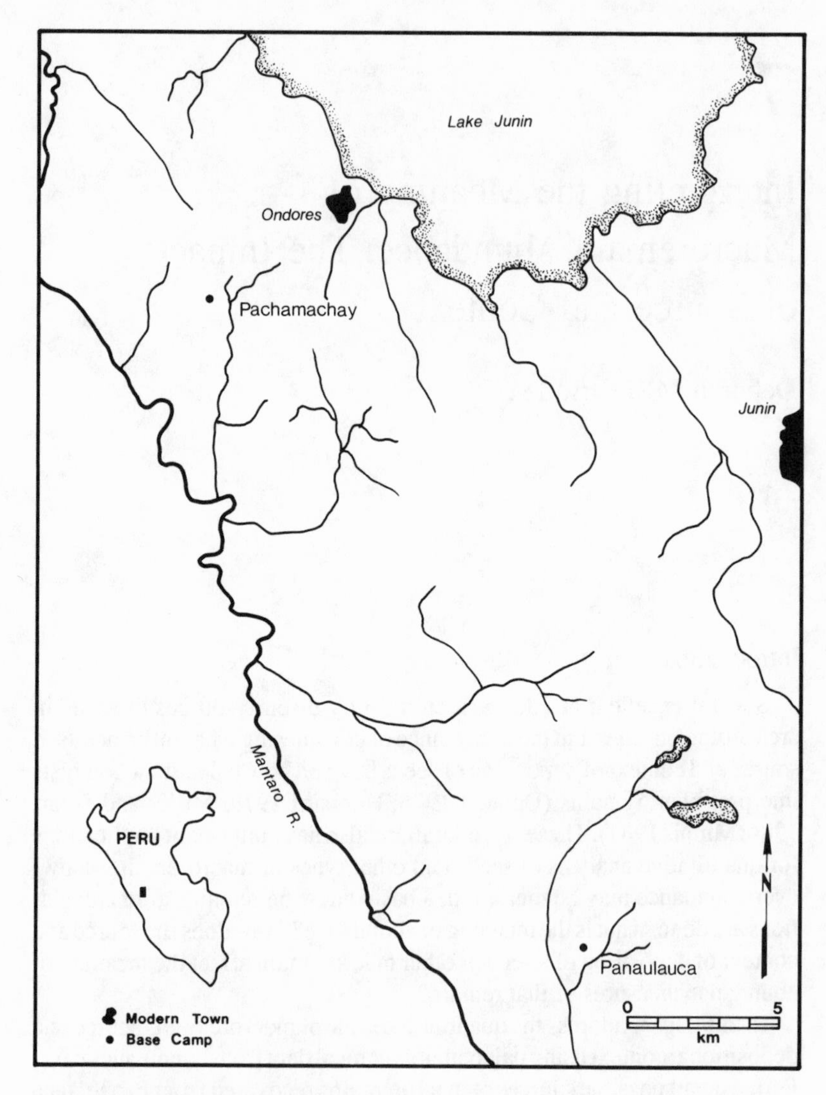

Figure 7.1. Map of the project study area.

depositional context enhances our understanding of depositional processes at the site.

Panaulauca is a limestone rock shelter located at 4150 m on the land of S.A.I.S. Atocsayco, in central Peru (fig. 7.1). I use data from this site to illustrate the impact of macroremains source and depositional context on

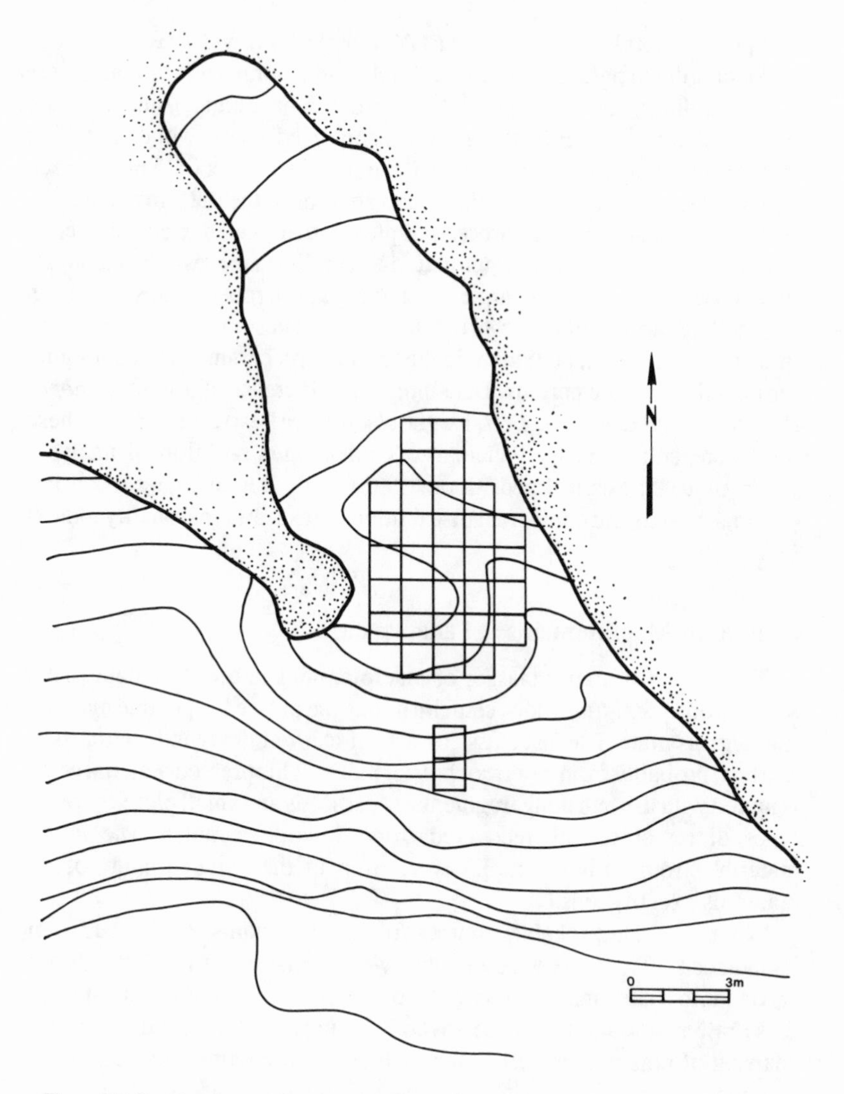

Figure 7.2. Panulauca cave, showing placement of excavation units.

interpretation of abundance measures, because it was during the Panaulauca project I realized these issues were vital to understanding paleoethnobotanical data. Excavations, directed by John W. Rick, consisted of 31 contiguous 1 x 1 m units, placed in the cave mouth, and two 1 x 1 m units on the talus slope (fig. 7.2). Data discussed in this paper come from strata dated from just prior to 3000 B.C. (level 22) to A.D. 500-600 (level 7)(Rick 1984).

Standardized paleoethnobotanical field and laboratory techniques were followed during this project. Only charred archaeological materials are preserved at the site. Flotation samples contained seeds, wood, and other materials ranging in size from about 0.5 mm to just under 0.25 in. Charred materials recovered in situ during excavation or in the 0.25-in excavation screens were designated carbon samples and included wood charcoal, whole taproots, and other larger materials. Preliminary results of analysis of seeds from flotation and larger charred *Lepidium* root remains have been reported (Pearsall 1983, 1984). I found evidence of changes in plant utilization at the site; beginning in the terminal preceramic and continuing through the ceramic periods. Data indicate an increase in use of *Chenopodium* seeds and *Lepidium* roots. I argue elsewhere (Pearsall 1986) that these taxa were cultivated by Panaulauca's inhabitants. Additional analyses (Pearsall 1985; Pearsall and Moore 1985) deal with changing wood use patterns, spatial and contextual distribution of taxa, and seasonality indicators.

Sources of Macroremains at Panaulauca

There are five major classes of macroremains at the Panaulauca site: seeds, wood, *Lepidium* roots, camelid dung, and pressed vegetable material (puna/grass mat). The last class consists of charred grass and compressed material probably from rosette or polster plants. This pressed material often is mixed with ash and dung fragments. Most seeds and small pieces of other types of remains were recovered from flotation samples. The larger materials from carbon samples were used in the detailed study of all materials except seeds.

What are the probable sources of macroremains recovered from Panaulauca? The issue of source has two aspects: how raw materials are carried into a site, and how charred, preservable remains are created from these raw materials. I propose several avenues for the introduction and charring of botanical materials for each class of remains recovered from Panaulauca.

Wood

1. Collected and burned as fuel
2. Used for tools, discarded, and burned
3. Used in construction and later dismantled and burned
4. Charred as the result of a sitewide conflagration

No evidence exists for a sitewide fire (no in situ burned posts, blanketing ash, etc.), so I assume that most wood charcoal recovered from Panaulauca came from burning firewood or from the occasional discarded wooden object or post in cooking or heating fires. The site is located above the modern tree line. Most identified wood is from small, local shrubs.

Camelid Dung

1. Collected and burned as fuel
2. Accidently burned in cooking or heating fires

Accidental deposition of charred dung would be an unlikely occurrence unless animals were corralled in the cave and the area then burned. There is no indication that this occurred in the periods under consideration here. It is far more likely that dung from wild, and later domesticated, camelids was deliberately collected as a fuel source in this cold, wood-scarce environment. Ethnographic data document use of camelid dung and dung from European domesticates as fuel in Peru (Winterhalder, Larson, and Thomas 1974).

Puna/Grass Mat

1. Cut as sod, or *champa*, and burned as fuel
2. Collected as individual plants and burned as fuel
3. Used in construction or for some other household purpose, discarded, and later burned
4. Accidently introduced and charred

Sod, generally containing *Distichia muscoides* polsters, is cut today as a source of fuel in the Andes. A number of other polster-forming plants and the bunchgrasses which dominate the puna landscape may also have been cut for fuel prehistorically. Pressed vegetable material recovered from Panaulauca is a mix of grass stems and other amorphous plant material not easily identified. If the Panaulauca inhabitants used earth ovens (*pachamancas*) for cooking meat and tuberous roots, they probably needed plant materials of various kinds to line these cooking pits and to cover food to protect it from the earth overburden.

Seeds

1. Gathered for food and accidently charred during cooking, parching, or other food preparation activities
2. Brought in as part of plants gathered for food and discarded as a waste portion
3. Brought in with plants gathered for nonfood purposes and discarded as a waste portion

4. Present in camelid dung or corral debris burned as fuel
5. Present in sod burned as fuel
6. Blown or carried in accidently and charred

These six processes probably charred different seed taxa. Ethnographies provide information on seeds used as foods and seeds which are discarded from edible fruit. Presence of seeds in human coprolites also indicates food use. I examined camelid dung and puna sod samples, both archaeological and modern comparative specimens, to determine what seeds would be charred when dung and sod were burned for fuel. Table 7.1 summarizes possible sources of seeds recovered at Panaulauca. While some taxa have only one likely source, others have several sources. It may be difficult to attribute a seed to only one of the several possible sources.

Roots

1. Gathered or grown for food and charred in the process of roasting
2. Present in sod cut for fuel and charred

The probable source for charred roots present in the upper strata of Panaulauca cave depends on their identification. Gross morphology and internal structure of remains indicate that they are probably enlarged taproots of *Lepidium* (Pearsall 1983, 1984). My examination of many other rosette plants using scanning electron microscopy showed that a small number of taxa resemble the archaeological type in some aspects of internal structure. However, these taxa differ in other respects (for example, size, growth habit). If, as I suggest, these remains are incipient cultivars of *Lepidium meyenii,* they are unlikely components of puna sod cut for fuel; their wild habitat is open, disturbed ground.

Interpreting Macroremain Abundance: Impact of Source

As discussed above, Panaulauca macroremains come from many sources. Analyzing Panaulauca seeds and Lepidium roots illustrates how knowledge of these sources affects interpretation of macroremain abundance. I will now examine how abundance of seeds varies through time (levels 21, 18, preceramic 16, ceramic 16, and 11) in one context, general midden deposit. I use two abundance measures: presence or ubiquity and frequency. Taxon presence is calculated by determining how many units (1 x 1 m squares) (fig. 7.2) on each floor contained the taxon. Presence is expressed as a percentage (number of units with taxon/total number of units

Table 7.1. Sources of seeds in the Panaulauca deposit

SEEDS USED AS FOOD

Festuca
Gramineae (large) [1]
Chenopodium
Amaranthus
Portulaca
Trifolium
Lupinus
Leguminosae
Polygonum
Zea mays

SEEDS BROUGHT IN WITH FOOD ITEM

Scirpus
Lepidium
Opuntia floccosa
Echinocactus
Solanum

SEEDS BROUGHT IN WITH NONFOOD ITEM

Festuca
Gramineae (large)
Scirpus
Relbunium
Galium
Compositae
Plantago
Labiatae

SEEDS PRESENT IN MAT

(1) Chupacancha observations
Gramineae (small)
Gramineae (medium)
Gramineae (large)
Relbunium
Cyperaceae

(2)Comparative mat observations
Gramineae (small)
Gramineae (large)
Luzula
Umbelliferae, ridged
Cyperaceae
Compositae

SEEDS PRESENT IN DUNG

(1) Chupacancha observations
Cyperaceae
Sisyrinchium
Relbunium
Calandrinia
Gramineae (medium)
Gramineae (large)

(2) Panaulauca observations
Calandrinia
Caryophyllaceae
Opuntia floccosa
Gramineae (small)

(3) Comparative vicuña observations
Sisyrinchium
Relbunium
Gramineae (small)
Gramineae (large)
Lupinus
Calandrinia

[1]Numerous grass seeds were observed in flotation and in comparative mat and dung samples which were difficlut to identify as to genus because of the great diversity of grasses in the puna zone. These are divided into small (ca. 0.5 mm), medium (0.5-1.0 mm), and large (> 1.0 mm) types.

in the level) (see Popper, chapter 4, on ubiquity). Taxon frequency is calculated by determining the total count of the taxon (five levels combined), then calculating what percentage of the total count occurs in each level (see Miller, chapter 5, on ratios). For *Lepidium* remains, I examine percentage presence per level for all completely excavated levels.

Seeds

The analysis groups seeds into four types of sources: (1) seeds whose probable source is camelid dung, (2) seeds used as food, or discarded from an edible fruit, (3) seeds from plants used for a purpose other than food, and (4) seed taxa with multiple sources (refer to table 7.1).

Seeds from Dung.

Of the seeds observed in camelid dung samples, *Sisyrinchium* (a low-growing herb) and small and medium Gramineae (grasses) probably only come from dung or perhaps burned puna mat. I know no other use for theseplants. *Calandrinia* (a small rosette) is another taxon probably deposited in the site from dung use. Figure 7.3 shows presence and frequency curves for these four taxa. The first three types are noteworthy for the lack, or near lack, of change in their presence over the five levels studied. *Calandrinia* shows no unidirectional change. Small and medium grass seeds also show little change over time when measured by frequency. The frequency curve for *Calandrinia* abundance parallels the presence curve. *Sisyrinchium*, by contrast, rises in frequency from level 21 to level ceramic 16 and declines in level 11.

Seeds from Foods

Chenopodium provides an example of seeds probably brought to the site for food. Abundant ethnographic and archaeological evidence exists for food use of *Chenopodium*, two species of which were ultimately brought under domestication in the Andes (*C. quinoa*, *C. pallidicaule*). Similarly, seeds of *Opuntia floccosa* and *Echinocactus* (polster-forming cacti) were probably deposited as waste from edible fruits. Puna inhabitants eat cactus fruits as a casual food source today. However, I did observe *Opuntia* seeds in one lot of camelid dung from the latest preceramic level (preceramic 16) at Panaulauca, suggesting the possibility of dung as an alternative source for Opuntia. I have not observed any *Chenopodium* or *Echinocactus* seeds in dung or puna mat samples. Figure 7.4 shows presence and frequency curves for these taxa. *Opuntia* shows little change in presence through time, remaining nearly ubiquitous. *Echinocactus* declines in ubiquity from earlier to later levels. *Chenopodium* shows the opposite trend: presence increases dramatically from level 18 to preceramic level 16 and remains high thereafter.

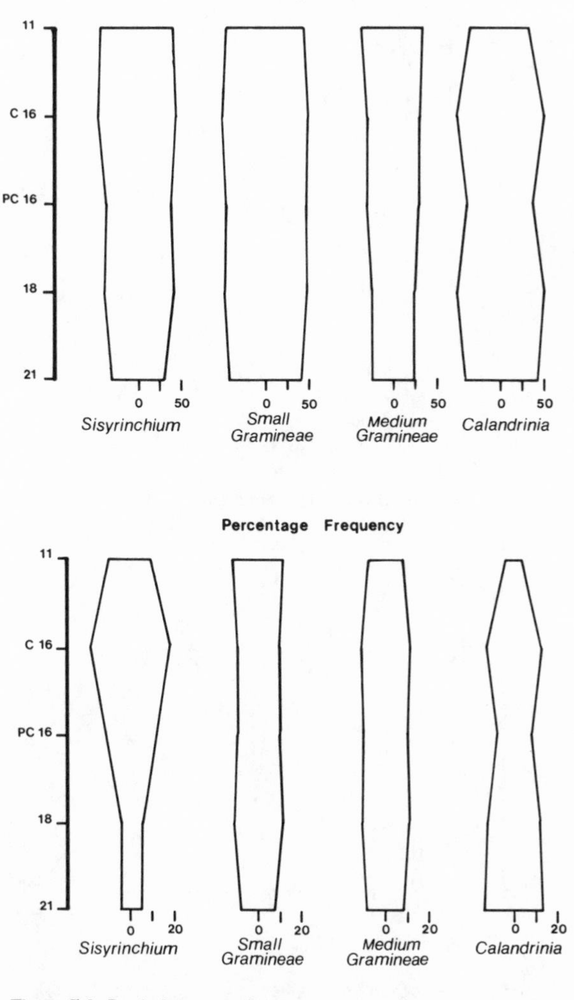

Figure 7.3. Seeds from camelid dung.

Frequency curves for *Opuntia*, *Echinocactus*, and especially *Chenopodium* show roughly the same pattern as presence curves. The frequency curve for *Echinocactus* indicates that seeds of this type are in fact concentrated by count in level 21, even though overall presence declines more gradually. The frequency curve for *Opuntia* is interesting in that it suggests a decline in abundance of this seed from level 18 onwards, rather than just in the final level, as indicated by the presence curve.

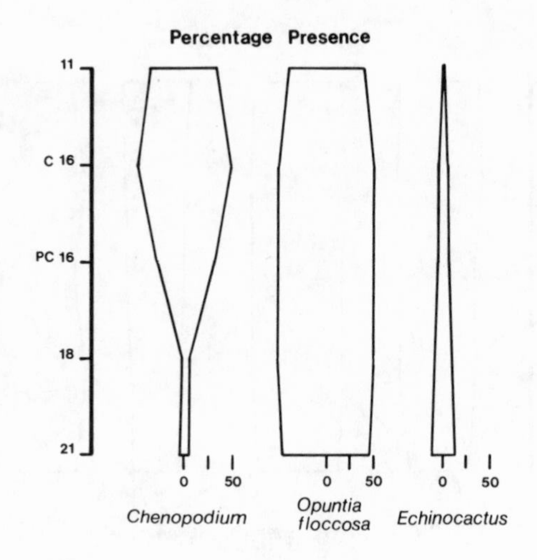

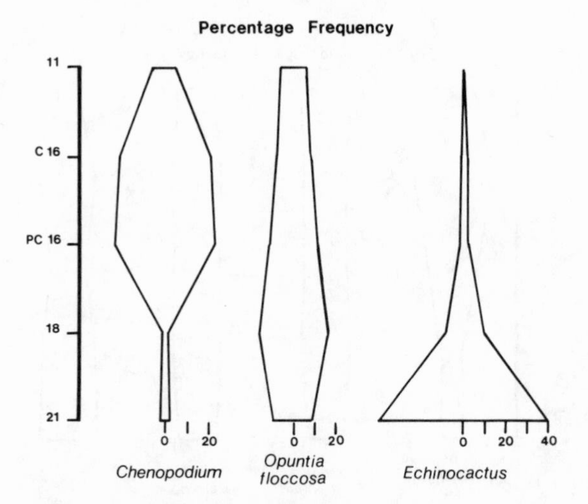

Figure 7.4. Seeds from food plants.

Seeds from Plants not used as Foods

I present Labiatae (mint family) and *Relbunium* (a small rosette) as examples of seeds likely brought in with plant material destined for nonfood use. Ethnographic accounts describe mint used to line tuber storage pits, and *Relbunium* is known to be a source of red dye (Soukup 1970; Towle 1961). Although I observed no Labiatae seeds in camelid dung or mat, *Relbunium* possibly came from this source (table 7.1). These taxa show variable

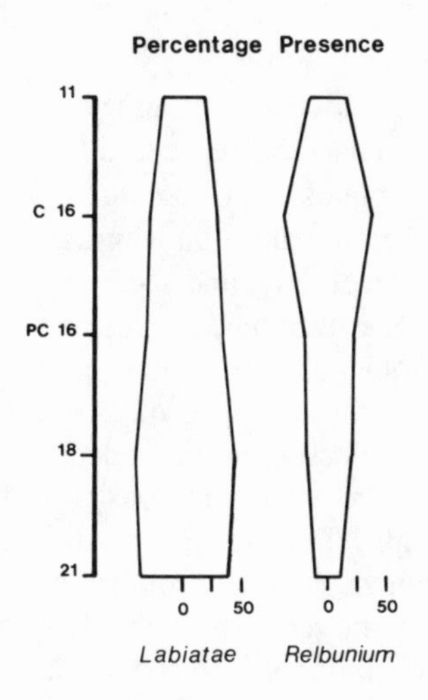

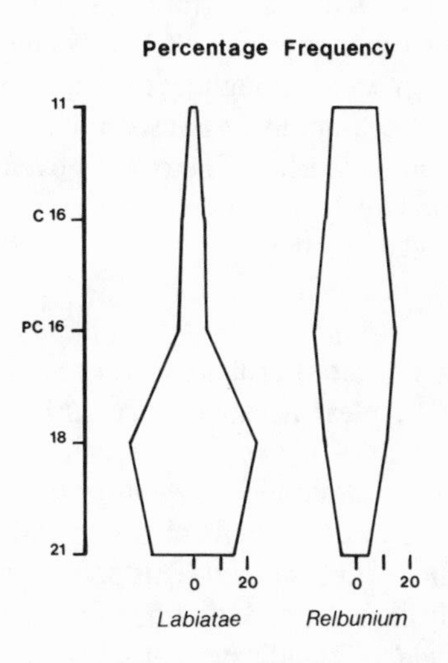

Figure 7.5. Seeds from plants used for household purposes.

abundance in the Panaulauca deposits (fig. 7.5). Labiatae presence falls gradually through time, while presence of *Relbunium* rises until ceramic level 16, then falls. The frequency curve for Labiatae parallels the presence curve but shows that most seeds of this taxon are concentrated in levels 21 and 18. The frequency curve for *Relbunium* shows a somewhat different trend from that of the presence curve, with the highest frequency of seeds in the preceramic 16 level.

Seeds with Multiple Sources

The final group of seeds I wish to discuss are four taxa with potentially multiple sources in the archaeological record (*Festuca*, large Gramineae, *Scirpus*, and small Leguminosae). One source is seeds brought in with nonfood uses. Seeds of *Festuca* (large bunchgrass), other larger grass seeds identified to the family level only, and seeds of *Scirpus*, or *totora* (giant bulrush) could have become deposited through use of their vegetative plant parts for some household purpose (thatch, mats, bedding, pit linings, baskets, etc.). Another source is seeds used as food. *Scirpus* rhizomes and grass seeds are edible. Collecting large-seeded grasses for food is documented in ethnographies from other regions (for example, Bohrer 1975; Doebley 1984). Although I have not observed *Festuca* seeds in camelid dung, I have seen other grass seeds and small Cyperaceae seeds (similar to *Scirpus*) there. Small legume seeds (probably from rosette taxa) also have several potential sources: food, burned sod, or dung.

The many potential sources of this group of seeds make interpretation of abundance measures particularly difficult. None of these taxa show a strong trend of change, being present throughout the deposit in varying quantities (Fig. 7.6). *Scirpus* and Leguminosae are somewhat more abundant in the later levels, *Festuca* in the earlier. The overall even abundance of these seeds may be explained by their many possible sources: sources may have varied from one period to another.

Discussion

To summarize the impact of probable seed source on interpretation of abundance measures, it is clear that abundance can have a different meaning depending on the source of the remains. Occurrences of *Sisyrinchium*, small, medium, and large Gramineae, *Calandrinia*, *Opuntia,* and Leguminosae were all characterized by high presence and frequency and little variation over the time periods studied. This pattern of seed occurrence for seeds which probably came from dung (*Sisyrinchium*, small and medium Gramineae, and *Calandrinia*) indicates consistent use of dung, or perhaps sod or corral debris, as a fuel source. It is interesting to note, however, that abundance of dung in the Panaulauca deposits, as measured by weight/cubic meter of deposit for dung recovered in carbon samples, is not consistent through time (fig. 7.7). When both dung and puna mat occurrence are considered, occurrence of nonwood fuel sources evens out somewhat. One explanation for this discrepancy is that dung and puna mat are underrepresented. Only carbon samples, containing whole dung pellets, large dung fragments, or masses of pressed vegetable material, were included in the calculation of weight/cubic meter of deposit. If highly fragmented dung and mat remains recovered in flotation samples had been included, a pattern

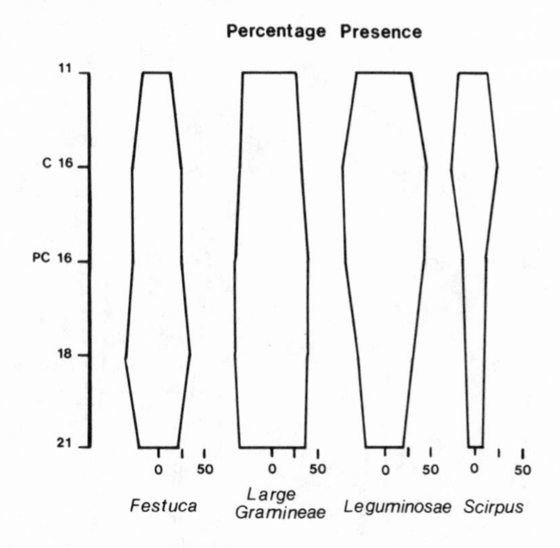

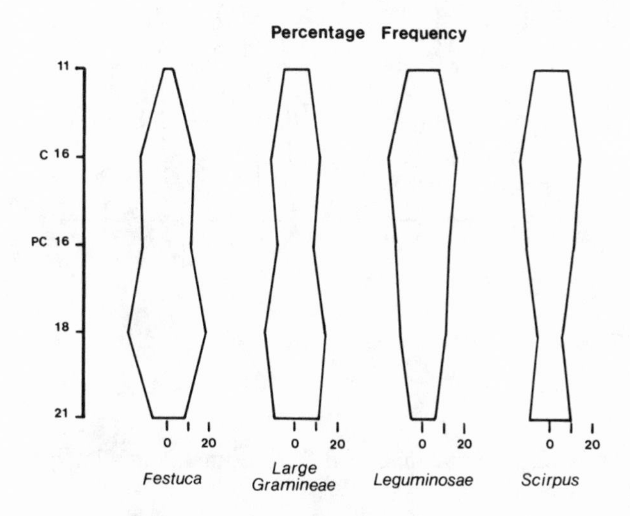

Figure 7.6. Seeds with multiple sources of origin.

of more even nonwood fuel abundance paralleling the pattern for abundance of seeds released from dung might have emerged.

A similar pattern of high presence and frequency for *Opuntia*, by contrast, indicates a consistent use of cactus fruits as a casual food source. The possibility of multiple sources for Leguminosae and Gramineae seeds,

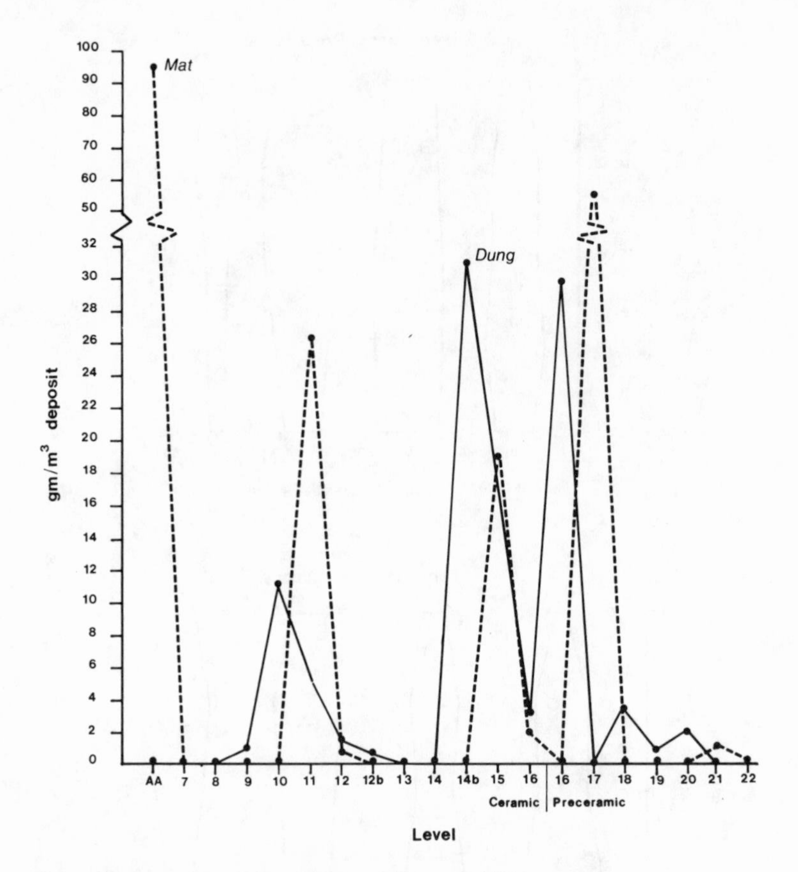

Figure 7.7. Occurrence of camelid dung and puna mat fuel.

as well as *Festuca*, *Relbunium*, and *Scirpus*, makes any interpretation of their abundance difficult.

Abundance of *Chenopodium* and *Echinocactus* seeds can be interpreted fairly securely as reflecting the importance or frequency of use of these resources as foods. These taxa show opposite trends, with *Chenopodium* increasing in use and *Echinocactus* decreasing in use, or perhaps in availability, over the time period studied.

In several of the cases described above, I note differences between abundance as measured by presence and frequency. It is beyond the scope of this paper to discuss why these measures differ or to assess which is the more accurate measure of abundance. Presence minimizes the impact of absolute quantity of remains, since 1 seed of taxon A/unit is equal to 100

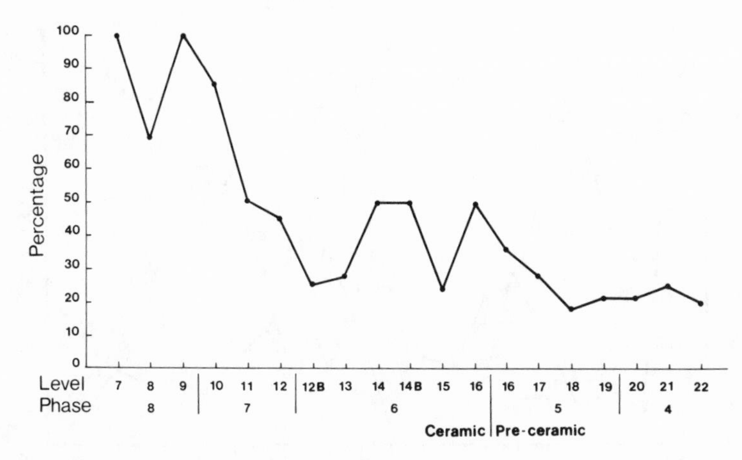

Figure 7.8. Percentage presence of *Lepidium* roots.

seeds of taxon A/unit. Since seed charring is accidental, minimizing the impact of absolute quantity seems a valid approach. Frequency as calculated here (summing each taxon through time, then calculating the percentage which occurs at each time level) is somewhat more subject to absolute quantity, since caches of seeds can skew a frequency curve.

Lepidium Roots

Considering the source of botanical remains is also important in the analysis of larger materials recovered during excavation. A brief discussion of *Lepidium* root abundance illustrates this point.

Figure 7.8 shows the abundance of *Lepidium* roots through time at Panaulauca cave as expressed by percentage presence in each fully excavated level. Overall, presence rises from level 22 to level 7, with several "plateaus" of abundance (e.g., 18-22, 11-preceramic 16, and 7-10). I have argued elsewhere (Pearsall 1983, 1984, 1986) that this pattern reflects increasing use of *Lepidium* roots as a food source and reflects an early phase of the process of domestication of *maca*.

Charring of *Lepidium* roots probably occurred during roasting. Is the abundance of these roots merely a function of the amount of burning activity going on at the site, or was use actually rising? Figure 7.9 shows the *Lepidium* presence curve graphed with the total weight of fuel (wood, dung, and mat) per cubic meter of deposit. There is little correspondence between these two curves. High values of *Lepidium* presence occur in levels where fuel remains are not abundant, and low values where fuel remains are abundant. It seems clear, therefore, that the *Lepidium* abundance reflects the importance and frequency of its use.

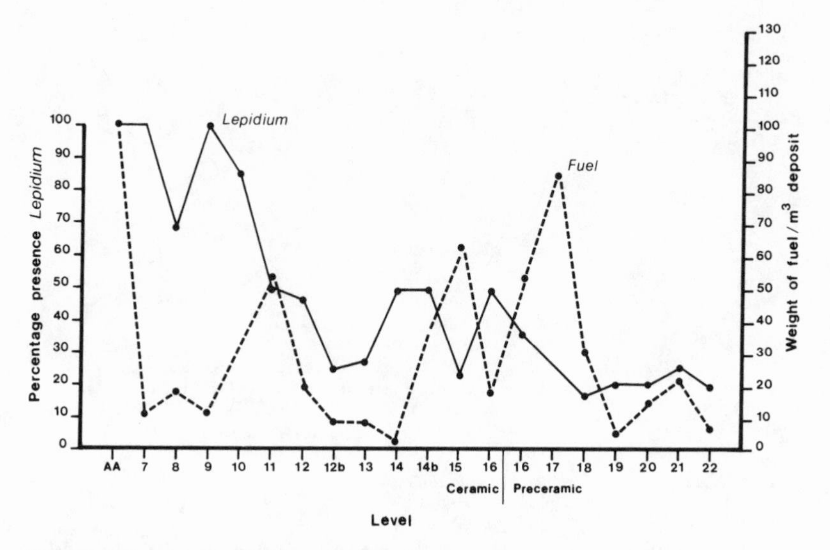

Figure 7.9. Comparison of abundance of *Lepidium* roots and total weight of all fuel sources.

Depositional Contexts at Panaulauca Cave

Because only charred botanical remains are preserved in the Panaulauca deposits, the ultimate sources of all macroremains were fires lit by the cave's inhabitants: surface cooking fires, fires lit for warmth or hide smoking, earth ovens, or similar contexts. Thus, the process of deposition of remains involves the outward movement of material from these primary burning contexts to other areas of the site, such as living floors, storage pits, and midden. It is also possible that fires were lit to burn garbage thrown onto the talus slope. The limited talus test excavation did not uncover evidence of this practice, however.

Redeposition of material was probably both deliberate and casual. The cave inhabitants probably cleaned out their hearths and dumped material outside the cave mouth area. Daily activities of a small band in the restricted cave mouth area also probably spread materials.

To examine variation in macroremain occurrence among different contexts at Panaulauca, I defined eight context types with the help of J. Rick: (1) general midden deposit within the cave mouth, (2) general midden deposit on the talus slope, (3) structures, (4) primary hearth features, (5) in situ ash lenses or other in situ burning features, (6) secondary ash deposition features, (7) pit features with no burning activity, and (8) burials (level 21 only). To illustrate variation in macroremain abundance among context types, I examine seed data from upper level 16, the initial ceramic period level at Panaulauca.

Interpreting Macroremain Abundance: Impact of Context

Table 7.2 summarizes distribution of seed types among the seven contexts occurring in ceramic level 16. For each context, I tabulated total seed count and expressed individual seed abundance as a percentage of that total. The number of flotation samples available for each context differed, varying from 1 talus midden sample to 17 samples from the cave mouth midden. Average seed counts per sample for each context also differed, varying from 38 seeds/sample for in situ ash deposits to 183 seeds/sample for structure F 129.

Summary of Seed Occurrences

The cave mouth midden context is characterized by high abundance of small Gramineae, *Opuntia*, and *Sisyrinchium*. *Chenopodium*, large Gramineae, and *Calandrinia* seeds are also fairly abundant.

The talus midden sample comes from one test square and has a relatively low seed count. Small Gramineae are most common, followed by *Opuntia* and *Calandrinia*. An unknown taxon named ("cf. *Chenopodium*"), a seed which looks like *Chenopodium* but is smaller, is also fairly common.

Structure F 129, which is a located in the cave mouth, incorporates six excavation squares and has several sublevels. Small Gramineae dominate the overall seed assemblage, followed by *Chenopodium*. *Calandrinia*, *Opuntia*, *Sisyrinchium*, and large Gramineae all occur fairly commonly.

Five hearths, all associated with structure F 129, were present in ceramic level 16. Small Gramineae dominated in this context, followed by *Chenopodium*. The next most abundant taxa were large Gramineae and *Opuntia*.

Three in situ ash deposits were examined. Small Gramineae were the most abundant seed in this context, followed by *Opuntia* and *Sisyrinchium*. *Calandrinia* and medium Gramineae were also fairly abundant.

Features judged to be areas of secondary dumping of ash and burned materials were dominated by *Opuntia*. Small and large Gramineae were also abundant. Moderate levels of Leguminosae, *Sisyrinchium*, and *Chenopodium* also occurred.

Two pit features characterized as having little evidence of burning activity or secondary deposition of burned material were examined. *Opuntia* seeds were the most abundant type present, followed by small Gramineae. *Calandrinia* and *Chenopodium* seeds, as well as a number of unknown taxa, were fairly common.

Table 7.2. Percentage seed occurrence among contexts (level 16 ceramic)

	Cave Mouth Midden	Talus Midden	F 129 Structure	in situ Hearth	in situ Ash	Secondary Ash	Feature Lacking Burning
Festuca	2.5	4.0	3.9	2.0		2.8	4.0
Gramineae (sm)	22.9	36.0	28.4	39.4	30.7	16.5	25.0
Gramineae (med)	4.5	5.9	3.4	7.9	4.2	4.0	
Gramineae (lge)	8.2	4.0	7.5	9.1	2.6	10.8	3.1
Scirpus	1.0		*				*
Cyperaceae	*						
Cyperaceae, thin			*		*		
Luzula	1.0		1.1	*	*	*	2.7
Sisyrinchium	11.3		7.4	6.2	13.2	9.4	*
Polygonum			*				
Chenopodium	8.7		12.0	14.7	5.3	8.0	6.7
Cf.*Chenopodium*		8.0			1.8	*	1.8
Amaranthus	*						
Portulaca	*		*				
Calandrinia	8.2	16.0	8.2	4.2	7.0	3.3	7.6
Cf. *Cerastium*							
Lepidium			*				
Cf. *Trifolium*	1.5		*	1.1	1.8	*	
Lupinus	*						
Leguminosae	3.7	4.0	3.1	3.1	1.8	9.4	1.8
Cf. Leguminosae							
Geraniaceae							
Malvastrum	1.4		1.2	1.4		1.9	*
Malvaceae	*		*				
Malvaceae, 2	*		*				
Opuntia floccosa	17.5	24.0	8.3	7.1	21.1	26.9	26.3
Echinocactus							
Umbelliferae, R.			*				*
Umbelliferae, P.	*						
Verbena	*						
Labiatae	2.3		2.4	2.5	*	1.4	1.3
Solanum							
Solanaceae							*
Plantago	*		*			*	
Relbunium	1.3	4.0	1.7	*	3.5	*	1.8
Galium							
Compositae	*						*
Compositae, 2	*		*				
Unknowns	3.4		6.7	4.5	*	*	10.7
Seed count	1,644	25	2,925	353	114	212	224
No. samples	17	1	16	5	3	4	2
Seeds/sample	97	25	183	71	38	53	112
Total seeds from dung	46.9	52.0	49.9	53.2	58.5	33.4	36.6

* less than 1% occurrence

Discussion

Several patterns of seed abundance emerge from these data and can be related to sample context. Structure F 129 and hearth samples associated with it are quite similar in relative abundances of major taxa. Note, for example, the higher percentage occurrences of *Chenopodium* and the lower levels of *Opuntia* in these two contexts. Since *Chenopodium* seeds probably came from accidental charring during cooking or parching of seeds, the similar abundance of this taxon in the hearth and structure contexts is not surprising.

The cave midden and structure F 129 contexts both have many rare seed types and an overall rich variety of taxa. The high seed counts of these contexts (i.e., the higher probability of recovering rarer types) probably account for this similarity.

Features characterized as areas of secondary deposition of ash and those showing little evidence of burning activity both exhibit high relative abundances of *Opuntia*. *Opuntia* is the most rugged seed in the Panaulauca seed assemblage and may have suffered less destruction than other seed taxa during redeposition or mixing with other refuse.

A final pattern of seed occurrence which may be related to sample context involves the relative abundances of seeds most likely deposited through dung burning. If percentages of small and medium Gramineae, *Calandrinia*, and *Sisyrinchium* are summed for each context (table 7.2), the primary burning contexts—ash lenses and hearths—show the highest levels of these seeds. Redeposited ash and features showing little evidence of burning activity have the lowest levels of these taxa.

I draw two general conclusions from this brief discussion of how seed abundances varied among contexts at Panaulauca. First, there is strong similarity in overall seed occurrence among the features and midden deposits of ceramic level 16. (This pattern is repeated in other levels [Pearsall 1985]). Overall, seed abundance varies more through time than through space at Panaulauca, a pattern probably related to the intensity of use of the small, sheltered, living area of the rock shelter. Activities of daily living have homogenized the deposits to the extent that all contemporaneous contexts are more similar to each other than to like contexts in earlier or later levels. At Panaulauca, variability of macroremain abundance among contexts depends not only on the original function of the context but its overall depositional history, which often included dispersal and mixing of remains.

Second although variation in seed assemblages and relative abundances of taxa among contexts is limited at Panaulauca, I discovered several informative patterns by grouping samples by feature type. The more ethnobotanists know about the cultural context of macroremains, the more information they gain in the final analysis.

Conclusions

In this paper I have addressed how the source of macroremains and the context of their deposition influence the meaning of abundance measures of macroremains. The realization that understanding sources and depositional histories of seeds is vital for interpreting macroremain assemblages is not new. The objective of this paper has been to extend this idea to quantification of botanical materials.

Using data from Panaulauca cave, Peru, I discussed sources of seeds, wood, *Lepidium* roots, camelid dung, and puna mat present at the site. Source has two aspects: how raw materials are introduced to a site and how charring occurs. The issue of seed source is particularly interesting because of the multiplicity of potential sources and the difficulty of distinguishing among sources in some cases. The Panaulauca example illustrates how the interpretation of abundance measures is dependent on the interpretation of the source. Abundance of some seeds indicates the importance of those taxa as foods, while other seed abundances indicate that dung or puna mat had been burned as fuel. In other words, the same pattern of abundance, for example high, consistent presence over time, may have a very different meaning depending on how the remains came to be introduced to the site.

The Panaulauca example also illustrates how the context of deposition of seeds can influence the interpretation of abundance. Although striking differences in seed assemblages across space (i.e., among contexts) were few at Panaulauca, a number did exist, such as variation in quantities of small Gramineae, *Chenopodium*, and *Opuntia*. I had to assess these differences among contexts not only in terms of the proposed function of the context (hearth, pit, structure, floor, etc.) but also in terms of the sources of the macroremains recovered. For example, understanding that certain seeds were likely components of dung burned as fuel led me to an explanation of why abundances of those taxa were higher in primary burning contexts. Although I considered sources of macroremains and contexts of their deposition separately in this paper, both form part of the process of incorporation of botanical remains into the archaeological record, and both must be understood before either taxa lists or abundance measures can take on meaning.

Acknowledgments

I thank J. Rick for the opportunity to participate in the Panaulauca project. Research was supported by a grant to Rick from the National Science Foundation and funding from the University of Missouri Research Council. Laboratory facilities and administrative support were provided by the University of Missouri, American Archaeology Division, M. J. O'Brien, Director. Figures were drawn by T. Holland.

References Cited

Bohrer, Vorsila L. 1975. The prehistoric and historic role of the cool-season grasses in the Southwest. *Economic Botany* 29(3):199-207.

Dennell, Robin W. 1976. The economic importance of plant resources represented on archaeological sites. *Journal of Archaeological Science* 3:229-47.

Doebley, John F. 1984. Seeds of wild grasses: a major food of Southwestern Indians. *Economic Botany* 38(1): 52-64.

Hubbard, R. N. L. B. 1976. On the strength of the evidence for prehistoric crop processing activities. *Journal of Archaeological Science* 3:257-265.

Miller, Naomi F., and Tristine Lee Smart. 1984. Intentional burning of dung as fuel: A mechanism for the incorporation of charred seeds into the archeological record. *Journal of Ethnobiology* 4(1):15-28.

Minnis, Paul E. 1981. Seeds in archaeological sites: Sources and some interpretive problems. *American Antiquity* 46(1):143-152.

Pearsall, Deborah M. 1983. Utilization of plant resources by prehistoric populations of the Junin Puna, Peru. Paper Presented at the eighty-second meeting of the American Anthropological Association, Chicago.

——. 1984. Prehistoric adaptation to the Junin Puna, Peru: The role of plant resources. Paper presented at the forty-ninth annual meeting of the Society for American Archaeology, Portland.

——. 1985. Floral background and data. In Hunting and herding in the high altitude tropics: The early prehistory of the Central Peruvian Andes, ed. John W. Rick.

——. 1986. Adaptation of prehistoric hunter-gatherers to the high Andes: The changing role of plant resources. Paper presented at the World Archaeology Congress, Southampton, England.

Pearsall, Deborah M., and Katherine Moore. 1985. Prehistoric economy and subsistence. In Hunting and herding in the high altitude tropics: the early prehistory of the Central Peruvian Andes, ed. John W. Rick.

Rick, John W. 1984. Structure and style at an early base camp in Junin, Peru. Paper presented at the forty-ninth annual meeting of the Society for American Archaeology, Portland.

Soukup, Jaroslav. 1970. *Vocabulario de los nombres vulgares de la flora Peruana*. Lima, Colegio Salesiano.

Towle, Margaret. 1961. *The ethnobotany of Pre-Columbian Peru*. Chicago: Aldine.

Winterhalder, Bruce, Robert Larsen, and R. Brooke Thomas. 1974. Dung as an essential resource in a highland Peruvian community. *Human Ecology* 2(2):89-104.

8

The Use of Paleoethnobotanical Data in Prehistoric Studies of Crop Production, Processing, and Consumption

Christine A. Hastorf

Plant remains recovered from archaeological sites provide unique data for economic studies of prehistoric cultures. Throughout prehistory, humans have obtained most of their food, fuel, and technological needs from the gathering of wild plants and agriculture. Plant remains have a direct link to these economic systems because plants are the actual results of these activities. Therefore, this paper examines three economic systems—crop production, plant processing, and food consumption—to assess how paleoethnobotanical data can and cannot contribute to our understanding of these systems.

The potential import of paleoethnobotanical research has not been adequately recognized. Plant data are not routinely applied to economic questions, let alone to questions of cultural meaning. Considering the relationship between plants and crop economics, in this paper I will examine some economic activities using paleoethnobotanical data. After a discussion of some of the constraints on paleoethnobotanical interpretation, I will define the three activities, including some examples from the literature as well as from my current research in the Peruvian Andes. The examples illustrate the direction I advocate for this type of research in paleoethnobotany. The Andean examples show the importance of paleoethnobotanical data in studies of prehistoric economies and also how those data can be supported and augmented with other archaeological data to improve our understanding of the economic issues.

Much of paleoethnobotany has been oriented toward the reconstruction of human diet (food consumption), operating under the assumption that remains of edible plants reflect prehistoric diet. However, not all plants found at an archaeological site relate to diet. Recognizing this, paleoethnobotanists have used their data to study other activities such as seasonal occupation (Bohrer 1970; Munson, Parmalee, and Yarnell 1971), site habitat (Bohrer 1970; Asch, Ford, and Asch 1972), land use (Minnis 1978; Hastorf 1983), and fuel use (Minnis 1978). Faced with the possibility that a particular botanical sample can reflect a wide range of activities, paleoethnobotanists have begun to develop methods for distinguishing one activity from another. Research shows that some activities are more visible than others in archaeobotanical data. Because not every activity that involved plant use left a record of its occurrence, inferring activities from the recoverable remains becomes one of the most crucial jobs in paleoethnobotanical research.

Can we distinguish the many activities which may be represented in a collection of plant remains? Several factors influence how accurately plant remains from activities are represented in archaeological data. First, activities may occur in locations which are not excavated by archaeologists (e.g., away from the habitation site). An excavated deposit will show only a subset of the total plant-related activities.

Second, cultural contexts cannot always be clearly defined, although it is important to try to identify the locations where the archaeobotanical data come from. As Pearsall (chapter 7) points out, the identification of excavated archaeological contexts greatly improves interpretation of the plant finds (which is why paleoethnobotanists must work in the field with or as the excavators). Many activities did occur in one archaeological context, however. For example, the plant debris at a winnowing/work area in a barnyard may represent many activities: chaff and seeds of domesticated plants from the winnowing, weed seeds that were mixed in with the winnowed crops, wood chips from chopping wood in the same location, and the remains of a lunch eaten there. Only through careful definitions of context based on all artifactual data including botanical remains can we decipher the range of possible activities at any given context (see Asch and Sidell, chapter 6).

Third, postdepositional cultural and natural processes ("C and N transforms," Schiffer 1976) play a crucial role in determining what prehistoric activities are recognizable in the paleoethnobotanical data. Some paleoethnobotanists, like Crawford (1983), who work with very poor plant preservation claim that individual activities are difficult to distinguish even if we know the archaeological context of the plant remains. He notes that charred plant remains could have entered the archaeological record by many routes:

for example as a mistake from activities like cereal grain parching; fortuitously as spills from cooking; or purposefully, as when a trash dump is burned. Although burning alters the data, it is also the key to interpretation, as it provides the preserved plant materials we have to work with in most circumstances. We should account for this by noting the different forms of burning and chart the history of burning activities on a site.

Fourth, plants are among the most fragile items in the archaeological record and do not consistantly withstand microbial decomposition. This creates an incomplete picture. Munson, Parmalee, and Yarnell (1971:422; also see Minnis 1981) sort food plants according to their chance of preservation through burial. Such analysis can improve our interpretation of archaeological finds. More work on differential preservation of different plant taxa is crucial (see Kadane, chapter 11).

By constructing a model of plant distribution in economic activities and of their potential for preservation, we can begin to link collectible data to events. Our goal is to work backward from the excavated plant assemblages to activities. It is through this type of analysis that we can discuss the economics of agricultural production. Because we cannot correlate excavated plant frequencies directly with the economic activities of a site's inhabitants, we must be explicit about the factors and events that affect the composition we see.

Let us begin by assuming that macrobotanical data found in cultural contexts got there primarily through human agency, although natural seed dispersal can also bring seeds onto sites (Minnis 1981:145). This entry can be by either purposeful/direct or unpurposeful/indirect means. An example of purposeful means is storing seed grain in some sort of granary or other designated location (Jones et al. 1986). Unpurposeful entrants might include unwanted weed seeds that end up in the same grain storage location.

Economic Activities

A goal of paleoethnobotanists is to use excavated archaeological plant remains to identify activities related to crop production, processing, and consumption. But as the discussion above outlines, frequencies of plant remains from archaeological sites cannot directly correlate with these activities. Trying to solve this problem, Dennell (1972, 1974, 1976), Hubbard (1976), and Hillman (1973, 1981, 1984) have been in the forefront of this inquiry. They differ in their approaches and methods, however. Dennell (1979:122) argues that paleoethnobotanical data is more suitable for modeling food production than food consumption. He bases this on the assumption that important plant resources are more commonly present in contexts of food production and processing than in contexts of consumption, since consumption removes plants from the record (Dennell 1976:234). Dennell generates theoretical models for production and processing at his site to discuss the possible plant distributions that could be uncovered. Hillman (1973) focuses his work on crop husbandry, both crop production and processing, as the effective economic focus of study. He builds his predictive model from ethnoarchaeological observations of crops being harvested and threshed. Consumption is actually not often addressed with macrobotanical data.

Production

Crop production refers to the activities that result in mature plants being harvested for use. Crops can include commodities other than food, such as fodder, construction materials, and fuel. An array of activities in the production of seed crops can include preparing the soil and terrain for planting (sometimes with the creation of irrigation ditches, mounds, terraces, etc.), planting the seed, turning over the soil, fertilizing the plants (often with domestic compost), perhaps recultivating the soil, watering, placing insecticide on the plants, weeding, and finally collecting the plant parts. Harvesting may entail reaping or beating plant tops to extract seeds, plucking off mature fruit, uprooting the whole plant, or furrowing for subsurface tubers, roots, or corms. Harvesting might occur more than once during a single growth cycle.

All of these activities, except seed storage, tool production and compost production, take place in the fields where the crops are grown, and that is where their material correlates are found. In excavations, fields are frequently overlooked, because excavators most often concentrate on habitation sites, passing over the loci of production in the archaeological record. Archaeologists therefore often use indirect data to study production. Four different research strategies have been applied to study production, each observing a different aspect of agriculture: mapping field systems, crop ecologies, excavation of fields for plant remains, and associations of harvested crops with their weed seeds collected from the habitation sites.

Consequently, to study production, the prehistoric fields themselves have become one focus of research. Some fields can be identified from artifact concentrations that result from the regular transport of domestic compost out to the fields (Wilkinson 1982). Geographers and archaeologists have discovered prehistoric field systems all over the world (see Farrington 1985 for 43 examples in the tropics alone). These diversified systems include valley floor drained fields, hillside terraces, soil mounds, irrigation canals, sunken gardens, and floating fields. Although all of these investigators study agriculture and agricultural production, the majority discuss only the field systems themselves—the technologies employed—

not the crops that are produced.

In some locations certain crops or technologies are restricted by ecological conditions (frost lines, slope, climate, etc.). In such places prehistoric crop taxa can be inferred from these constraints. These locations can provide production evidence of an indirect sort—crop ecology evidence. Golson (1981) demonstrates how the fields and climatic conditions in the Upper Wahgi Valley in Highland New Guinea can be used to predict the production of taro (*Dioscorea*) before the entry of the sweet potato in the swampy drained fields. These ecological studies do not yield evidence of the actual crops that were grown in the fields.

My research in the Andes of Peru shows that studying crop ecology provides evidence of prehistoric production that can be associated with prehistoric agricultural field systems. On the basis of modern evidence of crop distributions I discovered, restricted cropping patterns (Hastorf 1983). In the Upper Mantaro Valley I have suggested prehistoric agricultural production strategies for two major land-use zones—the valley floor and the rolling upland zones—by investigating what the zones can produce today. In this region the valley floor zone produces maize (*Zea mays*), among other crops. The nearby uplands surrounding the valley floor cannot produce maize, but yield the Andean tubers *oca* (*Oxalis tuberosa*), *ulluco* (*Ullucus tuberosus*), *mashua* (*Tropeolum tuberosum*), and especially potatoes (*Solanum tuberosum*). Two other indigenous crops, *quinoa* (*Chenopodium quinoa*) and the legume lupine, or *talhui* (*Lupinus mutabilis*), can be grown in both zones. From current studies of the paleoclimate in the region (Wright 1980, 1984) we judge that during the last thousand years the local temperature was at most 0.3°C cooler than today. This is not a major difference and so I believe that the modern crop information can be applied to the recent prehistoric periods. We know from the artifactual evidence from the nearby archaeological sites that the inhabitants used both of these zones in different proportions at different times.

Research conducted in 1982 and 1983 by, the Upper Mantaro Archaeological Research Project (UMARP), concentrated on the last two prehistoric phases, called the Wanka II and Wanka III periods (Earle et al. 1987). These represent, respectively, the final phase of local development by the Sausa people and the period when the Sausa were conquered by the expanding Inka state. In the Wanka II phase (A.D. 1300-1460) the population had aggregated into large walled towns located upon protected knolls just above the rolling upland zone. The evidence suggests that there was a great deal of internal, intersite tension during those years, and land use was probably restricted to a small area around the settlements. After the Inka conquest during Wanka III times (A.D. 1460-1532), the population was relocated into small villages down in the valleys.

From my reconaissance of the prehistoric agricultural field systems still visible on the landscape, especially the terraces and canals in the uplands, and of the settlement patterns of these two phases, I suggest that in the Wanka II period, during times of strife and defensive behavior, the population would have focused its production on the upland zone, producing mainly tubers and quinoa (*Chenopodium quinoa*). After the Inka conquest, with the relocation of the Sausa population into the valleys and with state-enforced peace, agricultural production was probably more of a mix between the upland and the valley crops, with an emphasis on the valley production of maize. From the small test excavations conducted in the valley drained fields no artifactual evidence was uncovered. In addition, many of the field areas are still in use today, and so recovering samples of prehistoric plant remains is difficult. The information used to test these land use propositions applies excavated plant data and is discussed below.

Only rarely do investigators excavate the fields themselves to uncover crops and other artifacts for direct production data, applying the third possible technique in studying crop production (Miksicek 1983; Parsons, Parsons, Popper, and Taft 1985). One such study took place in the Maya cultural area. Excavations of three raised fields at the Pulltrouser Swamp in Belize produced 36 identifiable macrofloral remains (Miksicek 1983). Out of that collection, potential domesticates were recovered, including two manioc family root fragments (perhaps not even the edible species), one *Zea mays* stem, and one avocado wood fragment (not the pit, which would have been a more direct link to food resources). As Miksicek (1983:103) states, the fragments' entry into the archaeological fields could have come from secondary deposition by mulching, building the raised fields, natural water transport, or cultivation. The maize stalk especially is tantalizing evidence for intensive maize production in this swamp environment. This suggestion fortunately was bolstered by a complementary study, which found maize pollen in the same swamp area (Wiseman 1983).

The fourth method in the study of crop production, pursued by Hillman (1981), is to correlate the weed seeds that are associated with certain crops and to compare their archaeological frequencies with the crop frequencies. Hillman (1981) studied British prehistoric farming practices (production and processing) by constructing a model of farming activities and their material correlates based on ethnographic field work. He did this by viewing traditional grain farmers in Turkey (Hillman 1972). He charted the different stages of crop production and processing in specific locations. From the farm procedures he outlined models of agricultural activities and their accompanying plant compositions: wild weed seeds, crop seeds, and byproducts. He assumed that "*if* the pattern of variation in composition is found to correspond with the distribution of certain classes of site context, and *if* it is possible to assign to each context-type specific activities concerned with crop processing, then . . . some progress may be made towards limiting the possible range of agricultural activities likely to have generated crop products of that type" (Hillman 1981:124-25, italics in original).

Using these models of activities and their weed and domestic seed distributions, Hillman described ways to distinguish prehistoric tilling methods for England. He predicted that in cultivation, a prehistoric ard plow destroyed different weed taxa from those destroyed by a moldboard plow. He also projected the sowing times of the various grain crops from the weed flora composition. Some weeds grow with the winter wheats, but others survive only in spring-sown fields. Further, he suggested that different weeding and harvesting methods also should be detectable in the plant samples from archaeological sites if the appropriate contexts (storage areas) are sampled. This type of production study can be pursued at habitation sites with adequate excavation strategies and certain crop types, but one must assume that all stored crops were grown by the inhabitants.

Optimally, of course, we would collect samples from both the fields and the associated habitation sites to form a more complete picture of production. Miksicek (1983) collected samples at the nearby archaeological habitation site of Kokeal as part of the Pulltrouser Swamp raised-field study. He did not conduct the detailed type of on-site collection that Hillman suggests, but he found that the habitation site and the fields shared some of the same species. A general species presence inventory showed that Kokeal yielded more economic species than the fields. The site evidence suggested that the villages had kitchen gardens of various tree species, and that somewhere nearby, maize was grown. As mentioned above, the fields yielded evidence of maize cultivation with avocado trees also growing near the swamps.

Processing

Processing covers preparation, storage, and cooking, with use and deposition of the edible, as well as the inedible, plant parts. It includes operations applied to harvested plants that remove them from the fields, prepare them for use, and store them, in addition to readying plant parts for their use as food, shelter, containers, tools, clothing, and so forth. These activities include transporting the plants to the settlement or other processing place, threshing (beating, tramping, hand rubbing), raking (of grain, chaff, leftover plant by-products), washing, drying, burning, parching, roasting, winnowing, sorting, sieving, grinding, dehusking, braiding, bagging, cutting up, boiling, baking, toasting, preparing a storage location, and placing the material in storage.

Most of these activities take place in the habitation area. Many activities, depending on the specific crop in question, also leave material remains in the archaeological record at a habitation site. In fact, some of these activities leave very distinctive combinations of botanical remains. Traces of processing, therefore, should be visible in the archaeological record if preservation is sufficient to permit plant presence.

Hally investigated crop processing, but he concluded that while archaeobotanical remains may provide a picture of production and processing, they may not always provide enough information to identify specific processing activities. At a site in Georgia, Hally (1981) tried to identify crop processing patterns from plant remains at the Little Egypt site. Even using ethnohistorical descriptions of processing methods from the Cherokee and the Choctaw, he found little patterned evidence of these activities in the macrobotanical record. His plant use predictions were general, focusing on seasonal plant availability, not on specific harvesting techniques. Because of the charring events, with one structure burnt at one time, Hally based his interpretation on the burning history. He found that the accumulated botanical data could provide a picture of composite production/processing but could not get at specific processing activities (Hally 1981:738).

The most specific models identifying plant processing in the archaeological record come from British paleoethnobotanists. Hubbard (1976), Dennell (1976), Hillman (1981, 1984), and Jones (1984) have tried to go beyond general plant use discussions by detailing the steps in crop processing, charring, and storage.

Dennell's (1974, 1976, 1978) approach to studying crop production began with constructing a general model of crop processing based on his knowledge of the grain processing stages in traditional Old World crop processing. He defined a sequence of processing steps and the probable composition of grain parts and wild seeds that could have been generated, deposited, and charred. This model was then applied at two early Neolithic sites in Bulgaria. As with Hally, one of his sites was consumed by fire. Using his model of grain processing stages and the likely composition of a collected sample, he separated the plant samples from the site into three types: fully processed crops ready for storage, partially processed crop residues (the crops along with chaff, spikelets, weed seeds, etc.), and crop processing residue (Dennell 1976:236). All samples contained the same crop species but had different quantities of weed seeds and chaff. He surmised from these differences that the fully processed crops were parched for storage and consumption. All but one of the fully processed samples were found in ovens. The partially processed samples were smaller and more heterogeneous, containing more weed seeds. These samples were found on floors of structures. A single chaff-enriched sample was found within a building; Dennell interpreted it to be from an area where chaff was stored for animal fodder, fuel, or bedding (1976:237).

By distinguishing partially processed samples from fully processed samples, Dennell felt that he could identify certain species as weeds and that these weed species had not been purposefully brought onto the site. In addition, using the first sample type only (the fully processed crop samples), Dennell discussed the importance of the domestic plant taxa in the Neolithic economy. He assumed that these samples represented the crops purposefully produced by the inhabitants. Dennell applied a theoretical model of crop processing and deposition including other archaeological data to identify the botanical samples with specific cultural contexts. He then could focus on samples from well-defined contexts to address specific cultural questions.

Hillman (1984) and Jones (1984) have been developing more thorough, predictive models of specific processing activities to identify collected plant samples with activities. Both have completed detailed ethnographic studies of traditional processing of Old World crops that established a sequence of events and material correlates for grain and legume processing. They recorded the frequencies of agricultural plant parts and wild species associated with cleaning, winnowing, parching, and storing. They also recorded the location, intensity, and outcome of charring to predict which plants would be preserved and in what frequency.

From the flow charts they generated of processing, plant deposition, and potential plant charring, and the associated plant frequencies, Hillman and Jones claim to be able to define specific stages and contexts in the processing sequence. These predicted stages can be matched to similar contexts in the archaeological record on the basis of plant frequencies. From this ethnographic research Hillman (1981:125) has proposed that when locations are sampled properly for macrobotanical remains, investigators can identify the past activity at a location more acurately from the plant samples than from the traditional visible discoveries revealed during excavation.

Hillman came to this conclusion in part because of the range of plant parts within the Old World assemblage. Old World grains have the advantage of generating a wide range of plant parts that can be deposited and preserved in the record. These parts provide evidence of the processing sequence that has been recorded by Dennell, Hillman, and Jones. Can a such a sequence be reconstructed for New World crops as well? New World crops, except for maize, rarely offer as many different fragments as the Old World grains. To see if reconstructing food processing in the New World is possible, two projects are in process. One is building a model of plant distributions to learn if paleoethnobotanical data can inform us about archaeological context identities. This is being attempted by applying a Bayesian probability model to contextual information gathered during the excavations and then testing to see if the paleoethnobotanical data can provide additional contextual information (Kadane and Hastorf 1988). Thus far the botanical data have been very informative; they identify storage areas, crop cleaning areas, and locations of consumption. A second study follows along the lines of Hillman and Jones's work. In 1986 Lynn Sikkink (1988) conducted an ethnoarchaeological study in the Upper Mantaro region of Peru to investigate the relationship of plant use activities with botanical assemblages.

Sikkink has observed the harvesting, processing, charring, consumption, and deposition of the crops, both indigenous and imported, currently grown in the region. She observed four families and their agricultural activities, located in the different microzones of the region. She has also collected soil samples from locations of these activities both in the domestic contexts and in the fields, in order to chart the deposition of plant remains as the activities take place. In this region, houses have one or more roofed rooms that face onto a walled patio area (the edges of the patio may be roofed, but most of it is open). The main door that leads to the outside opens from the patio. Hence the two main areas for study are inside the rooms and in the enclosed patio. Sikkink processed the collected soil samples with the same flotation procedure as UMARP used for prehistoric samples (a modified SMAP machine; see Earle et al. 1987 or Watson 1976 for a description). Although the laboratory analysis is not yet complete, tentative results show differences in the activities and deposited plant composition from various locations in the household compounds. These results provide useful models of crop processing patterns for Andean archaeologists.

First, quinoa seeds are found all over the household, in both the patio and the rooms. Farmers scatter quinoa on the floor to feed animals. It can also drop onto the floor or into the hearth during the process of cleaning and cooking. The quinoa seed is so small that it scatters easily when it is cleaned in the final winnowing stage as well.

Second, the hearth not only is a location for burning fuel (wood, grass, animal dung, and maize cobs), but also receives spilled food and sweepings. In the kitchen, food is dropped regularly on the dirt floor for the guinea pigs, *cuyes* (*Cavia* sp.), to eat. Against the walls in rooms used for storage, bags or piles of food are housed. The patio is used mainly for processing activities, grinding maize, final cleaning of beans, quinoa, and other foods, and the construction or mending of household items. This area is swept occasionally, and the remains are moved to the sides of the patio. Many plants are stored against the wall in the patio as well. Wild greens are brought in as fodder for dogs and cuyes; grasses and reeds are piled for making brooms, roofs, and other items, or to be used as fuel. Shrubs and wood are kept for building, for mending things, and for fuel. The location of these activities and their associated plant assemblages should help us to understand samples collected from prehistoric locations. One discovery from this documentation of Sausa household deposition is that the same plant taxa may reflect different activities in different contexts.

This ethnographic information and the field systems data from the Mantaro area, mentioned above, can be used along with paleoethnobotanical data to inform us about prehistoric crop production and processing in the Upper Mantaro Valley region. I would like to present here a small subset of the paleoethnobotanical data from our fieldwork there that points out how botanical data can be used to describe general production/processing as well as specific on-site processing activities. The research area, as outlined above, includes two major production locations, valley floor and uplands. For this illustration I will focus again on the Wanka II and Wanka III time periods. It should be remembered that the three sites excavated from the Wanka II period are on rocky knolls in defended positions, as are all of the Wanka II sites. The Wanka III settlements are lower down and dispersed in and around the edge of the maize-growing zone.

Figure 8.1 presents paleoethnobotanical data of the four major agricultural crops in a percentage presence (ubiquity) format (see Popper, chapter 4). A total of 668 flotation samples for the two time periods are included. We see that in Wanka III period, with a settlement shift to a lower elevation, maize and legumes increased in frequency, while tubers and quinoa decreased. In general, this is what was predicted from the agricultural field system data noted above. In this comparison the aggregated botanical data conform to the field systems production information.

A portion of these same data can begin to reflect household activities. Figure 8.2 presents a bar graph summation of the four major crop types from the Wanka II sites (N = 487). The three bars drawn for each crop represent presence in (1) all excavated proveniences, (2) floors, and (3) hearths. In this data set, the number of samples from floors is much greater than the number of samples from the hearths, and so this example should be viewed as tentative.

Floor contexts, however, should reflect a wider range of activities than hearth contexts. A floor is defined as the hard-packed surface within a walled household compound. A hearth is a well-defined burned zone within a structure. The two kinds of locations represent different stages in the processing sequence. The hearth should produce evidence of mistakes and spills from the final preparation and cooking stages of some of the crops. Floor contexts reflect a combination of winnowing, sorting, storing, and spills from hearths.

Bias enters into the percentage presence frequencies because of

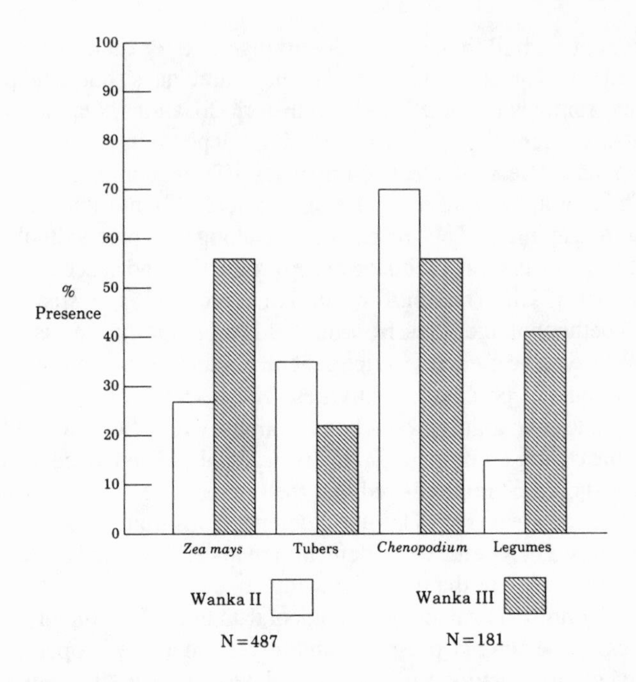

Figure 8.1. Percentage presence (ubiquity) of the four main food groups (crop types) in Wanka II and Wanka III times.

differences in preservation and plant part size: tubers are soft plant matter and decompose more easily than seeds. In addition, differences in fragment size affect the likelihood of loss during use. The regular presence of *Chenopodium* in all samples is likely due to its small size as much as to methods of processing and preparation. Maize, tubers, and legumes are larger items and would be harder to lose in the dirt. Over all, the data reflect more intensive household processing and storage of maize and tubers and greater loss of legumes in the cooking process.

To illustrate how one might look at prehistoric activities and the ability of plants to aid in interpretation, I have chosen one Wanka II household on Tunanmarca (J7) to study. There, 34 flotation samples and their plant ubiquities can be examined in relation to their specific locations in the household compound. With this illustration I want to point out how the same data in different contexts reflect different activities, how certain events leave more visible traces than others in the archaeological record, and how the contextual information combined with the botanical data can identify

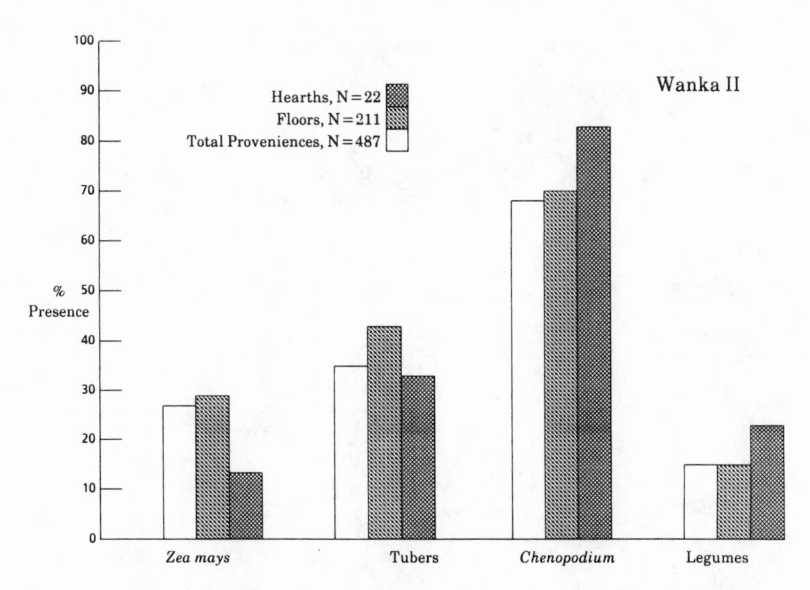

Figure 8.2. Percentage presence (ubiquity) of the four main crop types in Wanka II period.

the samples an investigator should apply to any given research question, whether it is production, consumption or processing.

The flotation samples were chosen from four locations assumed to represent certain contexts in the domesitc patio J7 = 2 (figure 8.3). These locations were determined from ethnographic observation of modern activities. The four are (1) hearths inside roofed round structures, (2) food storage against the walls within the structures, (3) work space in the central part of the patio, and (4) general storage against the patio walls. What can we learn about plant processing from these samples? Plants in each of the different contexts should represent different activities and be deposited for different reasons.

Figure 8.4 presents the plant data by context within the structures: hearths and storage areas. Because hearths are located in the floor, with material possibly moving between the two contexts, we might expect these two contexts to be similar in some categories, and in fact they are. A hearth is a very specific context; its purpose is to burn organic matter, mainly food and fuel. Therefore, the connection between activities and their material finds should be more precise in hearth than at other locations. We can assume that the four main food types found in hearths reflect food spills or loss. The grasses, wood, and maize cobs are likely to be residues of fuel use.

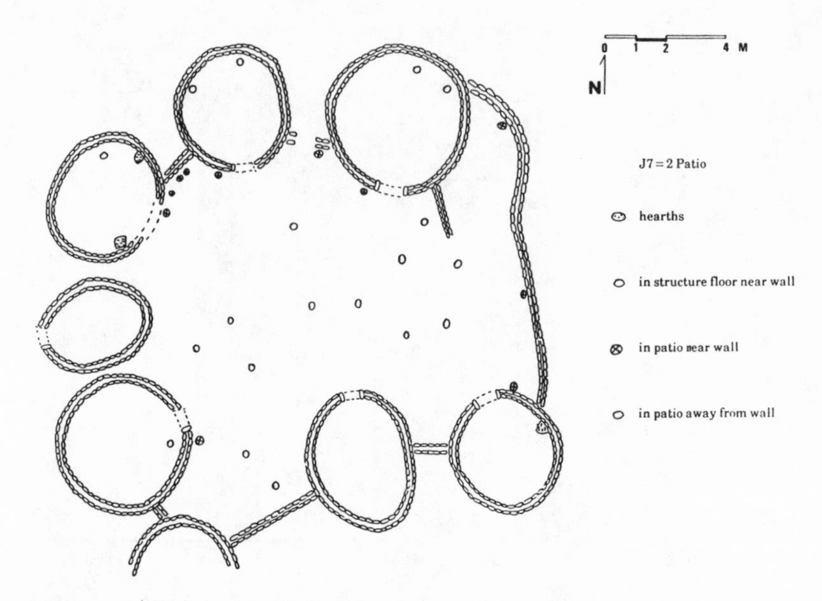

Figure 8.3. Flotation sample distribution in domestic compound J7 = 2.

The wild herbaceous plant seeds, *Scirpus*, *Amaranthus*, and *Trifolium*, could be guinea pig food that was swept into the fire, as it is today.

The structure floor contents are only slightly different from the hearth remains. The ethnographic data remind us that the food we see in these floor samples is very likely the spill scattered out from the hearth, leftovers dropped for the guinea pigs (cuyes) who live in the kitchen, as well as spills during eating or storage. The wild species, including the grasses, could be animal fodder or for food storage. The floor is less precisely correlated with specific processing activities. In fact the plant remains from the structures might be the best samples with which to study consumption. In these floor contexts we see the dominance of *Chenopodium* and tubers, with a significant amount of maize. These samples also look similar to the stable isotope consumption data from figure 8.6 for the same time period (see below).

Figure 8.5 portrays the macroplant presence in the patio contexts, viewing the plant deposition outside the structures. Because burning activities are not occur regularly in patios today, nor were distinct in situ burned areas uncovered in this patio during excavation, we would expect to find less-dense charred matter in the patio samples, and that is what we see. Ethnographic information predicts that these two patio contexts—in the center of the patio and against the wall—might be more easily distinguishable than those inside the structures. Remains found against the patio wall

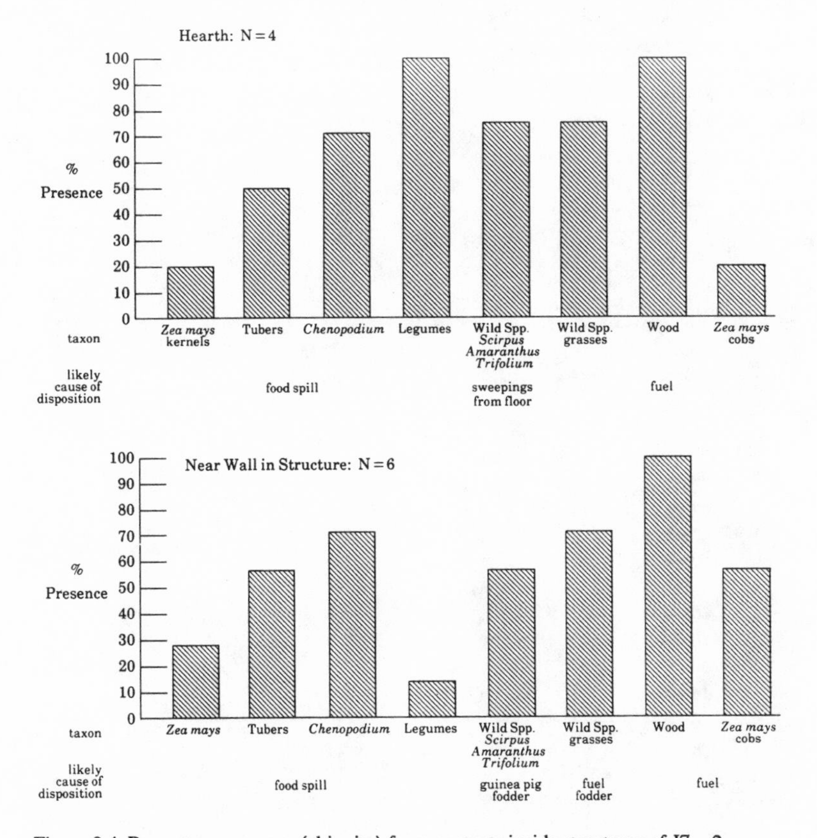

Figure 8.4. Percentage presence (ubiquity) from contexts inside structures of J7 = 2.

should reflect storage of fuel, raw materials, animal fodder, and tools evidence of plant processing—cleaning, winnowing, and sorting. These processing activities should be found also in samples from the center of the patio. Very little storage evidence should be identified in the center, as it is a place for activities and through traffic.

In the samples from the center of the patio, we see the same food taxa as are found inside the structures, but at a much lower density and frequency. The center of the patio has the sparsest deposits of the four contexts. Although some foods that could have been processed (*Chenopodium*) and especially materials for tool production (wood and grasses) are present, the evidence suggests that this area was probably trampled and swept clean periodically to remain clear for the many household tasks. This context is

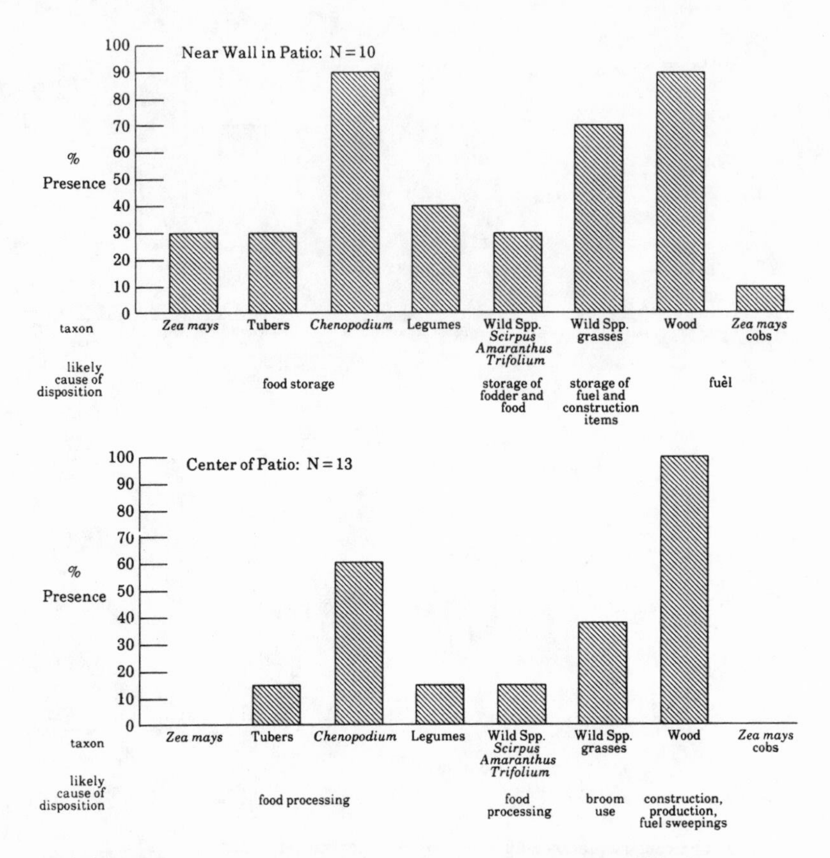

Figure 8.5. Percentage presence (ubiquity) from contexts in patio areas of J7 = 2.

probably the least informative for the ethnobotanist, as the many events that went on in this location are not well identified in the botanical data.

This experimental contextual example illustrates how (1) the same taxa in different contexts reflect different activities, (2) certain events leave more visible traces than others in the archaeological record, and (3) contextual information can identify the samples an investigator should use for a given research question. In this case, to study processing I would focus on the samples located against the patio wall.

Consumption

Food consumption can be defined as the dietary intake of plant and animal products by the household residents. The empirical evidence of consumption (direct and indirect) can be found in different data types, not strictly in the botanical data. Among the avenues of inquiry, consumption should be reflected in food preparation and cooking strategies. We may find evidence of consumption in the plant and animal remains within hearths, types of cooking vessels (i.e., flat toasters for dry grains, deep curved bowls for water based foods), heating techniques (stone *comales* for grilling or water-holding pots for boiling), charred residue on the cooking vessels, ovens or pits for roasting, and plant scatterings around the hearths and middens where food was prepared and leftovers were disposed of. Another less-common avenue is investigating diet within well preserved skeleton stomachs (Glob 1977), coprolites (Callen 1963; Bryant 1974), and more recently, bone chemistry (van de Merwe and Vogel 1978; DeNiro 1987). Although diet has been an important subject within archaeology, it has been elusive to study.

As I have said, identifying consumption at an archaeological site depends on our ability to associate specific contexts and artifact distributions with eating. Our problems with reconstructing diet from plant remains are not simply due to our inability to recover certain dietary components, such as milk products, saps, and foods consumed off the site. We see again the problem of differential preservation, especially with the loss of soft tissue in plants such as tubers, leaves, and fleshy fruits. By definition, things consumed entirely cannot show up in the archaeological record. Asch and Asch state the inverse relationship that "carbonized edible seeds represent only the portion *not* consumed" (1975:116; italics in original). Therefore, consumption can be represented in the archaeological record, but much of the evidence for consumption is not paleoethnobotanical in origin.

In an attempt to apply paleoethnobotanical data to the question of consumption, researchers have tried to quantify plants that represent prehistoric consumption. Traditionally, justification for equating crop frequencies and dietary consumption was based on the assumption that as the food is consumed, a portion of each item will be lost, discarded, or burned at each step in the processing and consuming activity. Further, the amount deposited will be proportional to the amount processed or consumed. Therefore, deposited plant remains have been claimed to represent diet. This reasoning could perhaps operate in very localized and well identified archaeological contexts such as an identified eating area. Within any particular excavated context, however, we should not accept these assumptions without careful thought. When we discuss consumption, I think that paleoethnobotanical data will have to be used in conjunction with other data.

The most prevalent method for quantifying consumption was developed by MacNeish (1967) and applied also by Flannery (1986:303). MacNeish tried to calculate the amount of each identified taxon (including animals) that was consumed during each phase of occupation in sites located in the

Tehuacan Valley of Mexico. His project included information from animal bones and plant remains from the excavations, and he associated those results with results from human coprolites (Callen 1967). He estimated sustenance by calculating the average live weight of each (food) plant taxon found in each excavated level. To do so, he measured one liter of modern mashed or compacted food by taxon and correlated those figures to the number of plant fragments that appeared in each archaeological excavation. For example, one kernel of maize represents one cob of maize kernels, which is 50 grams of maize, 170 calories, 3.25 grams of protein, and so forth. And for wild avocados, 60 pits represent 60 avocados, or one liter of avocado meat (MacNeish 1967:296). Through this method he calculated the edible amount of food for each plant taxon found in the excavations. He then tallied up the specimen counts by phase and calculated their live weight/food value. He converted these tallies to total food consumed by extrapolating the number of fragments that would have been recovered if the total occupation area had been excavated and then multiplying those fragments by their food value equivalents.

As Pozorski (1976:63) points out in discussing her modified use of this technique, plants will be underrepresented and animals will be overrepresented, and hence the analysis creates new problems. Differential preservation and lack of contextual differentiation were not built into the food value equations, so these formulas should not be used uncritically in an analysis of diet. A more specific method that applies paleoethnobotanical data to questions of food consumption may be to select very specific contexts for botanical viewing. This was illustrated in the Andean example, where the plant frequencies within the structures might be considered to give the best picture of the household diet.

Although plant remains can be included in the study of prehistoric diet, independent data sets and new techniques are being used more and more to study this aspect of past life. The newer techniques go beyond coprolite analysis to include such techniques as skeletal and soft tissue pathologies, dentition pathologies, trace elements in bone, stable isotopes in bone, population life tables, dietary stress, nutritional requirements, environmental reconstruction, tools, and procurement technologies (Gilbert and Mielke 1985). Researchers are turning to these methods to find data that can be collected regularly from archaeological sites, not only when a rare coprolite is preserved.

One technique that has recently been proposed to provide direct dietary information is the analysis of bone chemistry and, in particular, of stable isotopes from human bone samples. Recent research in geochemical stable isotopes has suggested that the isotopic composition of an animal's whole body reflects the composite diet of the animal (DeNiro and Epstein 1978,

1981; Schoeniger, DeNiro, and Tauber 1983; van der Merwe and Vogel 1978—to name only a few). People's average diets therefore will be reflected in their bones. The main stable isotopes involved in dietary reconstruction to date have been the carbon isotopes ($^{13}C/^{12}C$), which separate the two main photosynthetic pathways of plants: the Calvin cycle for so-called C_3 plants and the Hatch-Slack cycle called C_4 plants. These isotopes, with their different molecular weights, are deposited in bone collagen during life throughout bone growth and regeneration. This technique provides a composite picture of what was consumed. In this chemical analysis the isotopes are extracted from the bone collagen and identified using a mass spectrometer. In the process of bone growth and regeneration, bone collagen receives a relative frequency of the two plant groups (Bender 1971; Smith and Epstein 1971).

Because of possible invisible postmortem bone contamination from the environment (diagenesis) and misinterpretation of the isotopic values generated from sample processing, such analysis is still controversial and is being refined (DeNiro pers. com.). Yet as the technique is refined, many people think that it might provide a reliable reflection of overall diet in prehistoric groups. Although full critical discussion is needed to report properly on this technique of dietary reconstruction, we need not include such a discussion for the purposes of this paper, where the technique is used only as an illustration of exploring the paleoethnobotanical data (see Price 1988 for a current set of references on the technique).

On the Upper Mantaro material, Michael DeNiro, a geochemist, and I have been applying this technique. We know that the only C_4domestic crop is *Zea mays*, and that all other domesticates—legumes, tubers, a *Chenopodium*—are in the C_3 plant group. In our initial application of this technique, we analyzed 14 skeletons from the Wanka II period. To make the isotope data comparable to the macrobotanical material, the percentage of C_3 and C_4 plants in the diet was geochemically determined for each sample. Figure 8.6 shows, in addition to the same paleoethnobotanical data from Wanka II times as seen in Figure 8.2, two thin bars that represent the relative amounts of and C_3 plants, respectively, consumed by the sampled Wanka II adults (Hastorf 1985, 1986). Although the C_4 bar reflects *Zea mays*, the C_3 bar is a composite of tuber, *Chenopodium*, and legume consumption.

Comparing these isotope data with the paleoethnobotanical data from the same period, we see that the C_3 isotope values are approximately equivalent to the C_3 macrobotanical frequencies when the C_3 plant frequencies are adjusted for preservation and averaged. The C_4 bar is noticeably larger than the maize macrobotanical data, however. The maize data reflect a discrepancy that must be discussed, for if we assume that the isotopes reflect what was eaten, then the plant presence does not. One reason for the

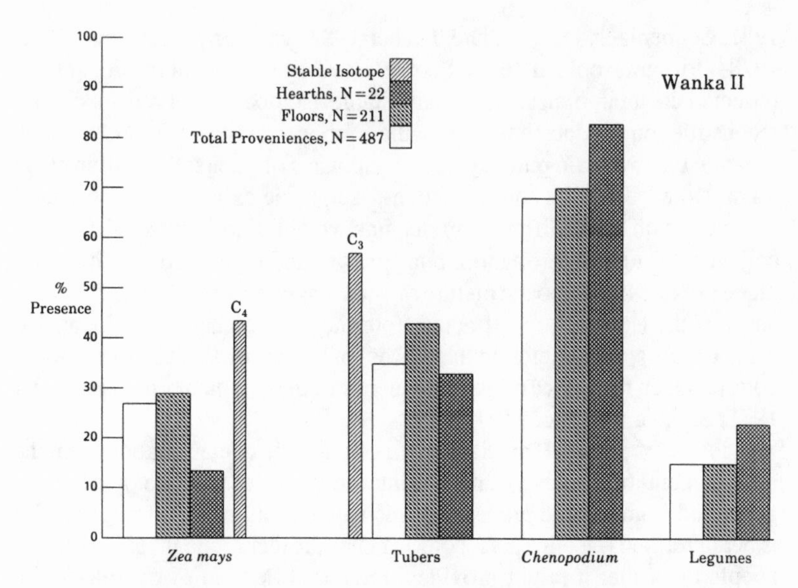

Figure 8.6. Percentage presence (ubiquity) of four crop types in the Wanka II period compared with summarized isotope consumption data from the same period.

difference between the maize in the samples and the C_4 data might be that the population ate more maize than they either produced or processed at the sites. The sites where these samples came from are not in the maize producing zone; the people may have eaten maize while they were away from their houses, either in another part of the settlement or at other sites. Alternatively, the C_4 enrichment in the human diet might have come from meat. From isotopic analysis of excavated animal bones from the same region, we know that llama, alpaca, and the hunted animals graze on C_3 plants. Cuyes and dogs did so as well, but their carbon isotope values suggest that they ate maize occasionally (although it would have been a small part of their diet).

A third interpretation might be that the botanical remains in this comparison probably do not reflect deposition during the whole lifespans of the inhabitants and might reflect only the last few years of occupation. The isotope data then portray a slightly different view from the paleoethnobotanical data, suggesting that maize might have been more regularly consumed at different times throughout the 30 or so years of the inhabitants' lives. A fourth explanation could be that the botanical quantification and/or the isotopic analysis are inappropriate for this comparison because of the sample size and the location of the flotation samples. Or finally, as Kadane (chapter 11) points out, perhaps the flotation data should be quantified in a different manner to make these two data sets truly comparable. If, however, we accept both data sets and the first interpretation, then we have to assume that these botanical remains do not reflect the full picture of consumption, but more closely correspond to household production and processing.

This example with the isotope data demonstrates the need to use more than paleoethnobotanical data to address food consumption questions, but it also shows a way we might be able to chart prehistoric diet. Just as MacNeish analyzed coprolites along with his plant and animal data, other data bases will fill in where the plant remains cannot provide complete answers to archaeological questions.

Conclusions

One purpose of this paper was to show how paleoethnobotanical data can and cannot be applied to economic questions. I have tried to point out how the use of more explicit models of plant deposition will require more conscious planning and control of botanical sample collection and their relations to hypotheses of plant use. Economic examples have been presented as well to demonstrate how the scope of paleoethnobotanical data and their contexts determine the types of conclusions that can be made with paleoethnobotanical data. General aggregated data cannot distinguish production from consumption, but specific context data begin to unravel different activities and therefore the causes and interpretations of the plant distributions in the archaeological record. Thus, until excavators make regular and detailed archaeological plant collections in specific locations and conexts, the discussion of plant economics will remain general. With integrated sampling and behavioral/depositional models, we will learn more about prehistoric economic activities.

The level of analytical detail will depend on empirical constraints, such as our ability to infer deposition activities from visible remains; to unravel differential preservation, age, and soil conditions of excavated sites; and to identify the cultural contexts where the samples are collected. Studies using only charred remains in poorly preserved, hard-to-identify contexts may have to operate at a more general level of interpretation. Natural and cultural conditions will always constrain archaeological interpretations. Paleoethnobotanists can study only the plants that are deposited in the archaeological record, yet by defining tasks and their locations by using supporting data that can be associated with plant remains we can increase our understanding of past activities, especially production, processing, and consumption. Although the constraint of incomplete data can never be eradicated, I hope that readers will see how archaeobotanical data can be applied to research questions that other data bases have traditionally dominated, but not addressed as fully.

Acknowledgments

The data presented in this paper were collected during the 1982-83 field seasons by many people associated with the UMARP project and supported by the National Science Foundation grant BNS8203723. The botanical analysis was further supported by National Science Foundation grant BNS845369. The isotope analysis was completed by Michael DeNiro at the Department of Earth and Space Sciences, UCLA. The writing of the paper was completed while I was a fellow at the Center for Advanced Studies in the Behavioral Sciences, partially supported by grant BNS8411738. Special thanks go to Jay Kadane, Ginny Popper, and an anonymous reviewer for encouraging me in areas I was unsure of. Thanks also to Ginny and Kathleen Much for help with editing.

References Cited

Asch, David, and Nancy Asch. 1975. Plant remains from the Zimmerman site-grid A: A quantitative perspective. In *The Zimmerman Site: Partner excavations at the grand village of Kaskakia*, ed. M. K. Brown, Illinois State Museum, Reports of Investigations, no. 32:116-20.

Asch, Nancy, Richard Ford, and David Asch. 1972. *Paleoethnobotany of the Koster site: The Archaic horizons.* Illinois State Museum Reports and Investigations, no. 24.

Bender, M. M. 1971. Variations on the $^{13}C/^{12}C$ ratios of plants in relation to the pathway of photosynthetic carbon dioxide fixation. *Phytochemistry* 10:1239-44.

Bohrer, Vorsila. 1970. Paleoecology of the Hay Hollow Site, Arizona, *Fieldiana* 63(1):1-30.

Bryant, Vaughn, Jr. 1974. The role of coprolite analysis in archaeology. *Bulletin of the Texas Archaeological Society* 45:1-28.

Buikstra, Jane, and James Mielke. 1985. Demography, diet and health. In *The analysis of prehistoric diets*, ed. R. Gilbert and J. Mielke, pp. 359-422. New York: Academic Press.

Callen, Eric O. 1963. Diet as revealed by coprolites. In *Science in archaeology*, ed. D. Brothwell and E. Higgs, pp. 186-94. London: Thames and Hudson.

_____. 1967. Analysis of the Tehuacan coprolites. In *The prehistory of the Tehuacan valley*, vol. 1, *Environment and subsistence*, ed. D. S. Byers, pp. 261-89. Austin: University of Texas Press.

Cohen, Mark, and George Armelagos, ed. 1984. *Paleopathology at the origins of agriculture*. New York: Academic Press.

Crawford, Gary W. 1983. *Paleoethnobotany of the Kameda Peninsula, Jomon*. Anthropological Papers no. 73. University of Michigan, Museum of Anthropology.

DeNiro, Michael J. 1987. Stable isotopy and archaeology. *American Scientist* 75(2):182-91.

DeNiro, Michael J., and Samuel Epstein. 1978. Influence of diet on the distribution of carbon isotopes in animals. *Geochimica et Cosmochimica Acta* 42:495-506.

DeNiro, Michael J. and Samuel Epstein. 1981. Influence of diet on the distribution of nitrogen isotopes in animals. *Geochimica et Cosmochimica Acta* 45:341-51.

Dennell, Robin. 1972. The interpretation of plant remains: Bulgaria. In Papers in economic prehistory, ed. Eric S. Higgs, pp. 149-59. Cambridge: University Press.

_____. 1974. Botanical evidence for prehistoric crop processing activities. *Journal of Archaeological Science* 1:275-84.

_____. 1976. The economic importance of plant resources represented on archaeological sites. *Journal of Archaeological Science* 3:229-47.

_____. 1978. *Early farming in South Bulgaria from the sixth to the third millennia B.C.* International Series 45. Oxford: British Archaeological Reports.

_____. 1979. Prehistoric diet and nutrition: Some food for thought. *World Archaeology* 11(2):121-35.

Earle, Timothy, Terence D'Altroy, Christine Hastorf, Catherine Scott, Cathy Costin, Glenn Russell, and Elsie Sandefur. 1987. *The effects of Inka conquest on the Wanka domestic economy*, Monograph 28. Los Angeles: UCLA, Institute of Archaeology.

Farrington, Ian S., ed. 1985. *Prehistoric intensive agriculture in the tropics*. International series 232. Oxford: British Archaeological Reports.

Flannery, Kent V. 1986. *Guilá Naquitz*. Orlando, Fla.: Academic Press.

Gilbert, Robert I., Jr. 1985. Stress, paleonutrition and trace elements. In *The analysis of prehistoric diets*, ed. R. Gilbert and J. Mielke, pp. 339-58. New York: Academic Press.

Gilbert, Robert, and James Mielke ed. 1985. *The analysis of prehistoric diets* . New York: Academic Press.

Glob, P. V. 1977. *The bog people*. London: Faber.

Golson, Jack. 1981. New Guinea agricultural history: A case study. In *A time to plant and a time to uproot*, ed. D. Denoon and C. Snowden, pp. 55-64. Port Moresby: Institute of Papua New Guinea Studies.

Hally, David J. 1981. Plant preservation and the content of paleobotanical samples: A case study. *American Antiquity* 46(4):732-42.

Harris, David R. 1984. Ethnohistorical evidence for the exploitation of wild grasses and forbs: Its scope and archaeological implications. In *Plants and ancient man: Studies in palaeoethnobotany*, ed. W. Van Zeist and W. Casparie, pp. 63-69. Rotterdam: A. A. Balkema.

Hastorf, Christine A. 1983. Prehistoric agricultural intensification and political development in the Jauja region of Central Peru. Ph.D. diss., UCLA. Ann Arbor: University Microfilms.

_____. 1985. The effect of Inka economics on northern Wanka agricultural production in the central Peruvian Andes. In Transformation of the domestic economy with Inka conquest of the Mantaro Valley. Paper presented at the fiftieth annual meetings of the Society for American Archaeology, Denver.

_____. 1986. Agricultura, alimentación y economia de los Wanka durante la epoca Inka. In *Actas y trabajos: VI Congreso Peruano: Hombre y cultura Andina*, ed. F. E. Iriarte Brenner, pp. 168-85. Lima: Universidad Inca Garcilasco de la Vega and the National Institute of Culture.

Helbaek, Hans. 1954. Prehistoric food plants and weeds of Denmark: A survey of archeo-botanical research. *Danmarks Geoligiske Unders II*, 80:250-61.

Hillman, Gordon C. 1972. Archaeo-botanical studies (Asvan 1971), under recent archaeological research in Turkey. *Anatolian Studies* 22:17-19.

_____. 1973. Crop husbandry and food production: modern models for the interpretation of plant remains. *Anatolian Studies* 23:241-44.

_____. 1981. Reconstructing crop husbandry practices from charred remains of crops. In *Farming practice in British prehistory*, ed. R. Mercer, pp. 123-62. Edinburgh: Edinburgh University Press.

_____. 1984. Interpretation of archaeological plant remains: The application of ethnographic models from Turkey. In *Plants and ancient man: Studies in palaeoethnobotany*, ed. W. Van Zeist and W. Casparie, pp. 1-41. Rotterdam: A. A. Balkema.

Hubbard, R. N. L. B. 1976. On the strength of the evidence for prehistoric crop processing activities. *Journal of Archaeological Science* 3:257-65.

Jones, Glynis. 1984. Interpretation of archaeological plant remains: Ethnographic models from Greece. In *Plants and ancient man: Studies in palaeoethnobotany*, ed. W. Van Zeist and W. Casparie, pp. 43-59. Rotterdam: A. A. Balkema.

Jones, Glynis, Kenneth Wardle, Paul Halstead, and Diana Wardle. 1986. Crop storage at Assiros. *Scientific American* 254 (3):96-103.

Kadane, Joseph B., and Christine A. Hastorf. 1988. Bayesian Paleoethnobotany. In *Bayesian Statistics III*, ed. J. Bernardo, M. H. DeGroot, D. V. Lindley, and A. M. F. Smith, Oxford: University Press.

MacNeish, Richard S. 1967. A summary of the subsistence. In *The prehistory of the Tehuacan valley*, vol. 1, *Environment and subsistence*, ed. D. S. Byers, pp. 290-309. Austin: University of Texas Press.

Miksicek, Charles H. 1983. Macrofloral remains of the Pulltrouser area: Settlements and fields. In *Pulltrouser Swamp*, ed. B. L. Turner II and P. D. Harrison, pp. 94-104. Austin: University of Texas Press.

Minnis, Paul. 1978. Paleoethnobotanical indicators of prehistoric environmental disturbance: A case study. In *The nature and status of ethnobotany*, ed. R. Ford, M. F. Brown, M. Hodge, W. L. Merrill pp. 347-66. Anthropological Papers no. 67. University of Michigan, Museum of Anthropology.

_____. 1981. Seeds in archaeological sites: Sources and some interpretive problems. *American Antiquity* 46:143-52.

Munson, Patrick, Paul Parmalee, and Richard Yarnell. 1971. Subsistence ecology at Scovill, a Terminal Middle Woodland village. *American Antiquity* 36:410-31.

Parsons, Jeffery R., Mary H. Parsons, Virginia Popper, and Mary Taft. 1985. Chinampa agriculture and Aztec urbanization in the Valley of Mexico. In *Prehistoric intensive agriculture in the tropics*, ed. I. S. Farrington, pp. 49-96. International Series 232. Oxford: British Archaeological Reports.

Pozorski, Sheila. 1976. Prehistoric subsistence patterns and site economics in the Moche Valley, Peru. Ph.D. diss., University of Texas. Ann Arbor: University Microfilms.

Price, T. Douglas., ed. 1986. *Studies in the chemistry of prehistoric human bone*. Cambridge: University Press.

Schiffer, Michael. 1976. *Behavioral Archaeology*. New York: Academic Press.

Schoeniger, Margaret, Michael DeNiro, and Henry Tauber. 1983. Stable nitrogen isotope ratios of bone collagen reflect marine and terrestrial components of prehistoric human diet. *Science* 220:1381-83.

Sikkink, Lynn. 1988. From field to house: Ethnoarchaeology and ethnobotany of harvest and crop-processing in Andean peasant households. M.A. thesis, Department of Anthropology, University of Minnesota, Minneapolis.

Smith, B. N., and S. Epstein. 1971. Two categories of $^{13}C/^{12}C$ ratios of higher plants. *Plant Physiology* 47:380-84.

van der Merwe, N. J., and J. C. Vogel. 1978. C-13 content of human collagen as a measure of prehistoric diet in Woodland North America. *Nature* 276:815-16.

Watson, Patty Jo. 1976. In pursuit of prehistoric subsistence: A comparative account of some contemporary flotation techniques. *Midcontinental Journal of Archaeology* 1:77-100.

Wilkinson, T. J. 1982. The definition of ancient manured zones by means of extensive sherd-sampling techniques. *Journal of Field Archaeology* 9:323-33.

Wiseman, Frederick M. 1983. Analysis of pollen from the fields at Pulltrouser Swamp. In *Pulltrouser Swamp*, ed. B. L. Turner II and P. D. Harrison, pp. 105-19. Austin: University of Texas Press.

Wright, Herbert E., Jr. 1980. Environmental history of the Junin plain and the nearby mountains. In *Prehistoric hunters of the high Andes*, ed. J. Rick, pp. 253-56. New York: Academic Press.

_____. 1984. Holocene glaciation in the Cerros Cuchpanga, central Peru. *Quaternary Research* 21:275-85.

9

Plant Remains and Culture Change: Are Paleoethnobotanical Data Better Than We Think?

Sissel Johannessen

Introduction

The analysis of plant remains from archaeological sites has many disadvantages as a means of reconstructing the conditions of the past. The preserved floral material that ends up in the laboratory is an extremely small sample of the original assemblage and one that is biased by many known and unknown factors of deposition, preservation, and recovery, as many careful studies have pointed out.

In spite of these disadvantages, however, the record of plant remains has several qualities that make floral analysis a unique and powerful tool for investigating the economic bases of culture change: (1) archaeological investigations allow consideration of the time dimension; (2) plant remains provide direct evidence of the basics of economic systems—food and fuel; (3) broad patterning in the plant remains, when discerned through comparative analysis of large systematic collections, is significant in terms of shifts in human-plant behavior; and (4) the principles of plant ecology provide an empirical basis for inferences from the plant remains about the evolving systems of human-plant interactions that produced them. These qualities make floral analysis of inestimable value in generating and testing hypotheses about the dynamics of the evolution of economic and cultural systems.

This chapter illustrates the utility of floral analysis with an example of a system as it developed over a 4,000-year time span in the central

Mississippi River valley. The large archaeology project from which the data are derived offers the unusual opportunity, through the standardized excavation of many sites of different time periods, of tracing the cultural transformations that occurred in one small area through time. The background of the project and the paleoethnobotanical methods are given in the first section of the chapter. Four major variables in the plant remains data are then examined as they change through time and are discussed in terms of their utility for discerning changing patterns of human-plant relationships.

Background and Methods

The American Bottom is a wide crescent of floodplain on the eastern side of the Mississippi River near the present location of St. Louis. The complex hydrology of the area contributes to a great variety of environments and habitats, including the broad floodplain with its shifting lakes and marshes, the talus slopes and limestone bluffs, and the stream valleys dissecting the adjacent uplands. The diverse habitats created by the varied conditions of moisture, river regime, soil, elevation, and slope allow the growth of a rich and varied flora, held by the hydrology in a state of dynamic stability (see Gregg 1975; Hus 1908; Telford 1927; Shelford 1963; Welch 1975; Yerkes 1987; and Zawacki and Hausfater 1969).

The FAI-270 Archaeological Mitigation Project, under the auspices of the University of Illinois at Urbana, the Illinois Department of Transportation, and the Federal Highway Administration, has examined some 80 archaeological sites on the floodplain and in the adjacent uplands which are to be affected by the construction of the FAI-270 highway (see Bareis and Porter 1984 for a summary of the project). Figure 9.1 shows the project area and the location of the sites from which plant remains were analyzed. The prehistoric sites cover a 4,000-year time span, from ca. 2300 B.C. (the Falling Springs phase of the Late Archaic) to ca. A.D. 1400 (the Sand Prairie phase of the Mississippian period) (see table 9.1). The plant remains from all excavated sites have been analyzed, and the results are summarized in Johannessen 1984. This section describes the methods of sampling, recovery, and analysis used.

All sites had the plow zone removed with heavy equipment, and all exposed features within the highway right-of-way were hand-excavated. Samples for flotation of a recorded volume (usually 10 liters) were collected routinely from each stratum of every feature excavated. All samples were water-floated by the Illinois Department of Transportation (IDOT) system, which is a method of tub flotation using 40-mesh screen (0.42 mm^2) (Wagner 1976). This resulted in an enormous number of samples, which

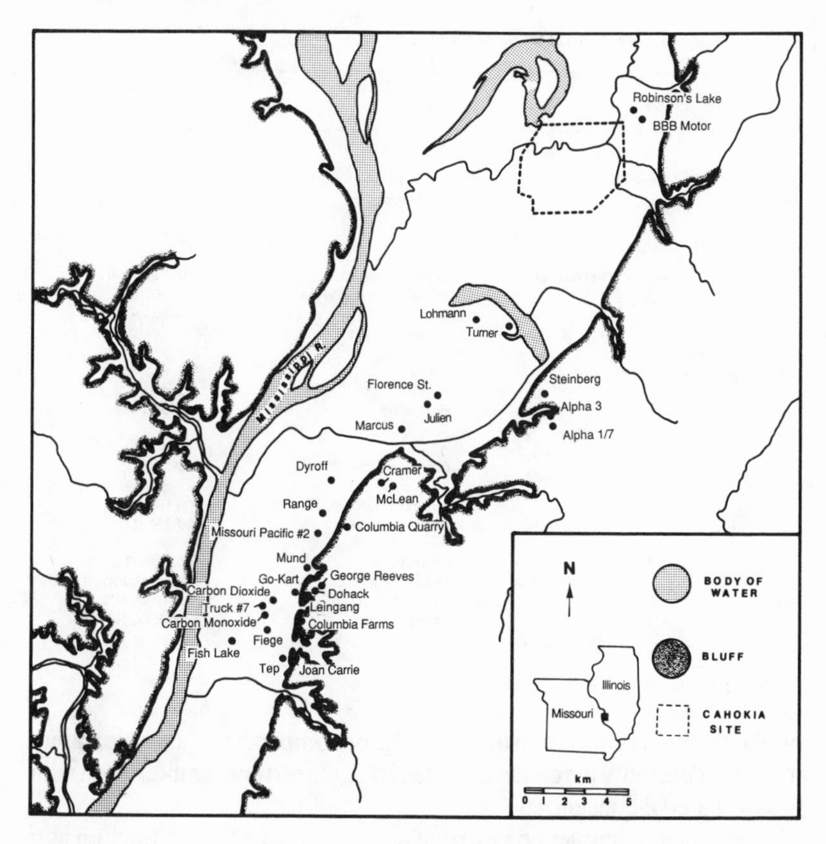

Figure 9.1. Project area and sites from which plant remains were analyzed.

then had to be subsampled to produce a manageable number for analysis of the plant material. The subsampling was accomplished in the following manner. First, all features making up a site (or a component if the site was multicomponent) were separated into gross functional and/or morphological categories, for example, structures, pits within structures, external pits, deep bell-shaped pits, shallow-basin pits, and so forth. Features with uncertain component association or those with excessive disturbance (e.g., by rodents) were rejected. Features were then selected randomly from each category to make up the number to be analyzed. Owing to the great variation in the number of features in the components, it was not feasible to analyze the same percentage of the total features at each component, but on the average 30% of the features making up each component were sampled. By this method of stratified random sampling, we hoped to recover a pattern

Table 9.1. American Bottom chronology

Period	Phase	Years
Mississippian	Sand Prairie	A.D. 1250-1400
	Moorehead	A.D. 1150-1250
	Stirling	A.D. 1050-1150
	Lohmann	A.D. 1000-1050
Emergent Mississippian	Edelhardt/Lindeman	A.D. 950-1000
	Merrell/George Reeves	A.D. 900-950
	Range	A.D. 850-900
	Dohack	A.D. 800-850
Late Woodland	Patrick	A.D. 600-800
	Mund	A.D. 450-600
	Rosewood	A.D. 300-450
Middle Woodland	Hill Lake	A.D. 1-300
	Cement Hollow	150-1 B.C.
Early Woodland	Columbia Complex	300-150 B.C.
	Marion/Florence	600-300 B.C.
Late Archaic	Prairie Lake	1000-600 B.C.
	Labras Lake	1900-1000 B.C.
	Titterington	2300-1900 B.C.
	Falling Springs	3000-2300 B.C.

From Bareis and Porter (1984), p. 12.

of plant remains characteristic of the site or component as a whole, rather than reflecting only the contents of special features, for example, those with heavy charcoal concentrations.

The selected samples consisted of a "heavy" and a "light" fraction as a result of water flotation. The heavy fraction was refloated, if necessary, in a zinc chloride solution to recover residual charcoal (Struever 1968). The total recovered botanical material was passed through a 2-mm screen, and each size fraction was sorted under low magnification (10X-30X). Only charred material was considered to be of archaeological origin. From the portion greater than 2-mm in size all plant remains were removed and sorted into categories, that is, wood, nutshell, seed, stem, maize, and so forth. The contents of each category were weighed, and the fragments were counted. The portion of the sample less than 2 mm in size was scanned carefully and all "seeds," seed fragments, and remains of domesticates (maize fragments and squash rind) were removed and counted.

Identifications were made with the aid of standard texts (Martin and Barkley 1961; Panshin and de Zeeuw 1970; Montgomery 1977) and ultimately by a one-to-one comparison to specimens in a modern reference collection. The plant remains were identified to the genus level where possible. Species-level identifications were made only if (1) only one species of the genus now exists in the area, or (2) all other possible species had been ruled out by a comparison of morphology.

The quantitative measures used for each sample included the size of the original soil sample (in liters before flotation) and the counts for the pieces in each of the several categories: nut, wood, seed (all disseminules, excluding maize kernels), tropical cultigens (maize, squash, and gourd), and other (grass stem, buds, fungus, amorphous fragments, etc.). Each of the categories nut, wood, and maize were weighed, but seeds were not, as their weight was generally negligible. Within the categories nut and seed, all pieces were examined, and counts were recorded for each taxon present (including unknowns and unidentifiables). Within the wood category, only 20 randomly selected fragments were examined for each sample, and this subsample was considered to be reasonably representative (Asch, Ford, and Asch 1972). For maize, counts of kernel fragments (kernels and germs) and cob fragments (cupules and glumes) were recorded, as well as the total maize weight. These sample data were added together for each feature, and the feature totals were also added to give a total for each component. The data presented in this chapter are derived from analysis of plant remains from 27,382 liters of fill from 984 features, which were distributed among 48 components of 29 sites.

Results

The concern of this chapter is to identify time trends in the pattern of plant remains that may reflect changes in the relationships between human and plant populations. We know that in the course of the 4,000-year time span covered by the data, human-land relationships changed from an extensive pattern depending mainly on gathered resources to an intensive pattern ultimately depending on maize agriculture. Therefore we want to examine aspects of the plant remains data which will best track the course of these changes. In this section I will examine four major variables which best reflect fundamental changes in the people-plant relationship through time. These four variables are (1) change in relative use of a major gathered food source, nuts; (2) change in the evidence of food production in terms of the indigenous seed plants; and (3) change in evidence of food production in terms of maize; and (4) change in the major fuelwoods used.

Table 9.2 presents data on the 48 site components, giving zone (floodplain coded 1 and upland coded 2), the approximate age of the component (given as the chronological midpoint of the phase to which the component is assigned, in years B.C. or A.D.), and the number of liters of feature fill processed for each. The table also gives standardized frequency data for each major class of plant remains, in mean numbers of wood

Table 9.2. Data summary

Phase and Midpoint	Site	Liters	Zone	Mean Wood	Upland Wood (%)	Mean Nut	Mean Seed	Star. Seed (%)	Feas. with Maize (%)	Nut : Wood Ratio
Falling Springs (2750 B.C.)	McLean	1080	2	14.7	95	161.0	1.5	0	0	10.95
Titterington (2200 B.C.)	George Reeves	60	2	20.3	14	20.3	0.3	0	0	1.00
	Go Kart	1607	1	2.0	16	45.9	0.4	9	0	22.57
Prairie Lake (800 B.C.)	Range	187	1	25.2	25	4.7	1.0	10	0	0.19
	Missouri Pacific	2304	1	16.6	12	12.5	0.5	14	0	0.76
	Dyroff	660	1	17.9	4	14.7	0.5	20	0	0.82
Marion/Florence (450 B.C.)	Tep	154	2	13.3	61	83.7	0.6	50	0	6.29
	Carbon Monoxide	110	1	4.9	0	0.0	1.4	17	0	0.0
	Fiege	150	1	3.0	0	11.6	0.5	0	0	3.78
	Florence	3903	1	2.6	2	1.0	0.3	33	0	0.39
Columbia Cmplx (225 B.C.)	Carbon Monoxide	340	1	6.9	19	38.8	2.6	0	0	5.57
Cement Hollow (75 B.C.)	Mund	628	1	33.8	31	44.4	6.6	43	0	1.31
Hill Lake (A.D.150)	Truck #7	693	1	38.0	58	16.2	7.1	72	0	0.43
Rosewood (A.D. 375)	Geo. Reeves	75	2	311.8	76	83.0	245.5	98	0	0.27
	Carbon Dioxide	435	1	143.7	76	108.4	1.5	29	0	0.75
	Alpha 1/7	340	2	121.8	84	8.3	4.6	67	0	0.07
	Leingang	516	2	152.3	88	50.4	1.1	55	0	0.33
	Dohack	210	2	299.5	95	10.7	3.8	92	0	0.04
	Steinberg	247	2	155.2	81	27.2	8.5	90	0	0.18
Mund (A.D. 525)	Geo. Reeves	90	2	292.1	95	15.4	18.8	96	0	0.05
	Columbia Quarry	370	2	223.4	88	15.5	9.4	82	0	0.07
	Mund	1496	1	164.6	62	29.7	64.0	94	6	0.18
Patrick (A.D. 700)	Fish Lake	420	1	11.4	19	17.0	38.8	53	0	1.49
	Alpha 3	210	2	40.3	84	17.4	0.7	82	0	0.43
	Dohack	280	2	386.1	89	196.1	43.3	95	0	0.51
	Julien	455	1	13.8	84	8.8	3.0	86	0	0.64
	Cramer	200	2	146.1	98	142.9	0.5	50	0	0.98
	Columbia Farms	251	2	186.4	82	89.2	7.1	69	0	0.48
	Range	1239	1	110.0	72	10.8	47.6	68	5	0.10
Dohack (A.D. 825)	Geo. Reeves	118	2	35.9	95	1.6	5.9	90	17	0.05
	Dohack	670	2	152.8	72	33.1	83.3	94	58	0.22
	Joan Carrie	164	2	61.8	88	9.0	102.1	97	46	0.15
Range (A.D. 875)	Range	720	1	175.4	90	5.6	47.5	93	79	0.03
Merrell /Geo. Reeves	Robinson's Lake	436	1	46.5	53	0.2	35.4	88	71	0.01
(A.D. 925)	Geo. Reeves	215	2	110.7	80	3.1	56.5	77	86	0.03
Lindeman/Edelhardt	Geo. Reeves	180	2	147.8	68	2.9	33.6	87	80	0.02
(A.D. 925)	Marcus	340	1	2.9	59	0.0	0.8	67	70	0.0
	BBB Motor	687	1	27.0	56	2.9	26.5	91	92	0.11
Lohmann (A.D. 1025)	Geo. Reeves	252	2	45.0	80	9.2	5.3	82	46	0.21
	Carbon Dioxide	607	1	45.1	42	11.1	8.9	83	75	0.25
	Lohmann	367	1	29.4	66	18.5	156.0	91	100	0.63
Stirling (A.D. 1100)	Range	736	1	64.8	76	48.4	51.9	80	90	0.75
	BBB Motor	726	1	56.4	20	3.4	38.2	86	92	0.06
	Julien	474	1	20.1	75	1.7	20.4	90	80	0.09
	Turner	1115	1	22.4	37	4.4	15.1	77	86	0.20
Moorehead (A.D.1200)	Julien	370	1	3.2	14	15.8	3.2	37	62	4.89
Sand Prairie (A.D. 1325)	Julien	305	1	58.7	46	6.5	3.9	42	80	0.11
	Florence St.	190	1	11.9	0	0.7	2.0	68	44	0.07

fragments, nut fragments, or seeds per 10-liter sample. The four remaining variables are those to be discussed in more detail below: nut-to-wood ratio (total number of nut fragments divided by total number of wood fragments); percentage of starchy seeds (percentage of total identifiable seeds belonging to the starchy seed complex—*Chenopodium* sp., *Phalaris caroliniana*, and *Polygonum erectum*); percentage of maize (percentage of the total features analyzed that yielded maize); and percentage of upland wood (percentage of the total identifiable wood fragments that were *Quercus* spp. or true *Carya*). These four variables will be examined in terms of major trends through time.

The variable nut-to-wood ratio was chosen as best reflecting the relative use of a major gathered food. The abundant nut-bearing trees of the area include the hickories (*Carya* spp.: six species of the true hickory group and two species of pecan hickories), oaks (several species of both the red and the white oak groups), black and white walnuts (*Juglans nigra* and *J. cinerea*), hazels (*Corylus americana*), and chestnuts (*Castanea dentata*). Nutshell fragments were recovered in varying amounts from all but 2 of the 48 components, with thick-shelled hickories being by far the most common throughout, with lesser amounts of acorn, black walnut, and hazelnut. Nuts appear to have been a valued resource throughout the prehistoric record; however, table 9.2 suggests that the relative, if not the absolute, contribution of nutshell to the total charcoal changes through time.

Figure 9.2 is a scattergram of the variable nut : wood ratio plotted against the age of the occupation. The nut : wood ratio was chosen as a measure of relative contribution of nutshell rather than simple mean nut frequency, since the ratio eliminates the effects of varying conditions of deposition and preservation. The correlation between the nut : wood ratio and age of occupation is strongly negative—$r = -.62$, and $r^2 = .384$; that is, almost 40% of the variation in the variable nut : wood ratio is explained by the age of the component. In other words, the relative contribution of a major gathered food, nuts, decreases with time.

Another strong trend in the data has to do with food production through the manipulation of seed plants. A phenomenon that has been noted throughout the Midwest is an increasing contribution through time of the seeds of several small-seeded native annuals, including marsh elder (*Iva annua*), sunflower (*Helianthus annuus*), chenopods (*Chenopodium* sp.), maygrass (*Phalaris caroliniana*), and erect knotweed (*Polygonum erectum*) (Gilmore 1931; Jones 1936; Kaplan and Maina 1977; Cowan, Jackson, and Moore 1981; Ford 1981; Asch and Asch 1985). This complex of plants, called the Eastern Agricultural Complex, begins to appear in quantity in the Early Woodland in Kentucky and Tennessee, and by the Middle Woodland farther to the northwest in Illinois (Watson 1985). Marsh elder and sunflower

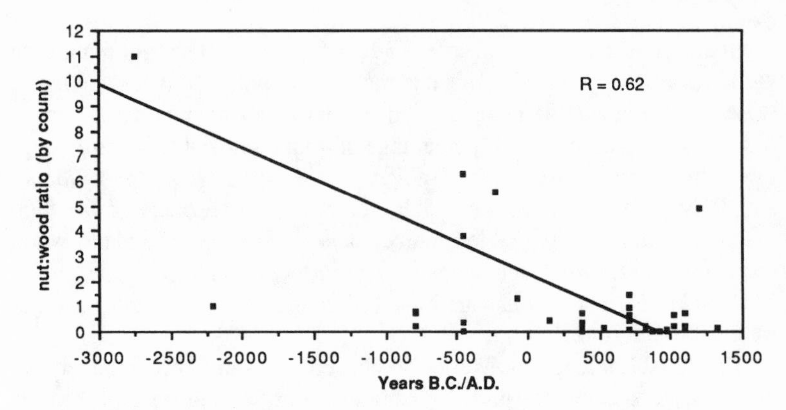

Figure 9.2. Change in nut : wood ratio.

exhibit morphological signs of domestication early in the record (Asch and Asch 1978; Yarnell 1978), and evidence for the cultivation and/or domestication of the three latter taxa is increasingly convincing (Cowan 1978; D. Asch and N. Asch 1985; N. Asch and D. Asch 1985; Fritz 1984; Smith 1985a, b, 1987; Fritz 1986).

The American Bottom data also reflect this trend, in the form of increasing abundance and frequency of these small seeds beginning in the Middle Woodland. The vast majority of this increase consists of the three taxa known as the starchy seed complex (maygrass, chenopod, and erect knotweed). The increasing contribution of this starchy seed complex is both absolute and relative, as can be seen in table 9.2. The scattergram in figure 9.3 shows the increase in the relative contribution of the starchy seeds, in terms of their percentage of the total identifiable seeds. The percentage of starchy seeds shows a strong positive correlation with the age of component ($r = .75$). About 56% of the variation in the percentage of starchy seeds is explained by the age of the component.

Another extremely important factor in the increasing dominance of food production is the advent of the widespread use of maize. Although the earliest use of maize in the Eastern Woodlands is problematic, it has been shown through carbon isotope analysis that it did not make a significant dietary contribution until about A.D. 800 or later (Bender, Barreis, and Steventon 1981; Lynott et al. 1986). The American Bottom data support this; maize occurs in negligible quantities until the Emergent Mississippian (beginning ca. A.D. 800), at which time it abruptly begins to appear in a majority of features. The scattergram in figure 9.4 plots the percentage of features yielding maize across time. It can be seen that maize makes what appears to be a rapid and abrupt leap to dominance.

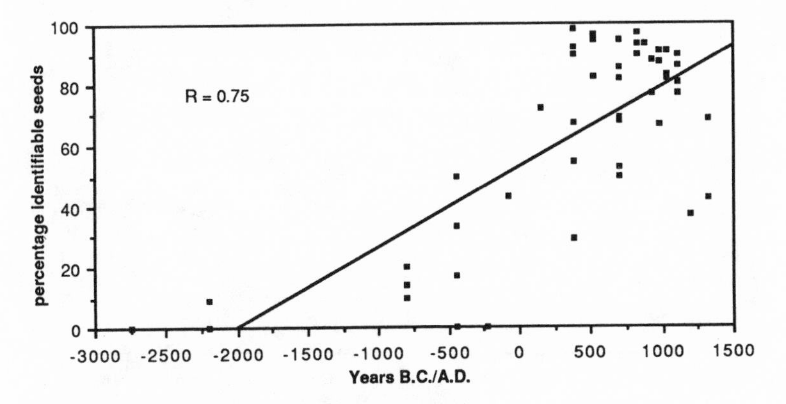

Figure 9.3. Change in percentage of starchy seeds.

We have seen in the variables examined thus far a decrease in the contribution of an important gathered resource—nuts, a relatively gradual increase in the contribution of starchy-seeded cultivated plants, and a further intensification of food production in a later rapid increase in maize. Certainly these are evidence that land use changed dramatically over this time. What other reflections of people's changing relationship to the land might the plant record show? Minnis (1978) and others have argued that changes in fuel use can indicate changes in the landscape. It was noted during the analysis of the American Bottom material that there were temporal shifts in the taxa that dominated the wood charcoal spectra. While the taxa dominant in the upland forest, oak (*Quercus* spp.) and true hickories (*Carya* spp.), were most common at sites that were located in the upland zones in all time periods, the sites on the floodplain did not exhibit this continuity. The wood charcoal of the earlier sites (before Middle Woodland) on the floodplain is dominated by such taxa as elm and hackberry (Ulmaceae), ash (*Fraxinus* spp.), honey locust (*Gleditsia triacanthos*), mulberry (*Morus rubra*), and Kentucky coffee tree (*Gymnocladus dioica*)—taxa that grow with greatest frequency in bottomland forests (Telford 1927). Beginning in the Middle Woodland, however, wood charcoal from these floodplain sites shows an increasing percentage of the oaks and hickories, dominants of the upland forest. To examine this trend across time, a scattergram was plotted (figure 9.5) of the percentage of oak and hickory (of total identifiable fragments) with the age of the component. Upland sites are differentiated from those located on the floodplain in figure 9.5. Since upland sites of all time periods yielded very high percentages of oak and

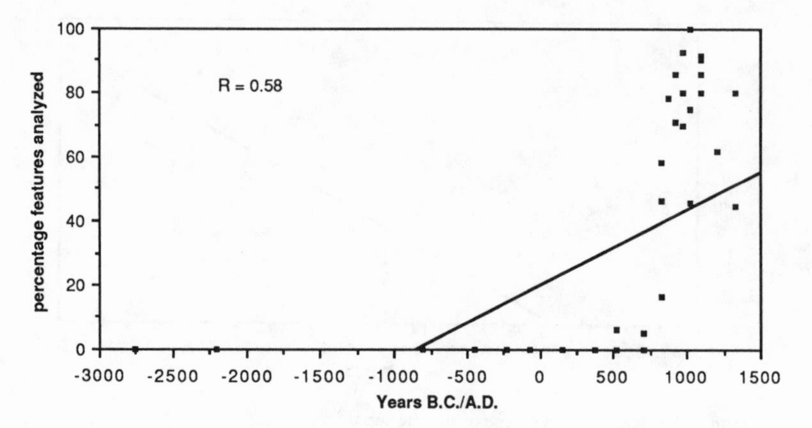

Figure 9.4. Change in percentage of features with maize.

hickory, the regression line describes only the data from floodplain sites. A gradual increase is seen, although some of the later Mississippian sites show a lowered percentage. In this case the correlation coefficient r = .50.

Discussion

In the previous section, I examined four variables that exhibit strong correlations with the age of the component. Before I discuss these trends further, it is necessary to consider the potential for bias in these time trends.

As stated previously, the major sources of bias in a record of plant remains are deposition, preservation, and recovery. These sources will be discussed in terms how they may have consistently affected the direction of the time trends—that is, are these time trends real or did spurious factors produce them?

Sampling, recovery, and analysis methods have been described as being kept constant as nearly as possible throughout the project so as to promote comparability. Some human error and variation are inevitable, but it is unlikely that they would have introduced a consistent bias that would have significantly affected the time trends seen above. Two procedural changes were made during the project to save time: (1) field crews began taking fewer flotation samples from each feature, and (2) zinc chloride flotation of the heavy fraction replaced hand sorting of the heavy fraction. The former change did not affect the selection of samples for analysis; at least one sample from each natural stratum of each feature was still available. The latter procedural change is unlikely to have affected the total amount of charcoal recovered, since recovery of residual charcoal by this method was

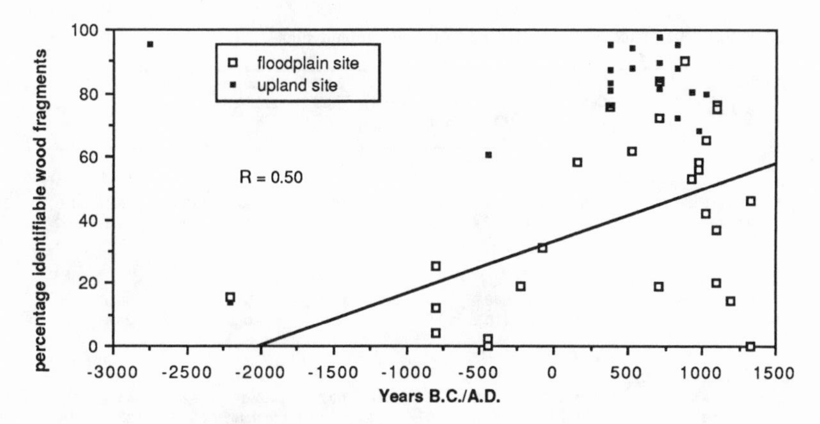

Figure 9.5. Change in percentage of upland wood types.

found to be close to 100%. Furthermore, even if these two changes did contribute slight biases to the data, they would not have caused a consistent skewing of the time trends in one direction or another, since the components were not analyzed in chronological order.

A second major source of bias is in preservation, both at the time the plant remains are charred and during the hundreds or thousands of years that the plant remains lie in the ground before they are recovered. It is well known that different classes of plant remains have different chances of being preserved through charring, so it is very difficult to reconstruct the relative contribution of each plant class to the aboriginal economy. However, this problem is not relevant in this study; here we are only concerned with comparing the varying proportions of plant classes among components, and we can assume that the properties of the plant classes that contribute to differential perservation of this kind remain constant.

A more difficult problem with preservation is what may happen to the plant remains between deposition and recovery. Factors contributing to this problem are very probably not constant from site to site and may include soil type, moisture conditions, and the actions of plants and animals. The fact that the American Bottom sites were all quite close to each other minimizes the probability that factors affecting preservation were extremely different between sites, but there is one major environmental difference: 28 of the site components are on the floodplain and 20 are in the uplands. To see if there are significant differences in the plant remains between the two groups of sites that may be due to differences in preservation, t-tests were run to assess the difference of means of the two groups on

Table 9.3. Difference of means of floodplain and upland sites

Variable	No. of Cases	Mean	Standard Dev.	Standard Error	F Value	2-tail Prob.	Variance Estimate	t Value	Df	2-tail Prob.
Mean charcoal weight (g)[a]										
Floodplain sites	28	0.9	1.1	0.2	4.71	.000	pooled	-3.79	46.0	.000
Upland sites	20	2.9	2.4	0.5			separate	-3.39	24.8	*.002*
Mean no. wood fragments[a]										
Floodplain sites	28	41.4	48.9	9.2	5.08	.000	pooled	-4.45	46.0	.000
Upland sites	20	145.9	110.2	24.6			separate	-3.97	24.4	*.001*
Mean no. nut fragments[a]										
Floodplain sites	28	17.3	23.0	4.3	6.41	.000	pooled	-2.62	46.0	.012
Upland sites	20	49.0	58.3	13.0			separate	-2.31	23.3	*.030*
Mean no. seeds[a]										
Floodplain sites	28	20.9	32.9	6.2	3.14	.007	pooled	-0.81	46.0	.422
Upland sites	20	31.6	58.3	13.0			separate	-0.74	27.6	*.464*
Percentage starchy seeds[b]										
Floodplain sites	28	55.1	32.7	6.2	1.25	.617	pooled	-1.92	46.0	*.061*
Upland sites	20	72.7	29.2	6.5			separate	-1.96	43.6	.057

Note: 2-tailed probabilities in italics indicate whether pooled or separate variance estimates were used based on the F-tests of the sample variances.

[a] Per 10 liters.
[b] of total identifiable seeds.

several variables: mean weight (in grams) per 10-liter sample, mean counts of wood, nut, and seeds per 10-liter sample, and percentage of starchy seeds. Table 9.3 shows that the values for mean weight, mean wood, and mean nut are significantly higher for the upland sites than for floodplain sites. The upland sites also have a higher mean number of seeds than the floodplain, although the difference is not significant. These quantitative differences may result from a better chance of preservation in the drier, better-drained soils of the uplands. Interestingly, for a primarily qualitative measure like percentage of starchy seeds, the difference of means and of variances of the upland vs. floodplain sites is not significant (at the .05 level); that is, these two groups could (statistically) have come from the same population. This makes sense, since these differences in preservation would be more likely to affect quantity than composition of a plant class.

This possible factor of better overall preservation at upland sites should not contribute a consistent bias to the time trends for two reasons: (1) there are sites of both early and late time periods in both environments, and (2) we have avoided using raw frequency data in examining time trends. The use of ratios and percentages should go some way towards obviating this factor of differential preservation.

We can then cautiously reject the likelihood that consistent bias has been introduced into the time trends through sampling, analysis, or differential preservation. The major remaining factor is deposition, that is, the different ways in which the plant remains entered the archaeological record. It was noted during the analysis that the distribution of the plant taxa across the sites was very homogeneous; most samples yielded very similar mixtures of taxa no matter what their feature context. The feature fills, then, do not appear to represent episodes of primary deposition, since one would expect a much more heterogeneous distribution with primary deposition, resulting from a variety of activities at different seasons. The contents of the features appear to be rather the results of a mixing of many daily episodes of burning, discarding of inedible parts, and accidental loss during parching and cooking. It is certainly possible that some of the variation we have seen through time in the proportions of certain plant classes result, not from changes in the overall importance of those plant classes in the economy, but from different processing techniques that resulted in different patterns of deposition. For example, it is possible that the observed increase in maize remains seen in the Emergent Mississippian results from the fact that people began to parch maize for storage or to use cobs for smudge rather than eating it green, and that it is this change in processing that is reflected in the plant record rather than an increase in maize's contribution to the diet. However, the latter explanation is more coherent; that is, it fits better into the archaeological picture of the time as a whole (e.g., the appearance of stone hoes and population nucleation at regional centers, as well as the carbon isotope studies on the dietary contribution of maize). In any case, whether the shifts in the plant record result from differences in processing or in relative consumption, they have nevertheless resulted from changes in basic behavioral patterns (i.e., culture change).

I have argued that the time trends of the four variables are real, that is, that they are reflections of changes in the plant-related behavior of the prehistoric people rather than spurious factors of preservation or recovery. Are the trends real statistically? In other words, given the great variation in the values of the variables for the 48 components, how much of that variation can be explained by the fact that the components are of different ages? We have seen that a certain percentage of the variation in the variables can be accounted for by the age of the component: 38% of the variation in the nut : wood ratio, 34% of the variation in the percentage of maize, 25% of the variation in the percentage of upland wood (at floodplain sites), and a very large 56% of the variation in the percentage of starchy seeds ($r^2 = .3$, .34, .25, .56, respectively). However, the significant correlation coefficients for these four variables with time ($r = -.62$, $r = .58$, $r = .50$, $r = .75$, respectively) are measures of linear relationships. It is clear from an

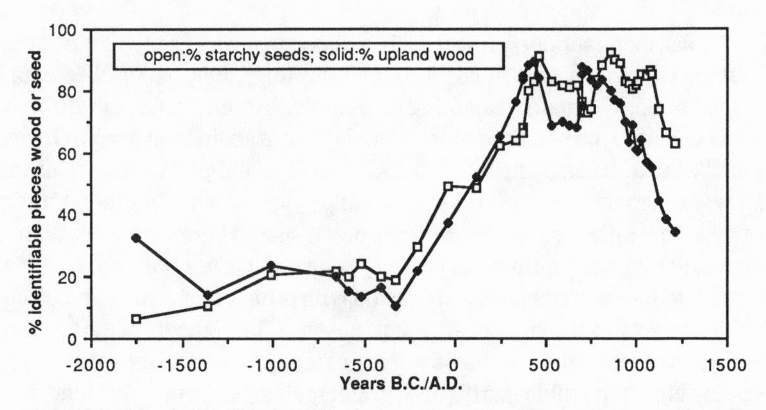

Figure 9.6. Smoothed data for percentage of starchy seeds and percentage of upland wood.

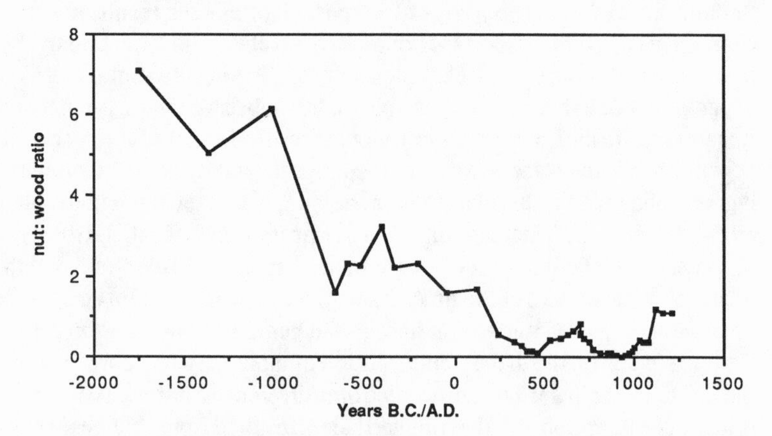

Figure 9.7. Smoothed data for nut : wood ratio.

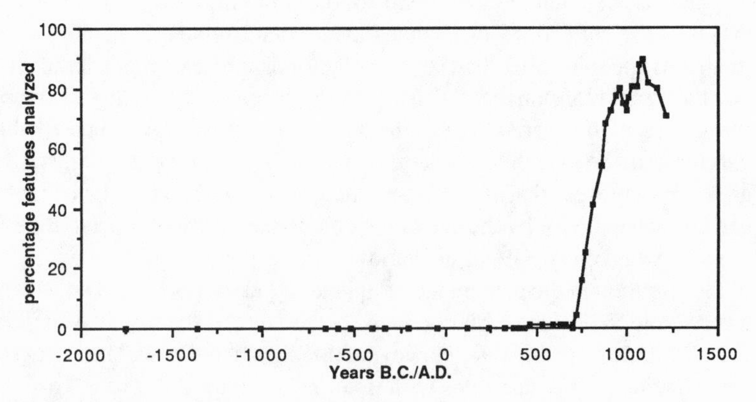

Figure 9.8. Smoothed data for percentage of features with maize.

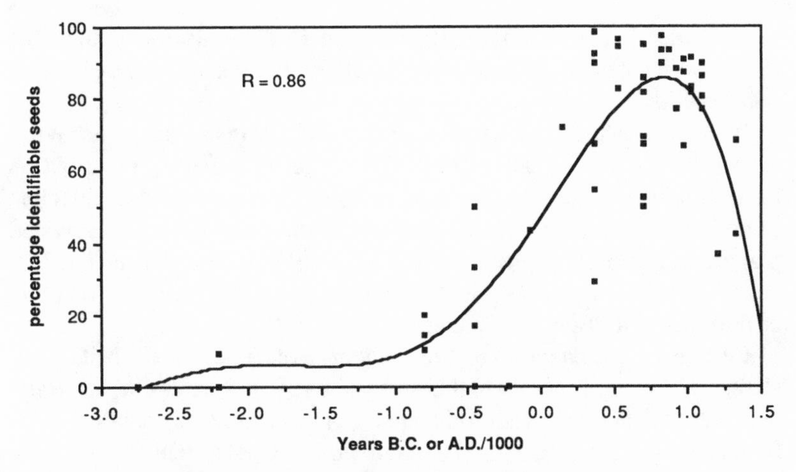

Figure 9.9. Fit of fifth-order polynomial curve to starchy seed scattergram.

examination of the scattergrams that the relationships between the four variables and the independent variable time are not linear; thus it is likely that the correlation coefficients have underestimated the true degree of the relationships.

It is possible to approximate the actual form of the relationship by smoothing the data. In this method, the line that best describes the relationship between two variables is derived by plotting running median. The median of the first five values of each variable is plotted. The next point is obtained by including the next value of each variable and dropping the first one, thus producing overlapping groups of five values and so on until the last five values in the entire series are used (Hartwig and Dearing 1979:36-39). A comparison of the approximate rates of change obtained by this method can be seen in figures 9.6, 9.7, and 9.8. Variables percentage of starchy seeds and percentage of upland wood (figure 9.6), and nut : wood ratio (figure 9.7) can be roughly described as having a long period of relatively slow change followed by a shorter period of rapid change which levels off and may even change direction at the end of the time span. The fourth variable, percentage of maize, has a different shape, jumping up rapidly and remaining high for the rest of the time (figure 9.8). The goodness of fit of the data to a curve describing such nonlinear relationships is likely to be better than to a linear model, and figure 9.9 illustrates the much-improved fit of a nonlinear curve—in this case a fifth-order polynomial. The nonlinear function explains 74% ($r^2 = .74$) of the variation in the percentage of starchy seeds—an improvement of 18% over the linear relationship ($r^2 = .56$).

Figures 9.6, 9.7, and 9.8, show the trends in the four variables in relation to each other. In the remainder of this section, I will discuss the significance of these changes as reflections of facets of the changing people-plant relationships.

It is clear that these trends reflect major changes in patterns of behavior. We have seen, starting in the Middle Woodland, an increasing contribution by a complex of cultivated indigenous plants, with a concomitant decline in nut remains. This increasing importance of the products of cultivated plants is very closely related to a replacement of bottomland wood types by oak and hickory. Maize came into widespread use only after some 700 years of development of this new pattern.

Certainly these patterns are direct evidence of some kinds of behavioral change; for example, we know that diet has changed over this time span, and that patterns of fuel collection changed. But the data also have other, more fundamental, implications. The nature of the plant remains imply a particular kind, in some cases specifiable, of relationship of people with those plants (cf. Harlan and de Wet 1965; de Wet and Harlan 1975). For example, we can say with some certainty that crops of maygrass (the most abundant small seed type in later time periods) must have been maintained by a set of behaviors including some kind of land clearance and tillage, sowing, tending, harvesting, and storage. Maygrass does not now grow in Illinois north of its southern tip, and yet it has been found at archaeological sites at least as far north as Jo Davies County (Katie Parker, pers. com.), 400 miles north of its present range, and thus must have been maintained by a relationship with humans. By knowing something about the behavior of maygrass in these northerly regions (which can be discovered by experiment), we can further specify the prehistoric human-maygrass relationship, for example, probable month of sowing and harvest, yield per hectare, and tillage requirements.

Another specifiable relationship can be derived from the morphological (genetic) changes seen in other members of the Eastern Agricultural Complex, such as marsh elder, sunflower, and chenopods (for the details of these morphological changes, see Asch and Asch 1978; Yarnell 1978; Smith 1985a and b). From these genetic changes it necessarily follows that the populations of the species were involved in a particular, quite intimate, relationship with humans—one which entailed sowing, seed selection and seed storage for next year's crop, and isolation from wild relatives. The genetic variants could not have developed and been maintained without this set of selective pressures from human behaviors. The cultural requirements of the tropical domesticates maize and tobacco (tobacco begins to appear in the Middle Woodland) are even more rigorous. Domesticated plants and people are tightly knit in a web of interdependence; they cannot survive (or at least cannot maintain the status quo) without each other. Thus, aspects of the patterns of plant remains have certain necessary behavioral correlates, at least in terms of fairly specific horticultural or agricultural practices (clearance, tillage, seed selection and storage) as well as work scheduling and the annual cycle of activities. We can quite safely say that the annual cycle of activities of a people who depend largely on nuts is quite different from that of a people who must sow, till, and harvest maygrass or maize, and we can also suggest specific ways in which they might be different, based on knowledge of the habits and the ecological requirements of the plants.

The change in wood use is another reflection of changing people-plant relationships. This shift in fuel gathering behavior has a number of possible explanations, but the most coherent one is systemic; that is, that this change is closely interrelated with the other changing facets of the system. Figures 9.6 and 9.7 show the very close correspondence between the increase in oak and hickory use and the increase in the percentage of starchy seeds, as well as the reciprocal trend in the nut remains. This may reflect a process in which the previously important and protected oaks and hickories (the major nut-bearing trees) are expended to make room and light for the increasingly necessary cultivated plants. The previous constraints on the expenditure of these nut-bearing trees were lifted—they were no longer so carefully spared when clearing or collecting fuel, and they became, in fact, the preferred fuel in view of their high fuel value, now that their value as food producers had decreased (Rindos and Johannessen 1984).

These new sets of relationships that had developed by the Late Woodland were important preconditions for the rapid incorporation of maize that marks the Emergent Mississippian, in that by the Late Woodland there already existed (1) a dependence on cultivated seed plants, (2) a long cultural history of the behaviors associated with plant husbandry, and (3) a landscape altered by human activities. It is doubtful whether without these preconditions maize agriculture would have achieved the extent or the impact that it did. Thus, although the incorporation of maize as a staple was abrupt and appears to have had a synergistic effect on the complexity of the economic system (if not the entire cultural system), it was firmly rooted in the previous 4,000 years of developmental history.

Across this time span, changes in the patterns of plant remains imply changes in diet, in the seasonal cycle of activities, probably in demographic potential and territory size, in practices of land tenure as use of the land became more intensive, and in the landscape itself, thus feeding back into changing ways of relating to that landscape. Surely these trends also indicate that cultural perceptions of important resources changed; in the Archaic the people were living in a nut grove, in the Middle and Late

Woodland they were living in a garden, and in the Mississippian they were living in a cornfield, not perhaps literally, but certainly in terms of their own cultural perceptions of their worlds.

Conclusions

In this chapter I have suggested that data from plant remains from a sequence of archaeological sites—with the very important provision that the sample is large and has been collected and analyzed systematically—is a unique and powerful tool for investigating the economic basis for culture change. With such a sample, variation damps out, and regularities and trends become evident in the data. These regularities and trends reflect patterns of normative, that is, rule-governed, behavior. The nature of these patterns of behavior can to some degree be specified, because some of the characteristics of the plant record can only have resulted from certain types of interactions of human populations with plants.

The regularities and trends we have seen in the American Bottom data are by no means isolated or local phenomena. There are major chronological, quantitative, and qualitative correspondences (as well as some interesting divergences) from throughout the Eastern Woodlands. It is exciting that as more large, systematic, quantified collections of plant remains are made, increasingly clear patterns are emerging over wide areas that will allow an unprecedented view into the processes and dynamics of culture history and culture change.

Perhaps the most important contribution that analysis of large collections of plant remains can make is to help us understand the ways in which agricultural systems develop, long a subject of (largely speculative) debate. In paleoethnobotanical data we have evidence with which to test theories about the processes of such development. One extended example may further illustrate the potential of paleoethnobotany in this direction. Rindos (1984) has proposed a model in which plant domestication and agricultural systems are consequences of the interaction of human populations and the plant populations that they use regularly. The same evolutionary principles can be applied to this interaction as to the coevolution of any two groups of organisms that have close and regular interaction. In Rindos's model, the unintentional selective pressures that human and plant populations exert on each other in the process of their interaction are sufficient explanation for the development of the system. This approach differs in important respects from other models that invoke exogenous variables (such as climate change or population pressure) in adaptationist explanatory frameworks.

Rindos proposes that three overlapping stages of domestication are the result of coevolutionary interactions between people and plants. The first—

incidental domestication—occurs as humans unconsciously protect and disperse in the general environment the plants that they use regularly. Specialized domestication comes about as human activities further change their local environments, resulting in a new niche, the agroecology, in which a new set of selective pressures prevail. These processes culminate in agricultural domestication, at which point there is a surge of growth in the system as crop plants evolve further in response to the new set of selective pressures that characterize the agroecology. Rindos's use of symbolic logic expresses the essential relationships of the model economically and allows the derivation of predictive statements, that is, of verifiable empirical claims that follow from the argument. This high degree of specificity in the model allows comparison to actual observations of developing agricultural systems. Many of the predictions of the model show a close congruence with aspects of the plant data from the American Bottom. The rates of change in the major variables (a long period of relatively slow change followed by rapid change which eventually levels off) is similar to the logistic curve that the model predicts for the rate of increase in the relative abundance of domesticates over time. The decrease in nut remains, the increase in the starchy seeds, and the accompanying change in wood types seem to reflect, in Rindos's terms, the predicted decrease in the contribution of wild foods and the growth of the agroecology. The change in wood types also illustrates an important feature of the model, which is that habitat in this case acts both as an independent and a dependent variable. The rapid and abrupt change in the contribution of maize is congruent with the model's prediction of explosive expansion of the system under agricultural domestication.

These suggestive correspondences require further examination, but the example stands as an illustration of the important function of large quantified paleoethnobotanical analyses in providing empirical evidence with which to test models of agricultural origins and development.

Acknowledgments

This research was made possible by Charles J. Bareis, the Department of Anthropology at the University of Illinois, Urbana, and the Illinois Department of Transportation. I thank especially Debby Pearsall, Lucy Whalley, and the FAI-270 ethnobotany lab workers for their contributions.

References Cited

Asch, David L., and Nancy B. Asch. 1978. The economic potential of *Iva annua* and its prehistoric importance in the Lower Illinois valley. In *The nature and status of ethnobotany*, ed. R. I. Ford, M. F. Brown, M. Hodge, and W. L. Merrill, pp. 301-41. Anthropological Papers, no. 67. University of Michigan, Museum of Anthropology.

_____. 1985. Prehistoric plant cultivation in west-central Illinois. In *Prehistoric food production in North America*, ed. R. I. Ford, pp. 149-203. Anthropological Papers, no. 75. University of Michigan, Museum of Anthropology.

Asch, Nancy B., and David L. Asch. 1985. Archaeobotany. In *The Hill Creek Homestead and the late Mississippian settlement in the lower Illinois valley*, ed. M. D. Conner, pp. 115-70. Kampsville Archeological Center, Research Series 1. Kampsville: Center for American Archeology.

Asch, Nancy B., Richard I. Ford, and David L. Asch. 1972. *Paleoethnobotany of the Koster site: The Archaic horizons.* Reports of Investigations, no. 24. Springfield: Illinois State Museum.

Bareis, Charles J., and James W. Porter, eds. 1984. *American Bottom archaeology.* Urbana: University of Illinois Press.

Bender, Margaret M., David A. Baerreis, and Raymond L. Steventon. 1981. Further light on carbon isotopes and Hopewell agriculture. *American Antiquity* 46:346-53.

Cowan, C. Wesley. 1978. The prehistoric use and distribution of maygrass in eastern North America: Cultural and phytogeographical implications. In *The nature and status of ethnobotany*, ed. R. I. Ford, M. F. Brown, M. Hodge, and W. L. Merrill, pp. 263-88. Anthropological Papers, no. 67. University of Michigan, Museum of Anthropology.

Cowan, C. Wesley, H. Edwin Jackson, Katherine Moore, Andrew Nicklehoff, and Tristine L. Smart. 1981. The Cloudsplitter rockshelter, Menifee County, Kentucky: A preliminary report. *Southeastern Archaeological Conference Bulletin* 24:60-76.

de Wet, Jan M., and Jack R. Harlan. 1975. Weeds and domesticates: Evolution in the man-made habitat. *Economic Botany* 29:99-107.

Ford, Richard I. 1981. Gardening and farming before A.D. 1000: Patterns of prehistoric cultivation north of Mexico. *Journal of Ethnobiology* 1(1):6-27.

Fritz, Gayle J. 1984. Identification of cultigen amaranth and chenopod from rockshelter sites in northwest Arkansas. *American Antiquity* 49(3):558-72.

_____. 1986. Prehistoric Ozark agriculture: The University of Arkansas rockshelter collections. Ph.D. diss., Department of Anthropology, University of North Carolina, Chapel Hill. Ann Arbor: University Microfilms.

Gilmore, Melvin R. 1931. Vegetal remains of the Ozark Bluff-dweller culture. *Papers of the Michigan Academy of Science, Arts, and Letters* 14:83-102.

Gregg, Michael L. 1975. Settlement morphology and production specialization: The Horseshoe Lake site, a case study. Ph.D. diss., Department of Anthropology, University of Wisconsin-Milwaukee. Ann Arbor: University Microfilms.

Harlan, Jack R., and Jan M. de Wet. 1965. Some thoughts on weeds. *Economic Botany* 18(1):16-24.

Hartwig, Frederick, and Brian E. Dearing. 1979. *Exploratory data analysis*. Quantitative Applications in the Social Sciences Series. London: Sage.

Hus, Henri. 1908. An ecological cross-section of the Mississippi River in the region of St. Louis, Missouri. *Missouri Botanical Garden, Annual Report* 19:127-258.

Johannessen, Sissel. 1984. Paleoethnobotany. In *American Bottom archaeology*, ed. C. J. Bareis and J. W. Porter, pp. 197-214. Urbana: University of Illinois Press.

Jones, Volney. 1936. The vegetal remains of Newt Kash Hollow shelter. In *Rockshelters in Menifee County, Kentucky*, ed. W. S. Webb and W. D. Funkhouser, University of Kentucky Reports in Anthropology and Archaeology 3:147-67.

Kaplan, Lawrence, and Shirley L. Maina. 1977. Archaeological botany of the Apple Creek site, Illinois. *Journal of Seed Technology* 2:40-53.

Lynott, Mark J., Thomas W. Boutton, James E. Price, and Dwight E. Nelson. 1986. Stable carbon isotope evidence for maize agriculture in southeast Missouri and northeast Arkansas. *American Antiquity* 51(1):51-65.

Martin, Alexander C., and William D. Barkley. 1961. *Seed identification manual*. Berkeley: University of California Press.

Minnis, Paul E. 1978. Paleoethnobotanical indicators of prehistoric environmental disturbance: A case study. In *The nature and status of ethnobotany*, ed. R. I. Ford, M. F. Brown, M. Hodge, and W. L. Merrill, pp. 347-66. Anthropological Papers, no. 67. University of Michigan, Museum of Anthropology.

Montgomery, Frederick H. 1977. *Seeds and fruits of plants of eastern Canada and the northeastern United States*. Toronto: University of Toronto Press.

Panshin, A. J., and Carl de Zeeuw. 1970. *Textbook of wood technology*. vol. 1. 3rd ed. New York: McGraw-Hill.

Rindos, David. 1984. *The origins of agriculture: An evolutionary perspective*. New York: Academic Press.

Rindos, David, and Sissel Johannessen. 1984. Human/plant interactions and cultural change in the American Bottom.

Shelford, Victor E. 1963. *The ecology of North America*. Urbana: University of Illinois Press.

Smith, Bruce D. 1985a. The role of *Chenopodium* as a domesticate in the pre-maize gardens of the eastern United States. *Southeastern Archaeology* 4(1):51-72.

_____. 1985b. *Chenopodium berlandieri* spp. *jonesianum*: Evidence for a Hopewellian domesticate from Ash Cave, Ohio. *Southeastern Archaeology* 4:107-33.

_____. 1987. The independent domestication of indigenous seed-bearing plants in eastern North America. In *Emergent horticultural economies of the eastern Woodlands*, ed. W. Keegan, pp. 3-47. Center for Archaeological Investigations, occasional paper no. 7. Southern Illinois University at Carbondale.

Struever, Stuart. 1968. Flotation techniques for the recovery of small-scale archaeological remains. *American Antiquity* 33(3):353-62.

Telford, Clarence J. 1927. Third report on a forest survey of Illinois. *Bulletin of the Illinois State Natural History Survey*, vol. 16.

Wagner, Gail E. 1976. IDOT flotation procedure manual. Fairview Heights: Illinois Department of Transportation, District 8.

Watson, Patty Jo. 1985. The impact of early horticulture in the upland drainages of the midwest and midsouth. In *Prehistoric food production in North America*, ed. R. I. Ford, pp. 99-147. Anthropological papers, no. 75. University of Michigan, Museum of Anthropology.

Welch, David. 1975. Wood utilization at Cahokia: Identification of wood charcoal from the Merrell Tract. M.A. thesis, University of Wisconsin-Madison.

Yarnell, Richard A. 1978. Domestication of sunflower and sumpweed in eastern North America. In *The nature and status of ethnobotany*, ed. R. I. Ford, M. F. Brown, M. Hodge, and W. L. Merrill, pp. 289-99. Anthropological Papers, no. 67. University of Michigan, Museum of Anthropology.

Yerkes, Richard W. 1987. *Prehistoric life on the Mississippi floodplain*. Chicago: University of Chicago Press.

Zawacki, April A., and Glenn Hausfater. 1969. Early vegetation of the lower Illinois valley: A study of the distribution of floral resources with reference to prehistoric cultural-ecological adaptations. *Reports of Investigations*, no. 17. Illinois State Museum, Springfield.

10

Environmental Interpretation of Archaeological Charcoal

Tristine Lee Smart and Ellen S. Hoffman

Introduction

Charcoal is the most common plant material recovered archaeologically, yet it frequently remains unanalyzed. All archaeologists appreciate the importance of charcoal for radiocarbon dating. However, it also provides evidence of selection and use of wood at a site and of prehistoric vegetation and environment (Bohrer 1986:33; Minnis 1987:121). In this paper we present a guide to the use of charcoal for environmental reconstruction to help researchers take full advantage of this valuable source of data.

By charcoal we mean the charred remains of a plant's woody structures. While charcoal is predominantly from trees and shrubs, a few grasses and other monocotyledons have woodlike structures which can be preserved. We are excluding seeds and nutshell from the present discussion.

Any archaeological interpretation requires an understanding of the processes that create archaeological remains. Therefore we begin by examining the factors that produce an archaeological charcoal assemblage. We then consider how well a charcoal assemblage reflects the floristic environment in one particular historic case. Finally, we discuss the kinds of environmental interpretations that are made from archaeological charcoal data. The current state of the discipline presented here is the result of half a century of research by paleoethnobotanists interested in interpreting archaeological charcoal assemblages (e.g., Salisbury and Jane 1940;

Godwin and Tansley 1941; Western 1963, 1971; Dimbleby [1967] 1978; Asch, Ford, and Asch 1972; Conrad and Koeppen 1972; Willcox 1974; Schweingruber 1976, 1977; Minnis 1978, 1987; Ford 1979; Cowan and Smart 1981; Miller 1982, 1985; Zalucha 1982, 1983; Pearsall 1983; Kohler et al. 1984; Lopinot 1984).

Factors Producing a Charcoal Assemblage

A number of factors operating together produce an archaeological charcoal assemblage:

1. Cultural and natural mechanisms that bring woody plants to a site
2. Cultural and physical factors affecting burning and preservation
3. Field techniques used for the recovery and sampling of charred plant remains
4. Laboratory techniques used for sampling and identifying charred plant remains

We must consider how each factor affects the woody plant types recovered from a site to understand the relationship between charcoal assemblage and prehistoric environment.

Transport of Woody Plants

Cultural mechanisms

People bring wood to a site for specific purposes, such as building, making artifacts, or for fuel. Selection of a wood type, or taxon, for a particular use depends on a number of criteria, including the physical properties, form, and size of the wood; relative abundance and ease of collection; and cultural values.

Fuelwood. The use of a particular wood type as fuel can depend upon physical characteristics, such as heat content and quantity of smoke produced during burning. For example, the Ingalik (an Athapaskan group in Alaska) selected spruce (*Picea*) wood for fuel in the winter because of its heating qualities. In the spring, when less heat was required, they also burned willow (*Salix*) and cottonwood (*Populus*). Birch (*Betula*) never was burned inside because its bark gives off a black smoke (Osgood 1958:163). However, when smoke was needed for a woman's smokehouse, the Ingalik used rotten willow (*Salix*) for kindling (Osgood 1940:319).

Culture-specific aesthetic values can influence the selection of firewood. For instance, the Ingalik never used alder (*Alnus*) wood as fuel because they found its red sap offensive (Osgood 1958:163).

Availability affects the ease of collection of a taxon, which is a consideration in selecting firewood. In some cases availability is more important than the physical characteristics of a wood type for people gathering fuelwood. The Huastec (Mayan speakers in northeastern Mexico) use several woody taxa for firewood which produce very poor quality fuel. These types are all members of the fast-growing successional plant community found in fallow cornfields and thus are readily available sources of fuelwood. In fact, the amount of land devoted to cornfield-fallow cycled fields depends to a large extent on fuelwood requirements (Alcorn 1981:225-26). Sometimes, preference for relatively rare or distant wood types is overruled by the time and effort required to obtain them. If preferred types become scarce due to overcollection, other taxa are used (Collier 1975:43, 45; Devres, Inc. 1980:27; Heizer 1963:190-91). For example, among peasant households in the communal lands of Zimbabwe there is less reliance on preferred wood types and more indiscriminate use of species for both fuel and construction in areas with greater levels of deforestation (Campbell, Du Toit, and Haney 1985:9-10).

Yet when particular fuel characteristics are required for special purposes, local availability might not be a factor in selecting wood. For example, aboriginal men in the Murray River area of Australia traveled considerable distances to collect false sandlewood to illuminate their canoes. When burned, this wood produces a strong light, an agreeable fragrance, and almost no smoke (Nicholson 1981:67).

The form of wood is also considered in choosing firewood. Fuelwood collectors today generally prefer fallen trees and dead branchwood (Heizer 1963:189; Openshaw 1974:271). This affects the taxa selected, because some trees are more likely to drop their branches than others (Asch, Ford, and Asch 1972:6; Godwin and Tansley 1941:118). When dead trees or branches are no longer available, live tree limbs or young saplings are cut for fuel. Eventually mature trees are used, especially by individuals who produce charcoal to be sold for fuel in urban centers. When wood supplies are extremely scarce, tree stumps are uprooted (not an easy task) and even roots of living trees can be "mined" for fuel (Devres, Inc. 1980:27-28; Heizer 1963:189; Openshaw 1974:271).

Size is also a factor in fuelwood selection. Small pieces of wood serve as kindling to start a fire, while various larger sizes are used as fuel. For example, the aboriginal peoples of Australia would carefully select woods of different sizes and types to create fires for specific purposes, such as removing scales, fur, or feathers from animals; grilling small game; or heating stones for baking ovens (Nicholson 1981:63).

Other Uses. Wood also is used extensively in the construction of artifacts and structures. The particular wood type used is not critical for some purposes. For example, the Ingalik made rafts using dry logs of the proper size regardless of wood type (Osgood 1940:381). Other cultural activities require woods with specific qualities (such as flexibility, hardness, strength, or durability) found only in particular taxa (e.g., Coles, Heal, and Orme 1978:25-26). Cultural values can determine the characteristics desired in woody plants. For native peoples of western North America, the thorny qualities of taxa such as devil's club (*Oplopanax horridus*) are associated with protection against witchcraft and bring power and luck to the user (Turner 1982:27).

Wood types with qualities that people value might be protected from other uses or even imported when not locally available. For example, the Huastec only make houseposts of woods that have straight trunks and are strong and decay resistant. Trees of these taxa may be spared when land is cleared for agricultural fields (Alcorn 1981:226). At Chaco Canyon in the American Southwest, the preferred wood type for roof beams, ponderosa pine (*Pinus ponderosa*), had to be transported from forests over 20 miles upstream or over 40 miles to the south (Lekson 1983:276, 1984:13).

Summary. The assemblage of woody taxa brought to and used at a site is the product of cultural selection which takes into account the activities at the site; the physical characteristics, availability, form, and size of local wood types; and culture-specific factors. Clearly, it is far too simplistic to assume that the proportions of wood types in this assemblage reflect the relative abundance of these taxa in the local vegetation.

Natural Mechanisms

Wood and charcoal can be transported to a site by natural means. Wood fragments or charcoal from area forest fires might be desposited at a site before, during, or after occupation. Burrows, root holes, earthworms, and other disturbances also add wood and charcoal to (or disperse them within) archaeological deposits (Lopinot 1984:99-101; Stein 1983; Wood and Johnson 1978). In addition, subsurface burning of roots during forest fires produces buried charcoal deposits (Brunett 1972:87-88). Such wood and charcoal fragments are not subject to cultural selection. Factors including proximity, size, and portability of fragments may determine which pieces are deposited at a site.

Charcoal brought to a site by natural mechanisms provides information about area vegetation but probably is not contemporary with site occupation. It is important to recognize charcoal from these sources. Site sediment collected away from specific cultural contexts (such as features, structures, and middens) can be examined to determine the amount of "background charcoal" deposited in part by natural mechanisms (Cowan and Smart 1981:28). Also, disturbances such as burrows and root holes are often recognized during excavation.

Wood Burning and Preservation

As with other types of plant macroremains, wood is more likely to be preserved if it is charred. Therefore we are focusing our discussion on charcoal rather than unburned wood.

Burning

Archaeological charcoal is produced by catastrophic burning of all or part of a site and on a smaller scale by the intentional or accidental burning of the wood itself (Miller and Smart 1984:15). Of these three processes, intentional burning is most likely to occur (Miller 1982:130-31, 139); therefore charcoal remnants of fuelwood are common. Other cultural practices, such as intentional burning of garbage or ceremonial burning of goods (as sometimes occurs in death rituals), can increase the potential for finding woods used in manufacture or construction.

Yet accidental burning does occur and may account for some charcoal at a site. Cultural practices involving the use of wood near or in conjunction with fire are more likely to result in accidental burning (cf. Miller and Smart 1984:16). For example, spruce (*Picea*) sticks used by the Ingalik to broil fish over a fire could accidently fall into the flames (Osgood 1940:175-76). In addition, the type of materials used in construction can increase the chances of accidental burning of an entire structure. Thatch will catch fire more easily than adobe brick.

Understanding why wood burned helps us determine how it was used. This in turn allows us to investigate cultural preferences for different wood types. The archaeological context of samples is critical for this analysis. Features identified as hearths, ovens, and roasting pits indicate intentional burning of firewood. Debris from intentional burning is likely to be recovered from ash dumps, middens, and other secondary deposits as well (Miller 1985:4; Minnis 1978:359). Variation in charcoal taxa from different types of thermal features at a site might indicate selection of specific fuelwoods for particular purposes (Cowan and Smart 1981:27). Remnants of accidental burning can be left in their original locations, providing evidence of use. For example, wall or roof debris (including charcoal) from a burned structure might remain where it fell until it is recovered archaeologically. Such charcoal provides evidence of the woods selected for construction purposes (e.g., Cowan et al. 1978:139).

Off-Site Burning

People intentionally burn area vegetation away from the site. Fire is commonly used to clear vegetation for agricultural plots. Hunters use fire both on a large scale for surrounds or drives and on a smaller scale to flush animals from burrows or undergrowth. Burning underbrush improves visibility for hunting, aids the gathering of roots or tubers, and makes travel easier. Setting fire to vegetation also can stimulate growth of foods preferred by wild prey or domestic herding animals (Gade 1985:109; Hudson 1978:276-77; Nicholson 1981:66-68; Powell 1982:207).

Cultural factors can promote off-site burning of vegetation. For example, people in Madagascar burn vegetation to express political or social discontent (Gade 1985:109). The aboriginal peoples of Australia set some fires to "clean up the country," returning it to its original state and cleansing it of evil spirits. This practice could have reduced the threat of serious fires occurring naturally in the area (Nicholson 1981:69).

Charcoal remnants of off-site fires can be recovered in soil or sediment samples from previously burned areas, such as former agricultural plots (e.g., Albert and Minc 1987:47-56). Charcoal from these fires also can wash into local bodies of water or bogs, to be recovered in sediment cores (e.g., Simmons and Innes 1987; Singh, Kershaw, and Clark 1981).

Charring and Preservation

Burning does not guarantee wood preservation. Some wood burns completely, leaving ash rather than charcoal. Whether or not a particular piece of wood is reduced to ash depends on the heating rate; the length of exposure to heat; the final wood temperature; the amount of oxygen present; the size, moisture content, and chemical composition of the wood; and other factors (Baileys and Blankenhorn 1982:20; Juneja 1975:201, 203-4; Panshin and de Zeeuw 1970:214-15).

Charcoal is a product of the chemical reactions that occur when wood is heated (i.e., thermal decomposition). Researchers have described general stages in the processes of thermal decomposition and combustion of wood, although the initial temperatures and products of these stages vary in specific cases. At temperatures up to ca. 200° C wood dries out, evolving water vapor and perhaps traces of gases. Charring can take place even at these low temperatures, given enough time. As the temperature of the wood increases to ca. 200-280° C, thermal decomposition produces primarily noncombustible gases and char. At higher temperatures (ca. 280-500° C), thermal decomposition produces not only char but also volatile components, including flammable gases and tars. These volatiles burn by flaming when sufficient oxygen is present. The relative proportions of gases, tars, and char produced vary widely depending on many factors, including the rate of heating and the moisture content of the wood. At even higher temperatures (above ca. 500° C), charcoal glows and is itself consumed during combustion, leaving a residue of ash (the inorganic products of charcoal combustion). If enough oxygen is not available, charcoal is formed without combustion even at these higher temperatures (Beall 1972:102-3; Browne 1958:1-7, 19; Juneja 1975:201-4; Knudson and Williamson 1971:176-77; Lopinot 1984:92-93; Tillman, Rossi, and Kitto 1981:93).

Within the same fire, some pieces of wood can burn to ash while others are left as charcoal, because of variation in heating conditions and differences in the wood. Wood at the center of the fire heats faster (Slocum, McGinnis, and Beall 1978:43) and therefore is more likely to burn completely, while charcoal buried in ash at the bottom of a hearth might not be consumed because of lack of oxygen. A small piece of wood (such as kindling) ignites easily and is likely to burn to ash because only a small quantity of heat is required to raise the temperature of the entire stick (Panshin and de Zeeuw 1970:214-15). However, wood with a high moisture content takes longer to heat and tends to produce more charcoal and less tar during thermal decomposition (Forest Products Laboratory 1961:89-90; Schaffer 1966:24; Tillman, Rossi, and Kitto 1981:79, 93). Thus, it is more likely to be left as charcoal.

Even when wood is charred it might not be preserved. Charcoal preservation varies tremendously from site to site, because of such factors as the rate of sediment deposition, depth below surface, freeze-thaw, soil moisture, burrowing, trampling, and archaeological recovery techniques (Brunett 1972:88; Gifford 1978:81-82, 91-92; Lopinot 1984:98-99; Western 1971:34).

Recovery of Charcoal in the Field

Charcoal is usually recovered archaeologically in two ways. Archaeologists often pull out large pieces of charcoal either during excavation or from a screen. In addition, charcoal may be found in sediment processed specifically to recover plant remains, using flotation or other techniques. (See Wagner, chapter 2, for a discussion of recovery techniques.)

Sampling

Today, controlled sampling is a fact of life in all aspects of archaeological fieldwork, including the collection of archaeobotanical remains. Plant macroremains are subject to three different sampling schemes in the field:

1. Usually only a portion of a site is excavated
2. With very few exceptions, only samples of the excavated deposits are processed to recover charred plant material
3. Only the larger pieces of charcoal are pulled out during excavation or caught by a screen

Together these sampling strategies determine how well the recovered material represents the charcoal from the entire site.

Laboratory Analysis of Charcoal

Sampling

Archaeobotanical remains are subject to additional sampling during laboratory analysis. Often time or cost constraints prohibit analyzing all archaeobotanical samples from a site. Therefore some portion of the samples must be chosen for analysis. Thoughtful selection of these samples is imperative for useful results.

Variation in Taxa Size. Often when a sample contains large quantities of charcoal, a subsample of the charcoal pieces is chosen for identification. The strategy used for selecting pieces is especially important because the size distributions of charcoal fragments can vary among taxa. Willcox (1974:124) found that taxon abundance varied with fragment size in charcoal samples from sites in eastern Anatolia. Zalucha (1982:32-36) provided a rigorous demonstration of this variation in his analysis of charcoal from four Mill Creek sites in northwestern Iowa. Taxon counts in four size fractions (> 6.30 mm; 6.30-3.33 mm; 3.33-1.0 mm; and < 1.0 mm) for each of eight charcoal taxa were analyzed using logistic regression. Statistically significant differences were found for seven of the eight charcoal taxa. Zalucha (1983:119-25) also found significant variation in fragment size for some of the taxa in charcoal samples from the Helb site in South Dakota. However, size variation might not be a major problem for all charcoal assemblages. Asch, Ford, and Asch (1972:3) reported only slight variation in size and shape distributions for fragments of identified charcoal taxa from the Archaic levels at the Koster site (located in the Illinois River valley in Illinois).

Some size variation among charcoal taxa could be due to the sizes of the woods used at the site. Certain wood types may be preferred for jobs requiring small pieces, such as kindling. In addition, some woody taxa are naturally smaller than others (i.e., types that grow as shrubs rather than trees).

Variation in charcoal shrinkage and fragmentation also could account for size differences among taxa. Numerous experiments have shown that the amounts of charcoal shrinkage and mass reduction vary among taxa and are primarily dependent on heating rate, exposure time, and wood temperature (Baileys and Blankenhorn 1982; Forest Products Laboratory 1961:91-94; Lopinot 1984:123-32; Rossen and Olson 1985; Slocum, McGinnis, and Beall 1978; Zalucha 1983:115-19). It is difficult to compare the specific results of these studies because of differences in experimental parameters (including heating methods and the sizes and shapes of the wood samples). However, even the ranking of specific taxa in terms of shrinkage and mass reduction varied in these experiments. For example, mass loss was consistently greater for hickory (*Carya ovata*) than for white oak (*Quercus alba*) over a range of temperatures in one experiment (Slocum, McGinnis, and Beall 1978:42-43), while *Quercus alba* experienced greater mass loss than *Carya ovata* at some but not all temperatures in another study (Lopinot 1984:125, 129).

Researchers have related variation in both shrinkage and mass reduction to differences in wood density or specific gravity (Forest Products Laboratory 1961:91-92; Lopinot 1984:130; Rossen and Olson 1985:449; Zalucha 1983:110, 116); to differences in wood structure (Rossen and Olson 1985:450; Slocum, McGinnis, and Beall 1978:44); and to differences in the chemical composition of wood taxa, including wood extractive content (i.e., gums, resins, oils, alkaloids, etc.) and the proportions of cellulose, hemicellulose and lignin (Baileys and Blakenhorn 1982:22; Lopinot 1984:131; Rossen and Olson 1985:450-51; Slocum, McGinnis, and Beall 1978:42-44, 47). Various researchers have suggested that woods with high extractive content (Rossen and Olson 1985:450-51); greater density (Forest Products Laboratory 1961:91-92; Rossen and Olson 1985:449; Zalucha 1983:110, 116); or a ring-porous or semidiffuse-porous hardwood pore pattern, a characteristic of wood stucture (Rossen and Olson 1985:450), will experience less of both shrinkage and loss of mass. Others suggest that woods with more lignin and hemicellulose will lose less mass (Slocum, McGinnis, and Beall 1978:44, 47). However, none of these factors alone is an infallible predictor of relative shrinkage and mass loss.

Charcoal can break while burning, and pieces that are friable or fissured can fragment when exposed to postdepositional processes. Zalucha (1982:28) related variation in charcoal fragmentation among woody taxa to differences in wood density. Friable charcoal has been associated with both rapid heating at high temperatures (Forest Products Laboratory 1961:89), and greater shrinkage and mass reduction (Rossen and Olson 1985:448). High moisture content or rapid heating at high temperatures also can produce fissures in charcoal (Minnis 1987:122).

Lopinot (1984:131-32) considered the problem of differential fragmentation in his controlled burning of 12 wood species at a range of temperatures. While there was very little fragmentation after burning, evidence of fissuring appeared in all specimens (especially in wood exposed to temperatures between 400° C and 600° C). Lopinot identified five species that showed the most fissuring and one species with the least fissuring in the 400-600° C temperature range. The most-fissured types lost moderate to large amounts of mass at these temperatures compared with other taxa in the experiment. The least-fissured taxon experienced less mass reduction (Lopinot 1984:129-31). In terms of wood densities, some of the most-fissured species and the least-fissured taxon are comparable (Panshin and de Zeeuw 1970:627-28).

Zalucha (1983:115-19) investigated differential fragmentation due to both burning and stress in his experiments with seven wood taxa. After burning, Zalucha subjected the charcoal specimens to stress by dropping them three times against a concrete surface from a uniform height. The resulting charcoal fragments were divided into six size fractions (> 1 in; 1-1/2 in; 1/2-1/4 in; 1/4-1/8 in; 1/8-1/16 in; and < 1/16 in). The percentages (by mass) of the seven taxa in each of the size fractions varied.

In summary, while the amounts of shrinkage and fragmentation vary among species, they are controlled primarily by the heating rate, exposure time, and final wood temperature. Therefore the size fraction in which a particular taxon predominates varies depending on the fire and cannot be predicted (Zalucha 1982:28-29). This implies that we must select a range of fragment sizes to obtain a representative charcoal assemblage. In addition, large fragments recovered during excavation might not be comparable to charcoal assemblages from flotation samples.

Subsample Selection. In order to include charcoal of all sizes in their analyses, paleoethnobotanists generally select either a random sample of charcoal fragments by splitting the sample (e.g., Willcox 1974:123), or a "grab sample" of pieces representing a range of sizes and shapes (e.g., Miller 1985:3). Sometimes a sample is passed through a series of graded sieves, and charcoal pieces are selected from each size fraction (e.g., Zalucha 1982:79, 1983:111, 114).

The analyst also determines the number of charcoal fragments selected for examination. The size of the subsample can affect profoundly the identified charcoal assemblage. In samples with great taxa diversity or a few pieces of a rare taxon, a subsample that is too small will not include all the wood types actually present. (See Zalucha 1982:39-49 for an examination of subsample variability.)

There is a simple method to determine an appropriate sample size for the taxa diversity in a charcoal assemblage. All charcoal fragments are examined in the first few samples. For each sample, the analyst plots the cumulative number of identified taxa for each additional fragment examined. The point at which the curve levels off indicates the number of identifications required to find all the taxa in the sample. If the curves for several samples are similar, the number of identified fragments at the leveling-off point determines the number selected in the rest of the samples. Yet charcoal taxa diversity can vary within a site, especially in samples from different contexts. This method cannot guarantee that all charcoal taxa will be recovered, and analysts should be alert for samples that do not follow the plotted pattern.

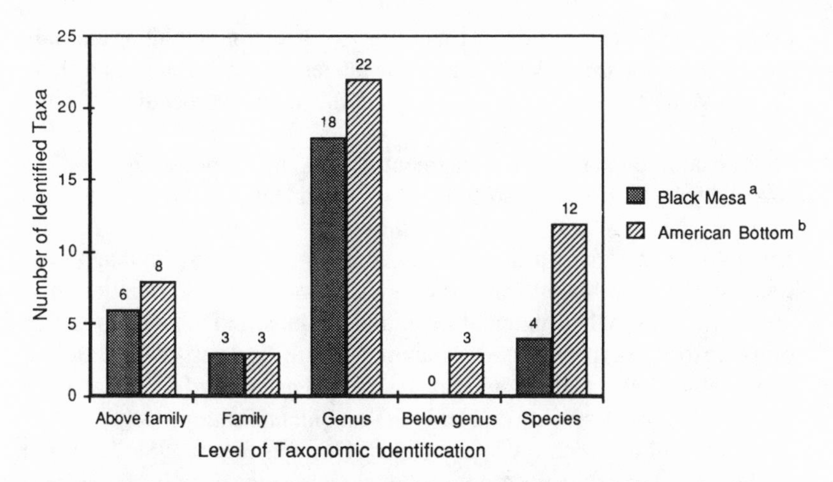

Figure 10.1. Taxonomic level of charcoal identifications for two multisite projects. (a) Charcoal identifications (excluding bark) for 45 prehistoric Anasazi sites (Archaic-Pueblo II-III) from Black Mesa in northeastern Arizona, excavated as part of the Black Mesa Archaeological Project of Southern Illinois University at Carbondale. Sources: Cowan et al. 1978; Ford et al. 1983; Wagner et al. 1984. (b) Charcoal identifications for 11 prehistoric sites (Archaic-Mississippian) excavated in the American Bottom, Illinois as part of the FAI-270 Archaeological Mitigation Project of the University of Illinois at Urbana-Champaign. Sources: Johannessen 1983a-e, 1984a-f; Whalley 1983, 1984.

Charcoal Identification

Paleoethnobotanists identify charcoal by comparing the form or presence/absence of various cellular structures in the unknown fragment with the structures found in known, modern wood taxa. Even the most experienced analyst cannot identify all charcoal to the species level. As figure 10.1 illustrates, charcoal often can be identified only to genus or family, and some fragments are completely unidentifiable. This is significant because even members of the same genus frequently live in very different habitats. The level of specificity of charcoal identifications is determined largely by the range of wood structures used for identification, the condition and size of the charcoal fragment, the diversity of the woody taxa in the region, and the availability of a good wood comparative collection and other reference materials.

Microscopic Examination. The wood structures used for identification are found along three different planes in the charcoal fragment. The cross section (transverse section) cuts perpendicular to the main axis of the wood, exposing the concentric growth rings. The radial section cuts along the main axis of the wood through its radius. The tangential section also cuts along the main axis of the wood, but not through the radius (perpendicular to the wood rays).

To examine charcoal, the fragment is broken (or more rarely cut) to reveal these sections. Microscopes with incident lighting are used to examine the structural features. In the cross section, the structures are generally visible using a standard dissecting microscope with magnifications of 10-30 X. Magnifications ranging from 50-150 X are required to view structures in the tangential and radial sections, and higher magnifications (up to 400 X) permit the examination of specific details. (See Barefoot and Hankins 1982; Côté, Côté, and Day 1979; Panshin and de Zeeuw 1970 for more information on wood structure and identification.)

Genus and occasionally species identifications are possible for some woody taxa using only the cross-sectional view of the charcoal. However, examination of the tangential and radial sections confirms the identification and can lead to greater specificity. For example, willow (*Salix*) and poplar (*Populus*) are distinguishable by the presence of heterocellular or homocellular rays in the radial section (Panshin and de Zeeuw 1970:549). Bohrer (1986:34) recently encouraged paleoethnobotanists to take full advantage of the tangential and radial sections when identifying charcoal. While this can improve identifications, it also increases analysis time (e.g., Willcox 1974:129) and requires appropriate microscopic equipment (see Minnis 1987:123, 129 for discussion).

Condition and Size. Wood structure is remarkably well preserved in charcoal. However, rapid heating at high temperatures can produce charcoal that crumbles during examination (Forest Products Laboratory 1961:89). Sometimes the structural features used to identify a charcoal fragment are distorted or even destroyed by burning or after deposition. For example, rays shrink less than other structures and tend to split during charring (Slocum, McGinnis, and Beall 1978:45; Rossen and Olson 1985:452), while spiral thickening can be destroyed at high temperatures (Knudson and Williamson 1971:183). After deposition, roots can penetrate charcoal fragments, creating holes that superficially resemble pores or resin ducts (Minnis 1987:122). These distortions can affect the specificity of identifications.

The size of a charcoal fragment is also a factor in identification. In general, smaller charcoal pieces are identified to a higher taxonomic level. As fragments become smaller, they become more difficult to break for examination, especially for the radial and tangential sections. Also, small pieces permit fewer exposures of each section, making it difficult to check features that are absent or unclear in the first break. In addition, structure varies within an individual plant because of differences in juvenile and adult wood and variation in growing conditions from year to year. With a larger charcoal fragment, this variability can be recognized and more specific identifications made.

The size required for even a genus identification varies among taxa. It will depend on the relative frequency of the diagnostic structure(s) within the charcoal fragment (Minnis 1987:122) and the distinctiveness of the structure(s) among the woody taxa in the region. For example, resin ducts occur infrequently in some conifers in the American Southwest and might be absent in a fragment that is less than 4 mm^2 in size (Minnis 1987:122). However, the very broad rays and arrangement of pores in oak (*Quercus*) are quite distinctive. Identification of small oak fragments is possible in regions (such as the American Great Lakes area and Britain) where these features are not common in other taxa (Dimbleby [1967] 1978:104).

This size bias in identification can affect the taxa identified within an archaeological assemblage. Wood types that are primarily found in smaller pieces because of greater fragmentation or other factors will tend to be underrepresented. However, structural idiosyncrasies of some taxa or the chance occurrence of diagnostic structures in a particular fragment might allow the identification of some smaller pieces of charcoal.

Diversity in Woody Taxa. The level of specificity of charcoal identifications is greatly affected by the diversity of woody taxa in the area. Species-level identifications are not a problem when only one species of a genus is native to the area. For example, 25% of the identified taxa from 11 sites in the American Bottom in Illinois are at the species level (figure 10.1). However, 7 of the 12 species identified are the only native members of their genera in this area (Jones and Fuller 1955).

Unfortunately, as the numbers of species per genus and of genera per family increase, it becomes much more difficult to identify charcoal to the species and even the genus level. There is tremendous variation in the diversity of woody plant types in different parts of the world, as demonstrated in figure 10.2. Thus, identifications of charcoal from regions with great floristic diversity, such as the tropical rain forests of the Philippines, might never achieve the level of specificity possible in other areas with fewer tree types.

Comparative Collections. The level of specificity of charcoal identifications also is determined by the availability of wood reference manuals and an extensive comparative collection for the region. Comparative wood material is especially important in areas where few descriptions of local

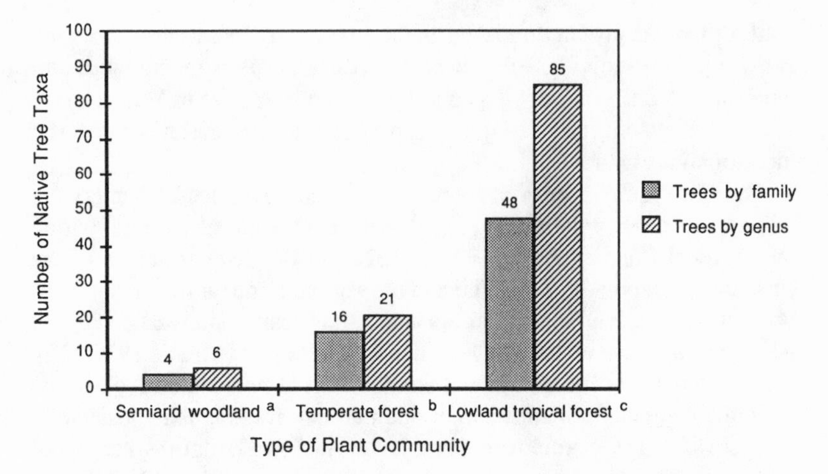

Figure 10.2. Comparison of the diversity of tree taxa for three plant communities. (a) Semiarid pinyon-juniper woodland from Black Mesa in northeastern Arizona. Sources: Espey, Huston, and Associates 1980, table 2.1; Moore 1979:189-213; Plog and Klesert 1978:6. Life forms based on Espey, Huston, and Associates 1980; Kearney and Peebles 1951. (b) Temperate forest of the American Bottom along the Mississippi River in Missouri and Illinois. Source: Hus 1908:216-51. Life forms based on Britton and Brown 1970. Families following Heywood 1978. (c) Tropical lowland rain forest in the Philippines. Source: Payawal 1981.

wood types and identification keys exist. A good comparative collection should contain more than one example of a species and include branches, trunk wood, bark, and roots (Dimbleby [1967] 1978:101-3). While such collections may be difficult and expensive to establish (especially in areas with complex vegetation), they are critical if genus and species level identifications are to be achieved.

How Representative is a Charcoal Assemblage?

The processes of transport, burning, preservation, recovery, and identification obscure the relationship between a charcoal assemblage and local vegetation. How well does an archaeological charcoal assemblage reflect the floristic environment?

Historic Navajo sites from northern Black Mesa in Arizona help us address this question, because the modern vegetation is an excellent approximation of the flora present during occupation. The modern landscape of the mesa top is characterized by dissected hills and complex systems of washes. An open woodland of pinyon pine (*Pinus edulis*) and juniper (primarily *Juniperus osteosperma*) with an understory of shrubs grows at higher elevations, while sagebrush (*Artemisia*), snakeweed (*Gutierrezia*), and other shrubs predominate at lower elevations along the washes (Nichols and Sink 1984:7-8; Espey, Huston, and Associates 1980, tables 2.1-2.33; Moore 1979; Plog and Klesert 1978:4, 6-9).

Charcoal identifications for 54 flotation samples from 24 historic Navajo sites are considered here (Wagner et al. 1984:G.297-G.329). While most of these sites were sheep camps or habitation sites (or both), there were three windbreaks, a sweat lodge, and one site of unknown type. One site was dated to the early 1800s; the rest were utilized for periods of time between the 1870s and 1980. All 54 flotation samples came from hearths or ash piles, many of which were associated with hogans, windbreaks, or shades (32 samples). One sample was collected from a fire-cracked rock and ash pile, associated with a sweat lodge. Charcoal fragments from these hearth and ash pile contexts are probably remnants of wood used as fuel (Dunlavey and Haley 1984; Estes, Hays, and Nelson 1984; Haley and Estes 1984; Michalik 1984a, 1984b; Rocek 1984; Semé and Joha 1984).

A grab sample of approximately 20 pieces of charcoal was examined from each flotation sample whenever possible, although 12 samples had fewer than 16 identified fragments. Seven charcoal taxa (excluding bark were identified from these 54 samples (Wagner et al. 1984:614, G.297-G.329). Two are species identifications (*Pinus edulis*) and *P. ponderosa*), three are genera (*Artemisia*, *Juniperus*, and *Pinus*), one is a plant family (Compositae), and one is above the family level (conifer). The identifications include the two predominant trees in the area woodlands, juniper (*Juniperus*) and pinyon (*Pinus edulis*).

Figure 10.3 compares the number of woody genera identified from the Navajo assemblages with the modern woody genera (including trees and shrubs) from northern Black Mesa. Only 9% of the modern woody genera were recovered from the historic Navajo sites. However, 33% of the modern tree genera were identified, the two most common tree types in the modern vegetation (*Juniperus* and *Pinus*). Only 3% of the modern shrubby genera were found.

Tree taxa were found at more sites and in more samples than the shrubby taxa (figures 10.4 and 10.5). The tree taxon conifer was identified in every sample, and at least one of *Juniperus*, *Pinus*, or *Pinus edulis* was found on every site. The two shrubby taxa, *Artemisia* and the family Compositae (which includes *Artemisia*, *Gutierrezia*, and four other modern shrubby genera), were found in only thirteen samples from eight sites.

The differences between tree and shrubby taxa in terms of presence at sites and ubiquity are not related to archaeological context. Shrubby taxa were recovered from a number of site types (habitation sites, possible sheep camps, a windbreak, and a sweat lodge) dating from the early 1800s to the

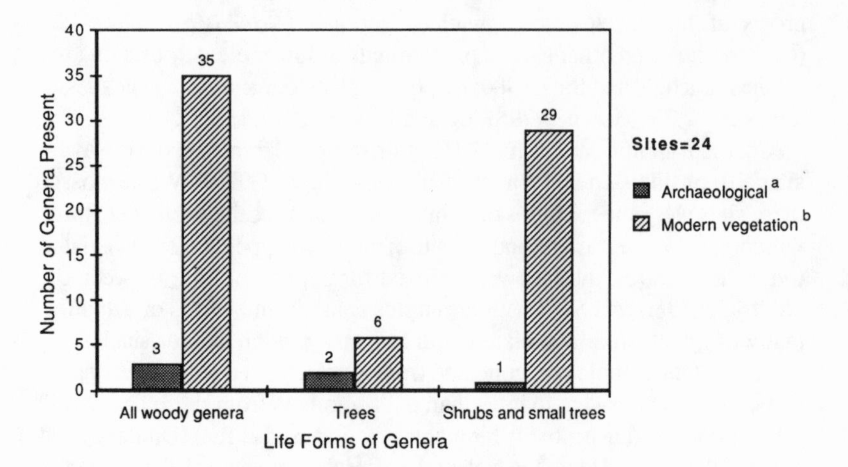

Figure 10.3. Comparison of identified charcoal genera from historic Navajo sites with the modern woody genera on Black Mesa. Life forms based on Espey, Huston, and Associates 1980; Kearney and Peebles 1951. (a) Identified charcoal genera (excluding bark) from 24 historic Navajo sites on Black Mesa in northeastern Arizona. One identified family is excluded. Source: Wagner et al. 1984:G.297-G.329. (b) Modern woody genera in the Black Mesa Archaeological Project area on northern Black Mesa. Sources: Espey, Huston, and Associates 1980, table 2.1; Moore 1979:189-213; Plog and Klesert 1978:6.

1960s. Samples containing shrubs came from both hearths and ash piles, some of which were associated with structures. Site location does not appear to be a factor in the presence of shrubby taxa either (although fine-scale differences in site environments were not examined). Sites with identified shrubby taxa and those with only tree taxa were located at a range of elevations including areas within the pinyon-juniper woodland (Dunlavey and Haley 1984; Estes, Hays, and Nelson 1984; Haley and Estes 1984; Michalik 1984a, 1984b; Nichols and Sink 1984; Rocek 1984; Semé and Joha 1984).

To summarize, while the identified charcoal from 24 historic Navajo sites included very few taxa (9% of the modern woody genera), the major trees in the modern woodland vegetation, juniper (*Juniperus*) and pinyon (*Pinus edulis*), were found at most of the sites. This low diversity in identified charcoal types should not be considered typical for other regions or even other cultures in the same region. Compare the number of identified genera from the prehistoric Anasazi sites at Black Mesa (figure 10.1) with the Navajo data (figure 10.3). However, the differential recovery of trees and shrubs from these sites demonstrates that important components of the regional vegetation can be missing from a charcoal assemblage. This is

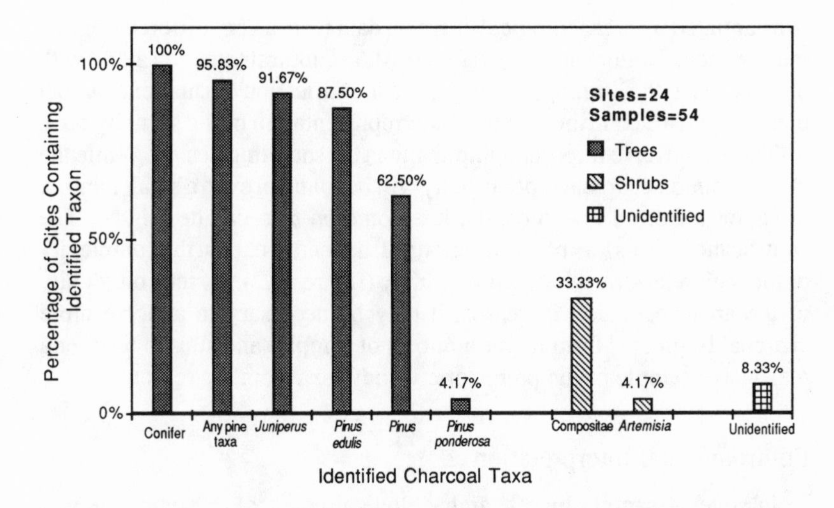

Figure 10.4. Percentage of Navajo sites with each identified charcoal taxon. Based on a total of 24 historic Navajo sites from Black Mesa in northeastern Arizona. Charred bark is not included. Source: Wagner et al. 1984:G.297-G.329.

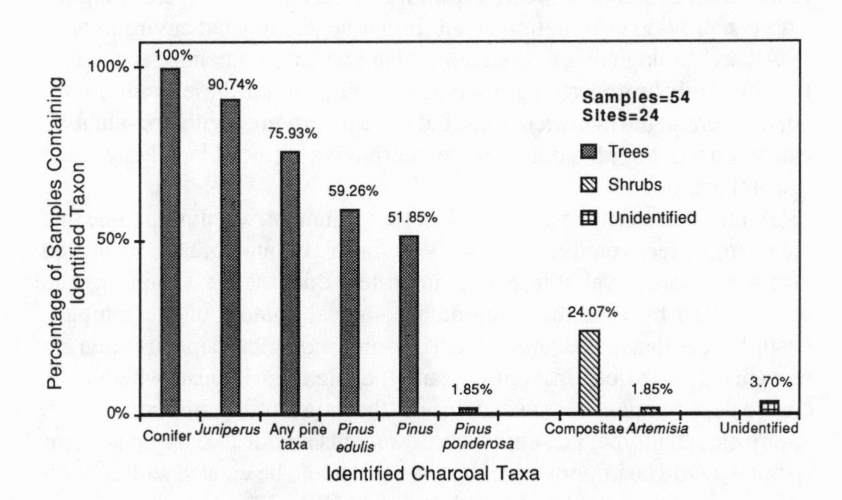

Figure 10.5. Ubiquity of identified charcoal taxa in 54 flotation samples from 24 historic Navajo sites on Black Mesa in northeastern Arizona. Charred bark is not included. Source: Wagner et al. 1984:G.297-G.329.

substantiated by archaeological charcoal data from a very different region, the American Bottom in Illinois (figure 10.6). Cultural selection along with differences in the burning, recovery, and identification of smaller charcoal pieces could all contribute to the underrepresentation of the shrubby taxa.

These data have important implications for sampling design. While the most-common charcoal types usually will be found in even a small number of samples from a few sites, the less-common taxa can be missed. The significance of this loss of information will depend in part on the complexity of the regional flora, which varies widely (figure 10.2). As the complexity of the area vegetation increases, it may be necessary to analyze more charcoal fragments from larger numbers of samples and sites to recover a reasonable sample of the prehistoric woody taxa from the region.

Environmental Interpretation

In spite of sample biases, archaeological charcoal is a valuable and commonly available source of data for reconstructing prehistoric and historic vegetation and environments. The identified charcoal taxa from a site are one source of information about paleoenvironments. Also, tree rings provide a record of the rate of growth of a woody plant, which is affected in part by external environmental factors. The problems and potential of the use of these growth rings for environmental reconstruction have been discussed extensively in other sources (see Fritts 1976; Hughes et al. 1982). In addition, charcoal recovered from locations outside of archaeological sites can provide information about former vegetation and environments.

All archaeological interpretation, including environmental reconstruction, must rely on underlying assumptions. We examine these assumptions, not to discredit the interpretations, but rather to promote critical evaluation and appropriate application of these interpretive methods by all interested researchers.

To interpret anything about the local environment, we must assume that the charcoal recovered from a site is not intrusive, and that the identified taxa were locally available and not imported. Both these assumptions can be evaluated by examining the archaeological context of the samples. Disturbances that introduce charcoal into archaeological deposits often are recognized in the field. In addition, sample context can indicate whether the charcoal is a remnant of a special activity that might utilize imported wood. A rare charcoal type, present in small amounts and/or in only one or two samples, could be imported or intrusive and should be viewed with caution when interpreting the data (e.g., Western 1971:36-37).

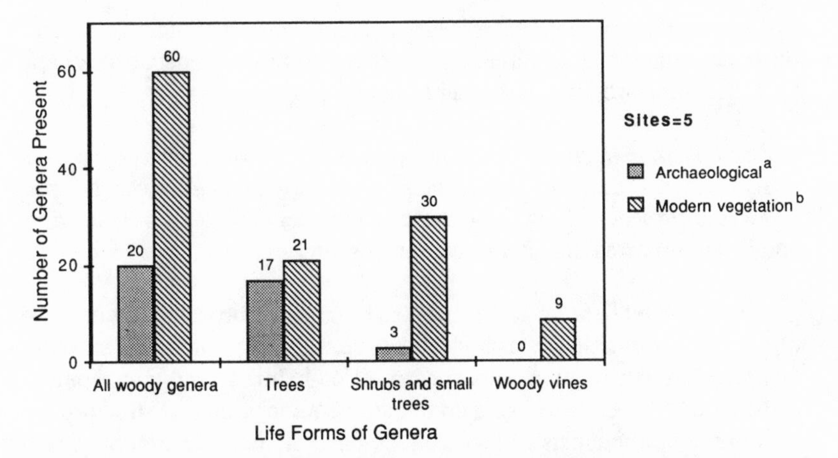

Figure 10.6. Comparison of identified charcoal genera from Mississippian sites with the modern native woody genera in the American Bottom. Life forms based on Britton and Brown 1970; Van Dersal 1938. (a) Identified charcoal genera from 5 Mississippian sites in the American Bottom, Illinois. Three identified families are excluded. Sources: Johannessen 1983b, 1984b; Whalley 1983, 1984. (b) Modern native woody genera in the American Bottom along the Mississippi River in Illinois and Missouri. Source: Hus 1908:216-51.

Identified Taxa From a Site

The charcoal taxa identified from an archaeological site provide valuable information about paleoenvironments. Analysts use taxa presence as well as ubiquity and relative amounts of charcoal taxa for environmental interpretation. These data are especially interesting when there are changes through time.

Taxa Presence

Paleoethnobotanists interpret charcoal taxa presence in a variety of ways. We have identified four kinds of interpretations commonly used for environmental reconstruction:

1. The identified taxa grew in the area
2. The identified taxa indicate the plant communities that grew in the area
3. Modern preferred habitats of the identified taxa indicate former environments in the area
4. Modern distributions of the identified taxa indicate the former locations of these taxa

The first two approaches reconstruct vegetation, while the latter two include other environmental variables. In practice, more than one of these approaches often are used in the same analysis.

Local Taxa in the Past. The first approach is the most conservative. The analyst suggests that the identified taxa were growing in the area when the site was occupied. As long as the charcoal is contemporary with occupation and is not imported, this interpretation is sound.

Modern Plant Ecology Data. The next three interpretive approaches rely on existing information regarding modern plant ecology, including autecology (i.e., growth requirements and preferred habitats) and geographical distribution of each taxon, and community composition and structure. In some regions, botanists and ecologists have studied the modern plant communities extensively. Outside the industrialized nations, such studies are less common, particularly for tropical areas. In many cases, limited information is available and local vegetation studies must be integrated into the archaeological project itself (e.g., Willcox 1974:117-18, 120-22).

In many parts of the world, the natural vegetation has been altered greatly by cultural activities. Examples of such drastic changes include the introduction of new species and plant diseases; selective cutting or intentional planting of commercially valuable forest trees; altering forest composition by burning; extensive clearance for agricultural fields and pastures; and deforestation due to urbanization, agriculture, grazing, or wood collection for fuel and construction (see chapter 14 in Spurr and Barnes 1973). In these situations, paleoethnobotanists must use other data to study local plant ecology. Sometimes relict stands of vegetation can be located and studied (e.g., Miller 1985:5, 7-8; Willcox 1974:118). In other cases, analysts use historical information, such as surveyors' records (e.g., Asch, Ford, and Asch 1972:6-7), photographs, travelers' accounts and other references to the area (e.g., Willcox 1974:123), and ancient texts (e.g., Miller 1985:14). Unfortunately, such historical sources often provide an incomplete picture of local plant ecology.

Plant Communities in the Past. In the second interpretive approach, identified charcoal taxa serve as indicators of the plant communities formerly growing in the site area. Often a number of the identified taxa are found in several modern plant communities (especially when identifications are not to species). However, some taxa primarily grow in a specific modern plant community, and these are considered indicative of former plant communities in the area.

The validity of this kind of interpretation will depend on the reliability of the taxon as an indicator of a particular plant community (sometimes called fidelity). Researchers have quantified the probability of finding a species in a given stand of a community in some regions, but generally the analyst must rely on more qualitative assessments of community composition (Zalucha 1982:8-9, 16-17, 24).

In this approach, the analyst also assumes that plant communities remain fairly stable through time. Yet changes in Pleistocene and Holocene vegetation, due to both environmental change and species migration (e.g., Davis 1976; Wright 1976; Delcourt and Delcourt 1981), make this kind of interpretation more tenuous as we move further back in time (King and Graham 1981:138). Vegetational stability through time varies tremendously from region to region. For example, the Delcourts (1983) recently identified three very different dynamics in the Late Quaternary vegetation of eastern North America. Areas north of ca. 43°N latitude have experienced continual vegetational instability and disequilibrium, while the vegetation in certain areas south of 33°N has been in dynamic equilibrium with a relatively constant flora. In the region between 33°N and 39 °N, the stability of the full-glacial vegetation was replaced by vegetational instability with the late-glacial climatic amelioration. Vegetational stability returned to this region after about 9000 B.P. An examination of regional pollen diagrams will help the analyst determine whether the assumption of vegetational stability is reasonable for a particular site.

Recent cultural influences on community composition and structure make some modern plant communities inappropriate analogs for vegetation in the past. Historic factors affecting vegetation should be considered before using modern analogs in vegetational reconstruction.

Pearsall's (1983:121-24) analysis of charcoal from the Real Alto and Rio Perdido sites (Early and Middle Formative sites, respectively, located in southwestern Ecuador) illustrates this approach. Using modern plant community data (from Pearsall's own reconnaissance and published botanical studies) and the results of interviews with longtime residents, Pearsall constructed plant community analogs for the area. Out of a total of seventeen taxa defined in this analysis, she identified four as members of the xerophytic forest and seven as members of the deciduous forest. The other six charcoal taxa were unidentified types. Pearsall suggested that both the deciduous and xerophytic forests were growing in the area when these sites were occupied. To support her vegetational reconstruction, she examined available paleoclimatological data and determined that the climate during Early and Middle Formative times was similar to modern conditions.

Habitats in the Past. In the third approach, the analyst suggests that the modern preferred habitats of the identified taxa were present in the site area during occupation. This allows the analyst to reconstruct not only area vegetation but also other aspects of the environment.

As was the case in the reconstruction of plant communities, this approach requires the careful selection of indicator taxa. Some wood types live in a wider range of habitats than others and are not as useful for this kind of analysis.

This approach requires that the preferred habitats of a taxon remain stable through time. This might not always be the case, because the range of a taxon is controlled in part by competition with other plants. For example, many forest species in central Europe are competitive only in a restricted portion of their potential range because of the enormous competitive ability of European beech (*Fagus sylvatica*; Spurr and Barnes 1973:382). If a new tree species were introduced, the distribution of a given taxon might decrease, while the elimination of a tree type could allow an expansion of its range (e.g., Willcox 1974:118). Regional pollen diagrams can be used to determine whether or not this might be a factor for a particular site.

An illustration of this approach is provided by Crites's (1987:3, 11-13, 24) analysis of charcoal from the Middle and Late Archaic levels in one excavation unit from the Hayes site (located in the Nashville Basin of Tennessee). Eighteen charcoal genera, subgenera, or species were identified from these levels. Using several lines of evidence, including modern distributions, autecology, and predominance in regional pollen spectra during periods of increasing dryness, Crites suggested that seven taxa were indicative of drier conditions. He identified black willow (*Salix nigra*) as a reliable indicator of wet habitats because of its consistent location on modern floodplains and other wet habitats. Two additional types also were considered local mesic indicators, presumably based on modern distributions. The remaining eight taxa occur in a variety of modern habitats. Interpretations based on charcoal from one unit at the site were necessarily tentative. However, Crites suggested the habitats associated with the indicator taxa were present in the site area.

Taxa Locations in the Past. In the last approach, the analyst uses the modern distribution of the identified taxa in the site area to determine the locations of the taxa when the site was occupied. Often this kind of interpretation appears as a discussion of the areas around the site that were utilized by its occupants (e.g., Johannessen 1983d:104).

This approach requires that conditions in the site area (such as climate, topography, water level, etc.) were similar enough to the modern environment to provide the same habitats in the same locations. Climatic changes in the Pleistocene and Holocene (e.g., Bryson, Baerreis, and Wendland 1970) could have altered the environment at a site and must be considered. The degree to which a particular site was affected by climatic change will vary depending on its location. On a more local scale, changes in colluvial and alluvial deposition, river regimes, or even tectonic activity could have affected the environment in the site area (e.g., Butzer 1978). The results of other environmental analyses, such as palynology, geomorphology, and sedimentology, can be used as a confirmation that past conditions resembled modern ones.

Lundström-Baudais's (1984:293-98, 301, 304) analysis of charcoal from Station III (a Late Neolithic site on the Lake of Clairvaux on the western edge of the Jura mountains in France) is an example of this approach. A total of 18 taxa (genera and one family) were identified from both uncharred posts and charcoal. Using modern natural distributions, Lundström-Baudais suggested that 17 of these taxa were growing near the site in Neolithic times. However, *Abies alba* becomes dominant in the modern natural vegetation of the region at higher elevations, which are found at a distance of ca. 5 km from the site. Based on this modern distribution and the relative scarcity of *Abies* pollen from the site, Lundström-Baudais concluded that this tree type was growing uphill from the site at a distance of at least several kilometers during the late Neolithic.

This interpretation was substantiated by evidence that only certain parts of the *Abies* trees were brought to the site. An estimate of the maximal diameter of *Abies* charcoal fragments (based on the form of the outermost tree ring) indicated that only the trunks (possibly cut to planks) and the extremities of branches of this taxon were utilized. Lundström-Baudais suggested that only those parts of the wood judged essential were transported to the site from the distant locations where this tree supposedly was growing (Lundström-Baudais 1984:297-98, 304).

Summary. Analysts use charcoal taxa presence for environmental reconstruction in a number of ways. The appropriateness of these approaches will vary from site to site depending on the availability of modern plant ecology data, regional pollen diagrams, and other paleoenvironmental data; the fidelity of the identified taxa; the stability of the regional vegetation through time; and the differences between the modern environment and past conditions. Even in the absence of ancillary studies, the identified charcoal taxa provide useful data for reconstructing area vegetation.

Quantified Taxon Data

Paleoethnobotanists describe a charcoal assemblage by quantifying the amount of each taxon present within a sample (using taxon count and/or mass) and the ubiquity of each taxon throughout the samples from a site. Some analysts use these quantities as sources of data for environmental reconstruction as well (See Popper, chapter 4, and Miller, chapter 5, for in depth discussions of quantification techniques).

The relative amount of a taxon in a charcoal sample is difficult to interpret for two reasons. First, it is difficult to relate the amount of charcoal to the amount of wood that burned. One log can produce many fragments of charcoal, and both the number and mass of these fragments can be distorted by differential fragmentation and mass reduction. Second, because the archaeological charcoal assemblage is a biased sample of the woody vegetation, it is difficult to relate relative amounts of identified taxa to actual vegetation (Miller 1985:4; Western 1971:34; Zalucha 1982:26, 31-32, 49-50).For these reasons, some analysts prefer not to use the relative amounts of charcoal taxa for environmental interpretation.

Ubiquity does not address the question of how much wood was burned. It merely indicates which types were present and will not include all the types if some burned completely, were not preserved, or were missed in sampling. As with the relative amounts of the taxa, it is difficult to relate ubiquity to actual vegetation. Some analysts are dissatisfied with ubiquity and choose not to use it in their analyses.

Yet cultural selection of woody taxa brought to a site can depend in part on local availability, especially for firewood. The bulk and weight of fuelwood along with the large amounts required by people who rely on wood as fuel can result in the selection of sources closer to the site regardless of type (Dimbleby [1967] 1978:110; Miller 1985:9; Minnis 1987:129; Western 1971:33; Zalucha 1982:7-8). Therefore some analysts assume that the proportions of woody taxa at the site (especially firewood) approximate the relative abundance of taxa in the area vegetation. Based on this assumption, the amount of a charcoal taxon within samples and ubiquity throughout the samples from a site are used as indicators of relative abundance in the local vegetation. The debate over this assumption was launched by one of the first charcoal analyses to attempt environmental reconstruction (Salisbury and Jane 1940:311 vis-à-vis Godwin and Tansley 1941:118) and has continued ever since.

The appropriateness of this assumption for a particular site can vary depending on cultural variables and the floristic environment. Today indiscriminate collection of fuelwood occurs in areas where preferred types are no longer available because of overcollection and deforestation

(Campbell, Du Toit, and Haney 1985:9-10; Collier 1975:43, 45; Devres, Inc. 1980:27; Heizer 1963:190-91). Length of occupation and population size can affect the availability of preferred fuelwoods in the site area over time. Also, the number and types of activities at a site that utilize fuelwood (such as heating, cooking, or craft production) affect the intensity of firewood collection in the area (Coles, Heal, and Orme 1978:33; Miller 1985:11-14). Depletion of preferred fuelwoods could take more time in densely forested regions than in more open environments. In addition, selection might be more of a factor in regions with greater woody plant diversity, which offer more possible choices for firewood (Cowan and Smart 1981:27). Thus, people living in temporary camps in a forested area might be more selective in their choice of fuelwood than residents of long-occupied, permanent settlements in an open woodland environment. Dimbleby ([1967] 1978:110) has suggested that corroborative evidence such as pollen can be used to determine whether selection was a factor for a particular site.

Even when this assumption is valid, other factors (including sampling design) affect the production of a charcoal assemblage and can result in a biased sample. Therefore some analysts prefer to consider only the relatively common charcoal taxa when interpreting quantitative data. The presence or predominance of a taxon in all or most of the samples suggests that it was fairly common in the woody vegetation of the area (e.g., Godwin and Tansley 1941:119). However, small amounts and/or presence in relatively few samples are not used or are considered only conditionally as evidence of relative abundance in the woody flora around the site (e.g., Willcox 1974:127-28). As the number of analyzed samples increases, this approach becomes less dependant on the assumption that the proportions of the wood types at the site reflect their relative abundance in the area vegetation. Instead we assume that a woody type must have been fairly abundant in the area if it is present or predominant in a large number of samples (even if selection was a factor).

Regardless of the underlying assumptions made, analysts using quantified charcoal data must take into account both sample context and the number of analyzed samples. Ubiquity and the relative amount of a taxon can be affected by cultural selection of different wood types for different jobs. Therefore it is extremely important to examine the archaeological context of the analyzed samples before making comparisons. Also, the number of available samples must be considered, and quantitative trends identified in only a few samples should be viewed with caution (e.g., Pearsall 1983:126-27).

Miller's (1985:1, 4, 14) analysis of charcoal from the ancient urban site of Malyan (located in the Kur River basin in southwestern Iran) illustrates the use of quantitative charcoal data. After considering sample contexts, Miller decided that most of the analyzed charcoal fragments were remnants of fuelwood. She suggested that the areas closest to the site would have been used first for firewood collection, because of the transport costs involved. Therefore she assumed that charcoal taxa percentages at Malyan reflected species availability near the site.

Because the Kur basin today is largely deforested, Miller examined remnant forests and used published studies of the regional flora to reconstruct the modern natural vegetation. A number of taxa identified in the Banesh period charcoal samples are members of the modern pistachio-almond steppe forest. Miller suggested that this plant community was growing in the area at this time, possibly on the lower slopes at the edge of the basin and extending onto the valley floor. In addition, Miller interpreted the relatively high proportions (by count and mass) and the ubiquity of juniper (*Juniperus*) in Banesh period samples as an indication that this taxon was a major component of the pistachio-almond steppe forest (although *Juniperus* is rare in the modern vegetation of the region). Thus, using quantitative charcoal data, Miller was able to reconstruct a forest community that differed from the modern vegetation in the region (Miller 1985:4-8, 10, 14-15).

Changes Through Time

Comparisons of charcoal assemblages from different strata at a site or from different sites are frequently made to assess environmental change through time. These studies seek not only to identify vegetational change but also to determine the causes of this change.

Identification of Vegetational Change. Analysts comparing charcoal assemblages from different components must first determine whether differences reflect an actual change or are the result of sampling. Some researchers have applied statistical techniques, such as chi-square (e.g., Pearsall 1983:124-26) and principal coordinates analysis (e.g., Prior and Williams 1985:465, 469), to quantitative data to assess the differences between components. Regardless of whether statistical analyses or qualitative comparisons are used, the number of analyzed samples must be considered. Temporal trends that are identified in relatively few samples may not be supported by additional analysis.

The analyst also must decide whether the differences in charcoal assemblages were produced by selection. Cultural selection can be a factor if the charcoal assemblages are remnants of woods used for different purposes. This can be checked by a careful examination of archaeological context. In addition, changes in wood preference or collection practices could result in differences between components. For example, Asch, Ford, and Asch (1972:8) suggested that differences in the relative amounts of the charcoal taxa in two Archaic levels at the Koster site (located in the Illinois River valley of Illinois) could have resulted from greater reliance on the upland forest for firewood collection in one of these levels (see also Pearsall 1983:126-27).

If sampling errors and selection are eliminated, differences in charcoal assemblages can be related to changes in taxa availability. This could result from differences in either the woody taxa growing in the area or the availability of dead branchwood (Kohler et al. 1984:105). Sometimes the condition of the charcoal provides evidence that dead wood was used. For example, charcoal may contain bore holes and other remnants of insect pests that attack dead wood (e.g., King and Hofman 1979:252; Salisbury and Jane 1940:310). In addition, Prior and Williams (1985:471-72) have suggested that higher mineral concentrations in decayed wood might be used to recognize dead branchwood.

Causes of Change. Changes in taxa availability can result from cultural activities (such as clearing agricultural fields, deforestation, etc.) or natural/physical factors, including climatic change or post-Pleistocene plant migration. Independent data regarding paleoenvironments (such as regional pollen diagrams) and cultural activities must be evaluated to select between these two possible interpretations. If this information is not available, the analyst can present alternative explanations. For example, Conrad and Koeppen (1972:52-53), in their analysis of charcoal from the Brewster site (a Mill Creek site in northwestern Iowa), suggested that changes in the total amount of charcoal and the relative amounts of taxa (by mass) could be the result of either a gradual desiccation of the area or the clearing of large tracts for agricultural fields.

Prior and Williams (1985:457-58, 472) suggested that climatic change led to the vegetational changes indicated by the charcoal from six Holocene levels of Siphiso Rock shelter (located in the Lubombo mountains of northwest Swaziland). They based their interpretations on changes in the total number of identified taxa and on modern preferred habitats and plant distributions. The lowest two analyzed levels (strata 6 and 5) and the three upper strata (strata 3, 2, and 1) contained relatively large numbers of taxa, including many types found in the area today. Prior and Williams considered this an indication of moist conditions during the periods these strata represented. By contrast, stratum 4 yielded a smaller number of taxa and an absence of riverine types. They suggested this represented an intermediate period of drier climatic conditions and reduced tree cover. This interpretation of the stratum 4 charcoal was substantiated by a relative increase in the amount of *Combretum apiculatum*, a taxon indicative of drier conditions. Prior and Williams supported their climatic reconstructions with the results of palynological and geomorphological studies in the region.

In contrast, Minnis (1978:351-55, 359-60) thought human activity was responsible for the vegetational changes evinced by charcoal taxa percentages (by count) from sites in the Mimbres valley of southwestern New Mexico. Most of the analyzed charcoal came from hearths or ash lenses, and Minnis suggested that all the charcoal fragments were remnants of fuelwood. Using modern plant distribution data, Minnis grouped the identified charcoal into taxa growing on the floodplains and taxa growing on terraces and mountains around the sites. He then compared the percentages of these two groups of taxa in five different time periods (Early Pithouse, Late Pithouse, Classic Mimbres, Animas, and Salido). Low percentages of floodplain types were found in the Early Pithouse and Classic Mimbres phases. These trends were corroborated by the relative amounts of charcoal taxa in the dendrochronological samples, which Minnis considered primarily remnants of wood used for construction.

The low percentage of floodplain taxa in the Early Pithouse period was related to the location of sites away from the floodplain. Sites from the four later periods were situated close to the floodplain, so location could not account for the differences in the Classic Mimbres charcoal. However, there was an increase in relative population size for this period (calculated from survey data). Minnis suggested that the low percentage of floodplain taxa during the Classic Mimbres period was the result of more extensive clearing of the floodplain for agricultural fields made necessary by the population increase (Minnis 1978:357, 359-61; see also Miller 1985; Willcox 1974).

Off-Site Charcoal

Charcoal remnants of vegetation that burned away from archaeological sites are another source of environmental data. Such charcoal could be produced by naturally occurring fires or by human-induced burning of area vegetation, which is of special interest to archaeologists. Both the total amount of charcoal and identified charcoal taxa are used for environmental interpretation.

Albert and Minc (1987:47-48, 52) used charcoal in soil samples from vegetation plots in the Colonial Point Forest (located in the northern lower peninsula of Michigan) to aid their reconstruction of the fire and vegetation history of the area. They suggested that greater total amounts of charcoal in certain plots indicated more severe fire histories in those areas. In addition, they used both ubiquity and the relative amounts (by mass) of identified genera to reconstruct the composition of the forest when it burned. Albert and Minc assumed that the relative amount (by mass) of a charcoal taxon was a crude measure of the amount of wood of that taxon in the area prior to burning. Therefore they suggested that the relative amount (by mass) of a charcoal taxon reflected the relative dominance of that taxon in the area vegetation (since calculations of relative dominance are based on basal area).

Albert and Minc (1987:52) identified three potential problems with this assumption. First, the relative amounts of the charcoal taxa could be distorted by differences in charring and preservation among woody species. Second, the prehistoric inhabitants could have removed some trees for cultural activities or avoided valuable forest tree types during burning. Third, because of the lack of chronological control for charcoal in soil samples, the remnants of multiple burns may be combined in a single sample.

Charcoal from off-site fires also can wash into bodies of water or bogs. Palynologists use charcoal in bog and lake sediments to help reconstruct the fire history of an area. Charcoal presence in a stratigraphic level is considered evidence of fire disturbance in the area at that time (e.g., Simmons and Innes 1987:394-95). The total amount of charcoal in a stratigraphic level is used as an indication of the relative severity of fire(s) during that period. For example, Singh, Kershaw, and Clark (1981:24-25) used charcoal surface area per unit volume of sediment as a measure of charcoal particle frequency in their analysis of a sedimentary core from Lake George in New South Wales, Australia. They assumed that relatively high or low charcoal particle frequencies reflected relatively high or low intensity and/or frequency of fire, respectively. When stratigraphic levels are well dated (such as varved lake sediments), analysts can calculate charcoal influx rates. Swain (1973:389-92) considered a peak in charcoal influx associated with increased varve thickness indicative of a local fire at that time in his analysis of sediment from Lake of the Clouds in northeastern Minnesota.

Unfortunately, it is not possible to determine whether or not a fire was caused by human activity from the paleoecological data alone (Simmons and Innes 1987:396). However, charcoal from off-site burning in conjunction with archaeological data can provide evidence of people's interactions with their environment, including subsistence-related activities (e.g., Simmons and Innes 1987:395-99; Singh, Kershaw, and Clark 1981:44-49; Tsukada and Deevey 1967:326-29).

Discussion

While an archaeological charcoal assemblage is a biased sample, it remains an important indicator of prehistoric and historic vegetation and environments. Our environmental reconstructions are enhanced by a careful consideration of the factors that lead to sample bias. Some of these factors, such as cultural selection, burning and preservation, and regional plant diversity, are beyond the control of the archaeologist and paleoethnobotanist. It is important for us to recognize these factors and understand how they affect the identified charcoal assemblage recovered from a site.

Yet some factors are controlled by the archaeologist and analyst. These include the sampling and recovery techniques used at the site, the sampling techniques used in the laboratory, the range of structural features used for identification, and the availability of an extensive comparative collection. In general, the larger the number of samples analyzed from a particular region, the more complete will be our understanding of the woody plant taxa of the area. This becomes increasingly important as the diversity of woody taxa in the area increases.

Large-scale archaeological projects that look at many samples from more than one site in a region should provide the most complete charcoal data for environmental reconstructions. However, not every project can be conducted on this scale, and poor plant preservation can limit the number of samples from some sites. In these situations, incorporating the results of other charcoal analyses can be helpful, as long as differences in sampling and methodology are considered.

The kinds of interpretations that are possible using archaeological charcoal vary from region to region, depending on the availability of ancillary data, the environmental and floristic stability of the area, and the diversity of the regional woody flora (which affects the specificity of identifications). For a particular analysis, the age and type of site also can affect interpretation. In general, the probability that environmental conditions at the site differed from modern conditions increases as we move further back in time, thus limiting the applicability of modern analogs for environmental reconstruction.

A synthetic approach, incorporating a variety of paleoenvironmental data (such as other plant macroremains, fauna, pollen, phytoliths, and sediment types) as well as archaeological charcoal, should promote sound reconstruction of paleoenvironments. However, even when these data are not available, identified charcoal taxa provide valuable information about vegetation in the past.

Acknowledgments

We would like to thank Susan Gregg, Christine Hastorf, Naomi Miller, Leah Minc, Virginia Popper, and our anonymous reviewers for their helpful comments.

References Cited

Albert, Dennis A., and Leah D. Minc. 1987. The natural ecology and cultural history of the Colonial Point red oak stands. University of Michigan Biological Station technical report no. 14.

Alcorn, Janis B. 1981. Factors influencing botanical resource perception among the Huastec: Suggestions for future ethnobotanical inquiry. *Journal of Ethnobiology* 1(2):221-30.

Asch, Nancy B., Richard I. Ford, and David L. Asch. 1972. *Paleoethnobotany of the Koster site: The Archaic horizons.* Illinois State Museum Reports of Investigations no. 24.

Baileys, Randall T., and Paul R. Blankenhorn. 1982. Calorific and porosity development in carbonized wood. *Wood Science* 15(1):19-28.

Barefoot, A. C., and F. W. Hankins. 1982. *Identification of modern and Tertiary woods.* Oxford: Clarendon.

Beall, F. C. 1972. Introduction to thermal analysis in the combustion of wood. *Wood Science* 5(2):102-8.

Bohrer, Vorsila. 1986. Guideposts in ethnobotany. *Journal of Ethnobiology* 6(1):27-43.

Britton, Nathaniel L., and Addison Brown. 1970. *An illustrated flora of the northern United States and Canada.* 2d ed., vols. 1-3. New York: Dover.

Browne, F. L. 1958. *Theories of the combustion of wood and its control: A survey of the literature.* U.S. Forest Service, Forest Products Laboratory Report no. 2136.

Brunett, Fel V. 1972. Wood from Schultz and other prehistoric sites in the Great Lakes area. In *The Schultz site at Green Point*, ed. James E. Fitting, pp. 87-90. Memoirs of the Museum of Anthropology, University of Michigan, no. 4.

Bryson, Reid A., David A. Baerreis, and Wayne M. Wendland. 1970. The character of Late-Glacial and Post-Glacial climatic changes. *Pleistocene and Recent environments of the central Great Plains.* Department of Geology,University of Kansas Special Publication 3.

Butzer, Karl W. 1978. Changing Holocene environments at the Koster site: A geo-archaeological perspective. *American Antiquity* 43(3):408-13.

Campbell, B. M., R. F. Du Toit, and R. A. Haney. 1985. Relationships between wood resources and use of species for construction and fuel in the communal lands of Zimbabwe. Paper presented at the 1985 AETFAT conference, St. Louis.

Coles, J. M., S. V. E. Heal, and B. J. Orme. 1978. The use and character of wood in prehistoric Britain and Ireland. *Proceedings of the Prehistoric Society* 44:1-45.

Collier, George A. 1975. *Fields of the Tzotzil: The ecological basis of tradition in highland Chiapas*. Austin: University of Texas Press.

Conrad, Lawrence A., and Robert C. Koeppen. 1972. An analysis of charcoal from the Brewster site (13CK15), Iowa. *Plains Anthropologist* 17(55):52-54.

Côté, H. A., W. A. Côté, and A. C. Day. 1979. *Wood structure and identification*. 2d ed. Syracuse Wood Science Series no. 6. Syracuse: Syracuse University Press.

Cowan, C. Wesley, Josselyn F. Moore, Richard I. Ford, and Michael T. Samuels. 1978. A preliminary analysis of paleoethnobotanical remains from Black Mesa, Arizona: 1977 season. Appendix 1 in *Excavation on Black Mesa, 1977: A preliminary report*, ed. Anthony L. Klesert, pp. 137-56. Southern Illinois University at Carbondale Center for Archaeological Investigations Research Paper no. 1.

Cowan, C. Wesley, and Tristine Lee Smart. 1981. Plant remains from the Hart site and the Kretz site: 1978 excavations. Appendix 4 in *Prehistoric foraging in a temperate forest: A linear programming model*, by Arthur S. Keene. Microfiche, pp. 24-45. New York: Academic Press.

Crites, Gary D. 1987. Middle and Late Holocene ethnobotany of the Hayes Site (40ML139): Evidence from unit 990N918E. *Midcontinental Journal of Archaeology* 12(1):3-32.

Davis, Margaret Bryan. 1976. Pleistocene biogeography of temperate deciduous forests. *Geoscience and Man* 13:13-26.

Delcourt, Paul A., and Hazel R. Delcourt. 1981. Vegetational maps for eastern North America: 40,000 yr B.P. to the present. In *Geobotany II*, ed. Robert C. Romans, pp.123-65. New York: Plenum.

______. 1983. Late-Quaternary vegetational dynamics and community stability reconsidered. *Quaternary Research* 19(2):265-67.

Devres, Inc. 1980. *The socio-economic context of fuelwood use in small rural communities*. A.I.D. Evaluation Special Study, no. 1.

Dimbleby, Geoffrey W. [1967] 1978. *Plants and archaeology*. 2d ed. London: Granada.

Dunlavey, Robert J., and Brian D. Haley. 1984. Navajo sites investigated in the J-9 mining area. In chapter 4 of *Excavations on Black Mesa, 1982: A descriptive report*, ed. Deborah L. Nichols and F. E. Smiley, pp.479-82. Southern Illinois University at Carbondale Center for Archaeological Investigations Research Paper no. 39.

Espey, Huston, and Associates, Inc. 1980. Vegetation and wildlife resources of the Black Mesa and Kayenta mine site. Report prepared for Peabody Coal Company, December 1980.

Estes, Byron M., Kelley Hays, and Elizabeth Nelson. 1984. Navajo sites investigated in the J-10 mining area. In chapter 4 of *Excavations on Black Mesa, 1982: A descriptive report*, ed. Deborah L. Nichols and F. E. Smiley, pp.483-88. Southern Illinois University at Carbondale Center for Archaeological Investigations Research Paper no. 39.

Ford, Richard I. 1979. Paleoethnobotany in American archaeology. In *Advances in archaeological method and theory*, ed. Michael B. Schiffer, 2:285-336. New York: Academic Press.

Ford, Richard I., Jean French, Janet Stock, Tristine Smart, Gretchen Hazen, and David Jessup. 1983. 1981 ethnobotanical recovery: Summary of analysis and frequency tables. Appendix 8 in *Excavations on Black Mesa, 1981: A descriptive report*, ed. F. E. Smiley, D. L. Nichols, and P. P. Andrews, pp.459-80. Southern Illinois University at Carbondale, Center for Archaeological Investigations Research Paper no. 36.

Forest Products Laboratory. 1961. *Charcoal production, marketing, and use*. U.S. Forest Service Forest Products Laboratory Report no. 2213.

Fritts, Harold C. 1976. *Tree rings and climate*. New York: Academic Press.

Gade, Daniel W. 1985. Savanna woodland, fire, protein and silk in highland Madagascar. *Journal of Ethnobiology* 5(2):109-22.

Gifford, Diane P. 1978. Ethnoarchaeological observations of natural processes affecting cultural materials. In *Explorations in ethnoarchaeology*, ed. Richard A. Gould, pp.77-101. School of American Research Seminar Series. Albuquerque: University of New Mexico Press.

Godwin, H., and A. G. Tansley. 1941. Prehistoric charcoals as evidence of former vegetation, soil and climate. *Journal of Ecology* 29(1):117-26.

Haley, Brian D., and Byron M. Estes. 1984. Navajo sites investigated in the J-8 mining area. In chapter 4 of *Excavations on Black Mesa, 1982: A descriptive report*, ed. Deborah L. Nichols and F. E. Smiley, pp.469-77. Southern Illinois University at Carbondale Center for Archaeological Investigations Research Paper no. 39.

Heizer, Robert F. 1963. Domestic fuel in primitive society. *Journal of the Royal Anthropological Institute of Great Britain and Ireland* 93(2):186-94.

Heywood, V. H., ed. 1978. *Flowering plants of the world*. New York: Mayflower.

Hudson, Charles M. 1978. *The southeastern Indians*. Knoxville: University of Tennessee Press.

Hughes, M. K., P. M. Kelly, J. R. Pilcher, and V. C. LaMarche, Jr. 1982. *Climate from tree rings*. Cambridge: University Press.

Hus, Henri. 1908. An ecological cross section of the Mississippi River in the region of St. Louis, Missouri. *Missouri Botanical Garden annual report* 19, pp.127-258.

Johannessen, Sissel. 1983a. Floral remains from the Early Woodland Florence phase. In *The Florence Street site*, by T. E. Emerson, G. R. Milner, and D. K. Jackson, pp.133-46. American Bottom Archaeology FAI-270 Site Reports, vol. 2. Urbana: University of Illinois Press.

_____. 1983b. Mississippian plant remains. In *The Florence Street site*, by T. E. Emerson, G. R. Milner, and D. K. Jackson, pp.200-203. American Bottom Archaeology FAI-270 Site Reports, vol. 2. Urbana: University of Illinois Press.

_____. 1983c. Plant remains from the Missouri Pacific no. 2 site. In *The Missouri Pacific no. 2 site*, by D. L. McElrath and A. C. Fortier, pp.191-207. American Bottom Archaeology FAI-270 Site Reports, vol. 3. Urbana: University of Illinois Press.

_____. 1983d. Plant remains from the Cement Hollow phase. In *The Mund site*, by A. C. Fortier, F. A. Finney, and R. B. Lacampagne, pp.94-104. American Bottom Archaeology FAI-270 Site Reports, vol. 5. Urbana: University of Illinois Press.

_____. 1983e. Plant remains from the Mund phase. In *The Mund site*, by A. C. Fortier, F. A. Finney, and R. B. Lacampagne, pp.299-318. American Bottom Archaeology FAI-270 Site Reports, vol. 5. Urbana: University of Illinois Press.

_____. 1984a. Plant remains from the Edelhardt phase. In *The BBB Motor site*, by T. E. Emerson and D. K. Jackson, pp.169-89. American Bottom Archaeology FAI-270 Site Reports, vol. 6. Urbana: University of Illinois Press.

_____. 1984b. Plant remains from the Julien site. In *The Julien site*, by G. R. Milner and J. A. Williams, pp.244-73. American Bottom Archaeology FAI-270 Site Reports, vol. 7. Urbana: University of Illinois Press.

_____. 1984c. Plant remains. In *The Fish Lake site*, by A. C. Fortier, R. B. Lacampagne, and F. A. Finney, pp.189-99. American Bottom Archaeology FAI-270 Site Reports, vol. 8. Urbana: University of Illinois Press.

_____. 1984d. Plant remains. In The Go-Kart North site, by A. C. Fortier, pp.166-78. American Bottom Archaeology FAI-270 Site Reports, vol. 9. Urbana: University of Illinois Press.

_____. 1984e. Floral resources and remains. In *The Dyroff and Levin sites*, by T. E. Emerson, pp.294-307. American Bottom Archaeology FAI-270 Site Reports, vol. 9. Urbana: University of Illinois Press.

_____. 1984f. Plant remains. In *The Robinson's Lake site*, by G. R. Milner, K. R. Cox, and M. C. Meinkoth, pp.124-32. American Bottom Archaeology FAI-270 Site Reports, vol. 10. Urbana: University of Illinois Press.

Jones, George Neville, and George Damon Fuller. 1955. *Vascular flora of Illinois*. Illinois State Museum Scientific Series, vol. 6. Urbana: University of Illinois Press.

Juneja, S. C. 1975. Combustion of cellulosic materials and its retardance—status and trends. Part 1. Ignition, combustion processes, and synergism. *Wood Science* 7(3):201-8.

Kearney, Thomas H., and Robert H. Peebles. 1951. *Arizona flora.* Berkeley: University of California Press.

King, Frances B., and Russell W. Graham. 1981. Effects of ecological and paleoecological patterns on subsistence and paleoenvironmental reconstructions. *American Antiquity* 46(1):128-42.

King, Frances B., and Jack L. Hofman. 1979. Plant remains from Twenhafel, a multicomponent site on the Mississippi River in southern Illinois. *The Wisconsin Archeologist* 60(3):249-59.

Knudson, R. M., and R. B. Williamson. 1971. Influence of temperature and time upon pyrolysis of untreated and fire retardant treated wood. *Wood Science and Technology* 5(3):176-89.

Kohler, Timothy A., William D. Lipe, Mary E. Floyd, and Robert A. Bye, Jr. 1984. Modeling wood resource depletion in the Grass Mésa locality. In *Dolores archaeological program: Synthetic report 1978-1981,* ed. David A. Breternitz, pp. 99-105. Denver: U.S. Department of the Interior, Bureau of Reclamation, Engineering and Research Center.

Lekson, Stephen H. 1983. Primer and glossary of Chacoan building. Appendix A in *The architecture and dendrochronology of Chetro Ketl,* ed. Stephen H. Lekson, pp.275-85. Report of the Chaco Center no. 6. Albuquerque: National Park Service, Division of Cultural Research.

_____. 1984. *Great pueblo architecture of Chaco Canyon, New Mexico.* Albuquerque: University of New Mexico Press.

Lopinot, Neal H. 1984. Archaeobotanical formation processes and the Late Middle Archaic human-plant interrelationships in the midcontinental U.S.A. Ph.D. diss., Southern Illinois University at Carbondale. Ann Arbor: University Microfilms.

Lundström-Baudais, Karen. 1984. Paleo-ethnobotanical investigation of plant remains from a Neolithic lakeshore site in France: Clairvaux, Station III. *Plants and ancient man,* ed. W. Van Zeist and W. A. Casparie, pp.293-305. Rotterdam: A. A. Balkema.

Michalik, Laura K. 1984a. Navajo sites investigated in the J-5/6-11/12 mining area. In chapter 4 of *Excavations on Black Mesa, 1982: A descriptive report,* ed. Deborah L. Nichols and F. E. Smiley, pp.463-68. Southern Illinois University at Carbondale Center for Archaeological Investigations Research Paper no. 39.

_____. 1984b. Navajo sites investigated in the J-15 mining area. In chapter 4 of *Excavations on Black Mesa, 1982: A descriptive report,* ed. Deborah

L. Nichols and F. E. Smiley, pp.503-9. Southern Illinois University at Carbondale Center for Archaeological Investigations Research Paper no. 39.

Miller, Naomi F. 1982. Economy and environment of Malyan, a third millenium B.C. urban center in southern Iran. Ph.D. diss., University of Michigan. Ann Arbor: University Microfilms.

_____. 1985. Paleoethnobotanical evidence for deforestation in ancient Iran: A case study of urban Malyan. *Journal of Ethnobiology* 5(1):1-19.

Miller, Naomi F., and Tristine Lee Smart. 1984. Intentional burning of dung as fuel: A mechanism for the incorporation of charred seeds into the archaeological record. *Journal of Ethnobiology* 4(1):15-28.

Minnis, Paul E. 1978. Paleoethnobotanical indicators of prehistoric environmental disturbance: A case study. In *The nature and status of ethnobotany*, ed. R. I. Ford, M. F. Brown, M. Hodge, and W. L. Merrill, pp.347-66. Museum of Anthropology, University of Michigan Anthropological Paper no. 67.

_____. 1987. Identification of wood from archaeological sites in the American Southwest. I. Keys for gymnosperms. *Journal of Archaeological Science* 14(2):121-31.

Moore, Josselyn. 1979. 1978 ethnobotanical and ecological research, Black Mesa, Arizona. Appendix 1 in *Excavation on Black Mesa, 1978: A descriptive report*, ed. Anthony L. Klesert and Shirley Powell, pp.179-215. Southern Illinois University at Carbondale Center for Archaeological Investigations Research Paper no. 8.

Nichols, Deborah L., and Clifton W. Sink. 1984. The 1982 field season. Chapter 1 in *Excavations on Black Mesa, 1982: A descriptive report*, ed. Deborah L. Nichols and F. E. Smiley, pp.1-86. Southern Illinois University at Carbondale Center for Archaeological Investigations Research Paper no. 39.

Nicholson, Phyllis H. 1981. Fire and the Australian Aborigine—an enigma. In *Fire and the Australian biota*, ed. A. M. Gill, R. H. Groves, and I. R. Noble, pp.55-76. Canberra: Australian Academy of Science.

Openshaw, Keith. 1974. Wood fuels in the developing world. *New Scientist* 61:271-72.

Osgood, Cornelius. 1940. *Ingalik material culture*. Yale University Publications in Anthropology no. 22. New Haven: Yale University Press.

_____. 1958. *Ingalik social culture*. Yale University Publications in Anthropology no. 53. New Haven: Yale University Press.

Panshin, A. J., and Carl de Zeeuw. 1970. *Textbook of wood technology*. 3d ed., vol. 1. New York: McGraw-Hill.

Payawal, P. C. 1981. Vegetation and modern pollen rain in a tropical rainforest: Mount Makiling, Philippines. Ph.D. diss., the University of Arizona. Ann Arbor: University Microfilms.

Pearsall, Deborah M. 1983. Evaluating the stability of subsistence strategies by use of paleoethnobotanical data. *Journal of Ethnobiology* 3(2):121-37.

Plog, Stephen, and Anthony L. Klesert. 1978. Introduction. Chapter 1 in *Excavation on Black Mesa, 1977: A preliminary report*, ed. Anthony L. Klesert, pp.1-20. Southern Illinois University at Carbondale Center for Archaeological Investigations Research Paper no. 1.

Powell, J. M. 1982. History of plant use and man's impact on the vegetation. In *Biogeography and ecology of New Guinea*, vol. 1, ed. J. L. Gressitt, pp.207-27. Monographiae Biologicae, vol. 42. The Hague: Dr W. Junk.

Prior, J., and D. Price Williams. 1985. An investigation of climatic change in the Holocene epoch using archaeological charcoal from Swaziland, southern Africa. *Journal of Archaeological Science* 12(6):457-75.

Rocek, Thomas R. 1984. Navajo sites investigated in the J-2 mining area. In chapter 4 of *Excavations on Black Mesa, 1982: A descriptive report*, ed. Deborah L. Nichols and F. E. Smiley, pp.451-62. Southern Illinois University at Carbondale Center for Archaeological Investigations Research Paper no. 39.

Rossen, Jack, and James Olson. 1985. The controlled carbonization and archaeological analysis of SE U.S. wood charcoals. *Journal of Field Archaeology* 12(4):445-56.

Salisbury, E. J., and F. W. Jane. 1940. Charcoals from Maiden Castle and their significance in relation to the vegetation and climatic conditions in prehistoric times. *Journal of Ecology* 28:310-25.

Schaffer, E. L. 1966. *Review of information related to the charring rate of wood.* U.S. Forest Service Research Note FPL-0145.

Schweingruber, Fritz H. 1976. Prähistorisches Holz, die Bedeutung von Holzfunden aus Mitteleuropa für die Lösung archäologischer und vegetationskundlicher Probleme. *Academia Helvetica* 2. Bern: Verlag Paul Haupt.

_____. 1977. Results of the examinations made on charcoal from Umingmak. In *Excavations at Umingmak on Banks Island, N.W.T., 1970 and 1973: Preliminary report*, ed. H. Muller-Beck, pp.105-11. Urgeschichtliche Materialhefte 1.

Semé, Michele, and Jon E. Joha. 1984. Navajo sites investigated in the J-13/14 mining area. In chapter 4 of *Excavations on Black Mesa, 1982: A descriptive report*, ed. Deborah L. Nichols and F. E. Smiley, pp.489-502. Southern Illinois University at Carbondale Center for Archaeological Investigations Research Paper no. 39.

Simmons, I. G., and J. B. Innes. 1987. Mid-Holocene adaptations and later Mesolithic forest disturbance in northern England. *Journal of Archaeological Science* 14(4):385-403.

Singh, G., A. P. Kershaw, and Robin Clark. 1981. Quaternary vegetation and fire history in Australia. In *Fire and the Australian biota*, ed. A. M. Gill, R. H. Groves, and I. R. Noble, pp.23-54. Canberra: Australian Academy of Science.

Slocum, D. H., E. A. McGinnis, Jr., and F. C. Beall. 1978. Charcoal yield, shrinkage, and density changes during carbonization of oak and hickory woods. *Wood Science* 11(1):42-47.

Spurr, Stephen H., and Burton V. Barnes. 1973. *Forest Ecology*. 2d ed. New York: Ronald.

Stein, Julie K. 1983. Earthworm activity: A source of potential disturbance of archaeological sediments. *American Antiquity* 48(2):277-89.

Swain, Albert M. 1973. A history of fire and vegetation in northeastern Minnesota as recorded in lake sediments. *Quaternary Research* 3(3):383-96.

Tillman, David A., Amadeo J. Rossi, and William D. Kitto. 1981. *Wood combustion: Principles, processes, and economics*. New York: Academic Press.

Tsukada, Matsuo, and Edward S. Deevey, Jr. 1967. Pollen analyses from four lakes in the southern Maya area of Guatemala and El Salvador. In *Quaternary paleoecology*, ed. E. J. Cushing and H. E. Wright, Jr., pp.303-31. Proceedings of the Seventh Congress of the International Association for Quaternary Research, vol. 7. New Haven: Yale University Press.

Turner, Nancy J. 1982. Traditional use of devil's-club (*Oplopanax horridus*; Araliaceae) by native peoples in western North America. *Journal of Ethnobiology* 2(1):17-38.

Van Dersal, William R. 1938. *Native and woody plants of the United States: Their erosion-control and wildlife values*. U.S. Department of Agriculture Miscellaneous Publication, no. 303.

Wagner, Gail, Tristine Smart, Richard I. Ford, and Heather Trigg. 1984. Ethnobotanical recovery, 1982: Summary of analysis and frequency tables. Appendix G in *Excavations on Black Mesa, 1982: A descriptive report*, ed. D. L. Nichols and F. E. Smiley, pp. 611-32 and microfiche. Southern Illinois University at Carbondale Center for Archaeological Investigations Research Paper, no. 39.

Western, A. Cecilia. 1963. Wood and charcoal in archaeology. Chapter 15 in *Science in Archaeology*, ed. Don Brothwell and Eric Higgs, pp.150-58. Bristol: Thames and Hudson.

_____. 1971. The ecological interpretation of ancient charcoals from Jericho. *Levant* 3:31-40.

Whalley, Lucy A. 1983. Plant remains from the Turner site. In *The Turner and DeMange sites*, by G. R. Milner and J. A. Williams, pp.213-33. American Bottom Archaeology FAI-270 Site Reports, vol. 4. Urbana: University of Illinois Press.

_____. 1984. Plant remains from the Stirling phase. In *The BBB Motor site*, by T. E. Emerson and D. K. Jackson, pp.321-35. American Bottom Archaeology FAI-270 Site Reports, vol. 6. Urbana: University of Illinois Press.

Willcox, G. H. 1974. A history of deforestation as indicated by charcoal analysis of four sites in eastern Anatolia. *Anatolian Studies* 24:117-33.

Wood, W. Raymond, and Donald Lee Johnson. 1978. A survey of disturbance processes in archaeological site formation. In *Advances in archaeological method and theory*, ed. Michael B. Schiffer, 1:315-81. New York: Academic Press.

Wright, H. E., Jr. 1976. The dynamic nature of Holocene vegetation: A problem in paleoclimatology, biogeography, and stratigraphic nomenclature. *Quaternary Research* 6(4):581-96.

Zalucha, L. Anthony. 1982. Methodology in paleoethnobotany: A study in vegetational reconstruction dealing with the Mill Creek culture of northwestern Iowa. Ph.D. diss., University of Wisconsin-Madison. Ann Arbor: University Microfilms.

_____. 1983. An analysis of charcoal from the Helb Site (39CA208), South Dakota. Chapter 9 in *Prairie archaeology: Papers in honor of David A. Baerreis*, ed. Guy E. Gibbon, pp. 109-29. University of Minnesota Publications in Anthropology no. 3.

11

Possible Statistical Contributions to Paleoethnobotany

Joseph B. Kadane

This paper was written at the invitation of the editors to explore some statistical ideas. I am a statistician, only superficially acquainted with paleoethnobotany. Consequently I apologize in advance for ways in which I may have misunderstood the subject or the writers in this volume.

I address two principal subjects: ubiquity versus frequency, and ratios. My final section is devoted to a variety of ideas occasioned by reading the other papers in the volume.

Absolute Counts Versus Ubiquity

Admiration for ubiquity, as contrasted to absolute counts, is rife in the papers in the volume. I shall concentrate on Popper's paper in this respect, because she discusses the reasons for this view, but others (Hastorf, Pearsall, Wagner) appear to share it.

Popper writes "Quantifying archaeobotanical data by absolute counts (the raw number of each taxon in each sample) assumes that the absolute frequency of plant remains accurately reflects prehistoric human-plant interactions. However, as the discussion above shows, absolute frequencies may reflect preservation, sampling, or various other factors. Thus, absolute counts rarely provide an adequate measurement for archaeobotanical remains" (chapter 4).

To make my position clear by contrast, I will propose that methods of quantifying data do not of themselves imply an particular assumptions. I therefore deny the correctness of her first sentence. The second sentence I agree with, but I contend that the same problems affect ubiquity data as well. Thus, for me her conclusion does not follow.

To begin an analysis, I will start with a simplest case model. To a statistician, the simplest model of count data is the Poisson distribution (see Feller 1977:156). It has a single parameter λ. The probability that a Poisson count with parameter λ takes the value x is

$$e^{-\lambda}\lambda^x/x\,!$$

for $x = 0,1,2,...$ Here e is the base of the natural logarithms, and $x!$ (pronounced x factorial) is the product of the first x integers. Thus $x\,! = x\,(x-1)(x-2)...\,(1)$, with the special rule that $0! = 1$. Thus, if C, the count of a burnt botanical remain at some provenience, has a Poisson distribution with parameter λ (where λ is any specified positive number), this means that the probabitity that C is zero is $e^{-\lambda}$, the probabitity is C is one is $\lambda e^{-\lambda}$, the probability that C is two is $\lambda^2 e^{-\lambda}/2$, the probability that C is three is $\lambda^3 e^{-\lambda}/6$, and so forth. The Poisson distribution has mean λ and variance λ, as well. Thus if the expected count λ is close to 0, most of the observations will also be small. However as the expected count rises, the variance of the counts around the mean rises as well.

Suppose that a count of a particular taxon at some site has a Poisson distribution with mean $\lambda = 3$. Then the probabilities of each possible count are given in the following graph.

Poisson distributions are as central to the analysis of count data as are normal, bell-shaped curves to the analysis of averages. The seed counts you expect to see should depend on the volume of soil you look for them in. Suppose, in a particular paleoethnobotanical context, that the count of a particular taxon is assumed to have a Poisson distribution with some mean λ, on the basis of a sample of 1% of a cubic meter of soil matrix. What might be the effect if, instead of sampling 1% of a cubic meter, one sampled 2%? If the taxon is distributed uniformly in the soil matrix, the expected seed count would double to 2λ. In general, if volume v is sampled, the expected seed count would be λv. Thus, if λ is the expected count per unit volume, λv is the expected count in a sample of volume v units. This argument suggests the assumption that counts of taxon remains should have a Poisson distribution with mean λv, where v is the soil volume examined, and λ is the expected seed count per unit volume of soil examined. The advantage of thinking this way is that now samples taken with different soil volumes can be compared.

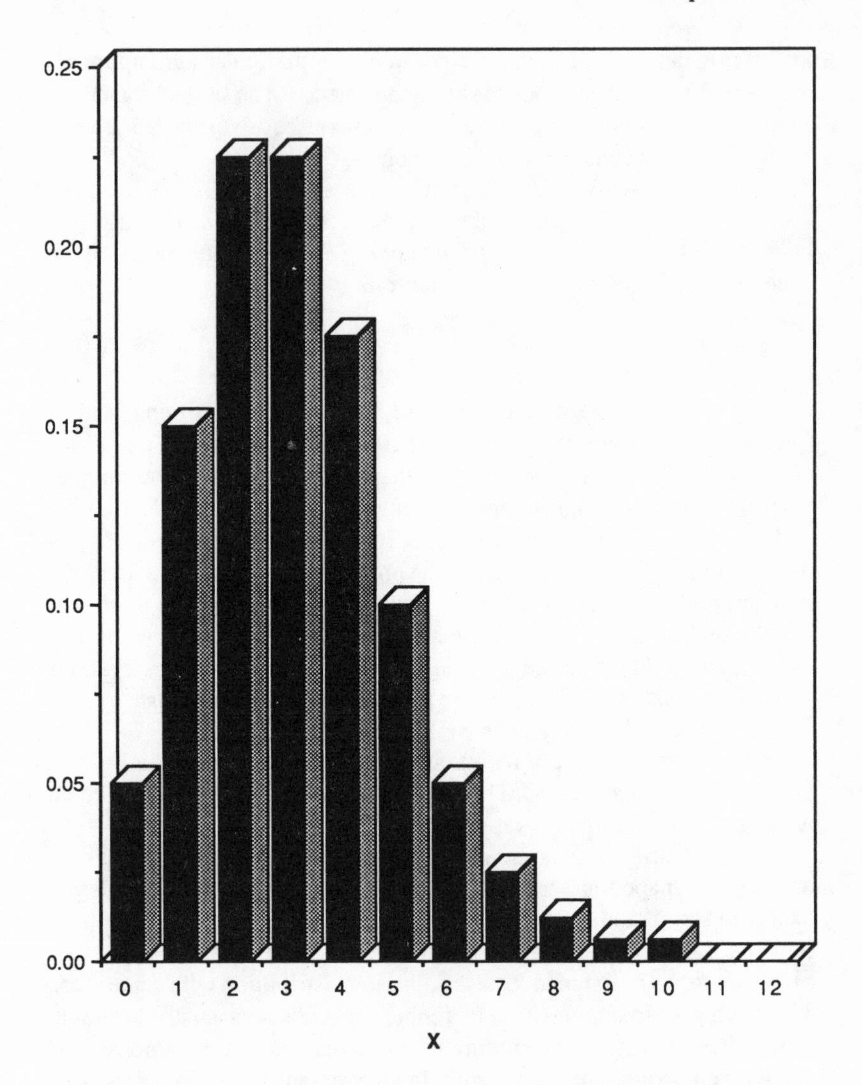

Figure 11.1. Probabilities of the Poisson distribution with parameter 3.

The Poisson assumption as it has so far been described does not take account of the passage of time and the question of preservation. Consider the fate of a single burnt botanical remain from the time of deposit to the time of excavation. It might survive and it might not. Suppose the probability that it survives is p . Now consider a second burnt botanical remain from the taxon deposited in the same provenience. It is reasonable to suppose that the probability that it survives is also p. However, to have described the probability structure of the preservation process requires more, namely, probabilities that both remains survive, or that neither survives. One possible (but extreme) assumption is that either both survive (which will happen with probability p), or that neither will (which will happen with probability $(1 - p)$. This would be the case if some common cause determined preservation. A second possibility is that the survivals of the two burnt remains have nothing to do with one another. In this case, the probability of both surviving is p^2, the probability that remain 1 survives but remain 2 does not is $p(1 - p)$, the probability that remain 2 survives but remain 2 survives but remain 1 does not is again $p(1 - p)$, and finally, the probability that neither survives is $(1 - p)^2$. A bit of easy algebra shows that the sum of these four probabilities is one, as it must be for these to be probabilities.

The latter assumption is called the assumption of independence. It can be applied to the survival of any number of burnt botanical remains. A useful mental model of it would be to think of the survival of each remain as if it were determined by the flip of a coin. If the coin comes up heads, which it will with probability p, the remain survives. If it comes up tails, which it will with probability $1 - p$, the remain will not survive. The assumption of independence is that each remain gets its own flip of the coin, and that the outcome of that flip is uninfluenced by the outcome of any other flip.

Assuming only that the probability of each botanical remain surviving is p, the expected number of surviving botanical remain is λpv. Under the additional assumption that survivals of botanical remains are independent, the distribution of surviving botanical remains is again Poisson, with, necessarily, parameter λpv. I regard the assumption of independence is the preservation process as quite dudious and am curious about the consequences of relaxing it. But for the sake of this argument, I shall assume it.

The consequence of this simple model is that if the initial process distributing burnt botanical remains is Poisson with mean count λ per unit volume, the preservation pocess is independent, with each remain having probability p of surviving. And if a volume v of soil is examined, the resulting observed botanical remains will have a Poisson distribution with parameter λpv. This confirms Popper's statement that taxon counts will depend on preservation and on sampling (if that is taken to mean the volume of soil matrix sampled).

Now consider ubiquity, namely, the average number of samples containing a positive count of the taxon. Again to take the simplest case, suppose that each sample is taken using the same volume v, that it has the same preservation probability p, and that the sample locations have the same rate, λ, of the presence of the taxon when the site was in use. Then as the number of samples gets larger, the ubiquity approaches the probability that the taxon was present in a sample volume v and survived. But this probability can be calculated. It is the probability that a random count having a Poisson distribution with parameter λpv take the value one, or two, or three, or. . . Since total probability is one, the probability sought is one minus the probability of a count of zero (i.e., one minus the probability that the taxon is unobserved at the provenience), which is $1 - e^{-p\lambda v}$. Thus, ubiquity depends on v and on p, just as do counts. There is no magic in ubiquity that takes away dependence on preservation and volume.

I think statisticians are likely to regard ubiquity with suspicion, because it involves such a radical reduction of the data. There must be some information in the fact that one provenience has remains of a particular taxon numbering one, ten, one hundred, one thousand, ten thousand, and so forth, especially when compared with other proveniences and other taxa. While paleoethnobotanists may believe that ubiquity reduces the effect of differential preservation, I can see no justification for that claim (which does not mean that no such justification is possible). Even in cases in which the estimation of p and λ is difficult, I would recommend addressing the difficulty head-on and doing one's best to assemble information about them. Lack of information about v, however, would be due to a failure to record field procedures properly.

The simple model given here has some useful implications, namely: (1) The volume v of soil matrix associated with a sample is an important part of the data and should be routinely recorded; (2) The preservation probabilities p are an inherent difficulty for paleoethnobotanical data. Their magnitude is a matter of opinion and conjecture. Even in such a circumstance, an appropriate statistical model for the data can permit the exploration of the consequences of a variety of views about preservation. Conclusions that are very sensitive to the precise form of an assumption should be viewed with greater caution than conclusions that are less sensitive. I regard such studies as an important area of possible contribution of statistics to paleoethnobotany.

The presence/absence model above may be useful in thinking about Hastorf's figure 8.6, in which she compares percentage presence with isotope data. It is not clear from the paper how the isotopes were obtained, and what their units are. But there is no particular reason to think that the units should work out so that $1 - e^{-\lambda vp}$ should equal the height of the isotope bars. Thus, I don't see that there is anything to explain about the discrepancy.

To go this far is only to say that the arguments for ubiquity over counts do not seem to bear up under scrutiny. But this does not say much about how to analyze paleoethnobotanical data. I believe that to do so requires a model for the data, perhaps developing from the Poisson count model suggested above. One example is given in Kadane and Hastorf (1988).

In that paper we used the Poisson model, except that because v was constant it was amalgamated into λ, so that λ is interpreted as the expected number of botanical remains of a particular taxon at deposition in a soil bag of the size Hastorf uses in her fieldwork. The data came from the Upper Mantaro Archaeological Research project in Peru (Earle et al. 1987), and were taken from a particular patio group that had been excavated to bedrock. There were 88 proveniences in the patio group. For each of them, Hastorf gave probabilities, based on digging notes, that the provenience, if inside a structure, has been used as a hearth, as indoor storage, or as an indoor living area; if outside structures, that it had been used as midden, outdoor storage, or patio activity area. Additionally Hastorf gave λ's for each of the six activities and 29 taxa used in the study. Finally she gave p's reflecting her view of the probability of preservation, by taxon, between deposition (ca. 1460) and excavation (1982). These ingredients permitted the computation of posterior probabilities (Lindley 1985) of use at each provenience. We concluded that the botanical materials had substantially changed her view of the likely activities provenience by provenience, and that she could interpret the patterns in an archaeologically meaningful way. We plan a more complete description of this work for an archaeological audience in a separate publication.

Ratios

Another method for trying to deal with preservation issues is to form ratios of counts. In fact ubiquity can be regarded as a kind of ratio, the ratio of the number of proveniences in which the burnt botanical remain was present to the number of all proveniences. While I find ratios too general a matter for me to discuss, forming a ratio does not in itself make preservation issue go away. As an example, consider Johannessen's (chapter 9) discussion of nut-to-wood ratios. Based on analysis of this ratio, she suggests that the late Archaic culture was based on gathering nuts for food. The observation of a ratio of nuts to wood found decreasing at sites in which deposition occurred closer to the present could be explained, if it were the case that nuts are preserved better than wood, even if at the time of deposition the nut-to-wood ratio were constant. Thus her analysis implicitly assumes something about the relative preservation of nuts and wood. Merely expressing the data in ratio form cannot obviate the need for a discussion of preservation assumptions, despite her claim that "the ratio eliminates the effects of varying conditions of deposition and preservation."

Miller also notes the use of ratios to charcoal "to control for likelihood of preservation." But all these protestations cannot obscure the fact that an important assumption is implicit here: that nuts and charcoal decay at equal rates. I am not in a position to know what evidence supports or contradicts this assumption, so I am not suggesting that Johannessen's conclusions are incorrect. I mean only to bring the assumptions to the attention of others in a better position that I to judge the extent to which it might be true.

Other Suggestions

Toll's excellent paper suggests that to use an obviously sensible strategy of two-stage sampling carries a high statistical price. "While clearly throwing any semblance of randomized sampling out the window . . . ". Fortunately this is not the case; she can complete two-stage random sampling and still compute variances. The way this works is that within each stratum (here strata are defined by screening sizes), random sampling is accomplished. Since the number of remains in each stratum can be counted or estimated, the proportion of a single taxon in the sample can be estimated too. Formulas for the resulting variances and for optimal sampling proportions for each stratum, are available. For a view of the statistical literature here, see Cochran (1977, chapters 10-12).

Johannessen gives a very interesting account of a time-series treatment of paleoethnobotanical data. I found her analysis quite convincing, with one possible exception. Looking at figure 9.2, it seems to me that the point in the upper left has an extreme influence on the regression line. If you hold a finger over that point, I think you can persuade yourself that the other points might present a nearly constant straight line of nut-to-wood ratio against time. In comparing figure 9.2 to the data given in table 9.2, it is clear that some sort of selection must have gone on between the table and the figure (what happened to the observation at 22.6?). Consequently I am not able to pursue the issue further. Points like this one are called "influential" or "leverage" points by statisticians. Some good general references about robustness of regressions are the books by Belsley, Kuh, and Welsch (1980). For further material on graphics in statistics, Kosslyn (1985) gives a comparative review of five recent books.

Smart and Hoffman raise the question of how to analyze data when identification of species cannot always be done without error. One method of conveying the information that can be gleaned by laboratory analysis is to give probabilities on species. A probability of 1.0 would mean that the analyst is satisfied with a species identification. Probabilities less than one, but positive, would indicate uncertainty. Data recorded in this way can be analyzed but would probably require statistical help.

A second way to handle this kind of problem is to think of the species data as missing, but higher categorizations, say by genus, are known. There is a large statistical literature on missing data, usually thought of as missing data in surveys of people. Some recent references are Rubin (1976), Little (1982), Dickey, Jiang, and Kadane (1987), and Little and Rubin (1987).

I found Wagner's paper, and in particular her figure 2.1, very interesting indeed. I wonder whether the tests reported there were run with comparable soils. It seems to me that tests of this kind are quite important for calibrating the machines being used and should be run for a variety of soil types and sizes of carbonized seeds. One obvious use of such information would be to correct for likely misses due to the machinery used. Yet Wagner specifically disavows this possibility, writing "they cannot provide quantifiable adjustments or corrections to the number and types of plant remains recovered." I wonder why she takes this position. I should think that even a not totally accurate adjustment would be better than none at all.

An approach to this problem would be to collect data from "similar" sites and use different recovery techniques. The major variables measuring soil differences would have to be recorded. Using data of this type, recovery techniques might be calibrated for how efficient they are, using, perhaps, linear regression techiques.

Conclusion

The papers in this volume provide an outsider like me with a fascinating glimpse at the world of paleoethnobotany. They raise many questions for me. Perhaps the time is right for serious collaborations between paleoethnobotanists and statisticians.

Acknowledgements

The Research for this chapter was supported in part by National Sceince Foundation Grant BNS 8411738 at the Center of Advanced Study in the Behavioral Sciences, and in part by Naval Research Contract N-00014-85-K-0539 at Carnegie Mellon University.

References Cited

Belseley, D. A., E. Kuh, and R. E. Welsch. 1980. *Regression Diagnostics.* New York: J. Wiley and Sons.

Cochran, W. G. 1977. *Sampling techniques.* 3d ed. New York: J. Wiley and Sons.

Cook, R.D., and S. Weisberg. 1982. *Residuals and influence in regression.* New York: Chapman and Hall.

Dickey, J. M., J. M. Jiang, and J. B. Kadane. 1987. Bayesian methods for censored categorical data. *Journal of the American Statistical Association,* 82: 773-81.

Earle, T., T. D'Altroy, C. Hastorf, C. Scott, C. Costin, G. Russell, and E. Sandefur. 1987. *The effects of Inka conquest on the Wanka domestic economy.* Los Angeles: UCLA Institute of Archaeology 28.

Feller, W. 1968. *An introduction to probability theory and its application.* vol. 1, 3d ed. New York: John Wiley and Sons.

Kadane, J. B., and C. A. Hastorf. 1988. Bayesian paleoethnobotany. In *Bayesian Statistics III.* ed. J. Bernardo, M. H. DeGroot, D. V. Lindley, and A. M. F. Smith, Oxford: University Press.

Kosslyn, S. M. 1985. Graphics and human information processing: A review of five books. *Journal of the American Statistical Association.* 80:499-512.

Lindley, D. 1985. *Making decisions.* 2d ed. New York: J. Wiley and Sons.

Little, R. J. A. 1982. Models for nonresponse in sample surveys. *Journal of the American Statistical Association.* 77:237-50.

Little, R. J. A., and D. Rubin. 1987. *Statistical analysis with missing data.* New York: J. Wiley and Sons.

Rubin, D. 1976. Inference and missing data. *Biometrika.* 63:581-92.

12

Commentary: Little Things Mean a Lot—Quantification and Qualification in Paleoethnobotany

Richard I. Ford

Paleoethnobotany is experiencing a methodological explosion. The papers in this seminal volume acknowledge the necessity for quantification because of the advances in field recovery and laboratory techniques. At the same time, the interpretation of archaeological plant remains continues to demand development of a synthesis between cultural and plant biology theories.

Less than a generation ago there was no need for a volume of this genre. Just as radiocarbon dating transformed prehistory, flotation revolutionized paleoethnobotany. Before flotation (i.e., water separation), the well-equipped archaeobotanical laboratory had occasional use for a monocular-compound microscope, a paraffin-embedding heater, and a microtome. Even comparative collections were quite small and restricted. Today most laboratories have stereozoom dissecting scopes, a research microscope, access to a SEM (scanning electron microscope), and in some cases a new morphometric laboratory complete with digestizer and graphic emulators. Why the change? Because the water separation of prehistoric plant fragments has given paleoethnobotanists more data to analyze and more opportunities for stunning discoveries than were possible 20 years ago. The tiny plant remains, the little things, which were once invisible in the field or lost through a wide-mesh screen, are the commonplace data base of contemporary paleoethnobotanists.

In addition to new field recovery methods and laboratory technology, an archaeological soil matrix yields more than macrofossils. Pollen grains and plant chemical crystals—truly microscopic plant remains—must be saved to answer anthropological questions. The complementarity of charred remains, pollen, and phytoliths for cultural and environmental interpretations is rarely appreciated. While the papers presented here discuss macrofossils, other botanical components of an archaeological site must not be forgotten.

The implications of the wealth of archaeobotanical data available today are well presented by the authors in this volume. The quantity has demanded statistical analyses of botanical remains for intersite understanding and for intersite comparisons. Patterns of plant use and change are better understood today than ever before. Exceptional examples are discussed by Toll (chapter 3) for the Southwest, Johannessen (chapter 9) for Illinois, and Pearsall (chapter 7) for Peru. The vast amount of data at hand increases the probability for identifying unusual plants as well as magnifying the problem of contamination. Before 1960 only rare sites had preservation which yielded statistically adequate samples; arithmetic description sufficed. With enormous samples available, the analytical methods now in use have given paleoethnobotanical conclusions credibility in archaeology.

Quantification

Various methods are available to paleoethnobotanists for the description of data and their statistical comparison. The authors have selected the simplest, most common, and—as Kadane comments—very appropriate statistics. Popper (chapter 4) provides a succinct review to orient the reader to statistical methods found in the paleoethnobotanical literature. Miller (chapter 5) and Pearsall (chapter 7) augment this introduction by discussing in essential detail the use of ratios.

Archaeobotanical data are highly constrained as Popper (chapter 4) and Hastorf (chapter 8) emphasize. No discussion of samples of plant remains can ignore soil volume (Wagner, chapter 2), preservation factors (Johannessen, chapter 9), or cultural processes for deposition (Hastorf, chapter 8). Unless these are controlled and appreciated, quantification will have little meaning and conclusions will remain only assertions.

Kadane (chapter 11) discusses the Poisson distribution of data. The outliers in a Poisson distribution may be widely separated and may be quite meaningless for statistical appraisal. Yet these rare little things are often significant for cultural interpretation. Their low probability of occurrence may highlight their actual importance. Archaeobotanists have long appreciated that plant anatomy will condition the potential for a taxon to be preserved in an open site (Munson, Parmalee, and Yarnell 1971). When few soil samples are processed, the plants with low probabilities will almost never be recovered. As the number of water-processed soil samples increases, the prospects of discovering a rare or unusual plant remain also rises. Poorly preserved taxa can only be discovered when numerous soil samples are analyzed. But they must be sought because they provide a greater cultural texture to a site's description. The number of soil samples processed does not change the Poisson distribution or the calculated mean, but it does change the species count. The two-level sampling strategy advocated by Toll (chapter 3) increases the chances for finding underrepresented taxa.

Kadane elevates this discussion from mere chance of discovery to the necessity for recognizing the actual probability that a taxon will be found in a site. His argument is imperative for the mathematic models he has developed. Unfortunately, insufficient botanical data are available to allow archaeobotanists to provide these figures without considerable research. But who will conduct it? Ethnoarchaeologists respond to social anthropologists's lack of interest in material culture by conducting the studies themselves. More recently, paleoethnobotanists have continued ethnographic studies by tracking the cultural processes which lead to the consumption, disposal, and deposition of plant products. As valuable as this research is, its emphasis has been on plant degradation from a cultural perspective. To determine the probability of archaeological plant survival, plant taphonomy must be studied from a biological perspective as well. Research must examine the geochemical, biological, and mechanico-environmental breakdown over time of each useful taxon in a specific soil matrix to explain why plants in the ground deteriorate. Archaeobotanists must do the experiments. It is not romantic science, but ultimately the missing probability estimates will become available to satisfy mathematical equations.

The context of plant macrofossils is a standardized volume of soil matrix. The recovery of plant macrofossils is ably discussed by several authors (e.g., Wagner and Toll), but how the plants got there in the first place is another matter. In open sites charred remains are the main evidence. Even after burning in a human-established reducing environment (oxygen depleted), the biological evidence continues to endure postdepositional destruction. The bulk of these samples are woody plant tissue, and perhaps 95% are a consequence of cultural behavior. Contamination by unburned plant debris is easy to recognize and to remove. Prehistoric contaminants (noncultural in origin) must be acknowledged even if they cannot always be factored out. Quantitatively, as far as we know they do not distort basic statistical analyses, although qualitatively they may inflate the taxa list from a site. However, in dry shelters and anaerobic wet sites the interpretation of samples is reversed. Under such conditions the exceptional preservation environment retains soft tissue resulting in 90% or more of the archaeobotanical data being derived from naturally transported (wind or water, respectively) or animal activity. Dry shelters in the eastern United States and Southwest contain predominantly naturally deposited plants, some even in statistically significant patterns, because pack-rat spatial behavior on prehistoric surfaces mimics human activity areas. These seemingly ideal circumstances for cultural reconstruction in reality can be an often-unrecognized paleoethnobotanical nightmare. In these situations, determining human-introduced plants is a very difficult necessity.

The quantitative procedures commonly applied to paleoethnobotanical data are discussed with authority in this volume. An alternative approach for analyzing archaeobotanical data mentioned in the Introduction and by Kadane has recently been employed by Margaret Scarry (1986). She has examined her prehistoric Moundville, Alabama, botanical data with Exploratory Data Analysis statistics (Tukey 1977). This approach accounts for the multimodality of many archaeological plant data sets and is not based on the assumption of normal distribution required by most descriptive statistics. Consequently, she eschews mean and standard deviation calculations and instead examines dispersion around the median. Furthermore, she standardizes her data with total plant counts rather than with weights. In her analysis of data structure and variability, she expresses her data graphically with scatter plots, box plots, and stem-and-leaf diagrams. The result is a visual understanding of the data in the process of analysis. Because paleoethnobotanists are in the regrettable position of not formulating the research designs of most excavations, her exploratory data analyses allows quantitative assessment of multiple data sets without the constraints imposed by soil volume differences or excavation unit discrepancies that undermine sample independence. The promise of this method for interpreting data should find widespread application by paleoethnobotanists.

The eloquence of a statistical analysis of a data base may not answer the question which was originally proposed. The most common example is edible plant food. As one example, many archaeologists assume that the presence of maize on a site indicates that maize was a prehistoric human food item. But this is an assumption based upon present-day use of the plant or ethnographic analogy. The alternative hypotheses that corn was raised to feed deer may sound ludicrous but must be disproven. Too often we accept conclusions without attempting to falsify them. For example, corn survives at most sites as cobs or detached cupules, with the best explanation being that cobs were used for fuel. (Surprisingly, for a long time the food value of this evidence was emphasized at the expense of fuel.) The consumption of kernels by humans is neither confirmed nor denied by their excavation, even in considerable quantity, from an archaeological site. Moreover, the assumption is often made that an increase in the number of kernels indicates maize's increased importance in the prehistoric human diet. In actuality, the quantified data and even trend analysis over time do not prove this conclusion. An independent analysis with isotopic chemistry on human bone is required to demonstrate the consumption of maize and its importance in the diet (e.g., Bumsted 1984; Hastorf, chapter 8). Our best efforts at quantification may not answer the original question that spawned the research.

Modeling of human diets by means of linear programming (e.g., Keene 1981; Reidhead 1979) or simulation (e.g., Dove 1984) are alternative methods of interpretation that rely upon the correct taxonomic identification of archaeobotanical data and that can suggest missing plant data. Both begin with the assumption that human nutritional requirements have changed little in the Holocene. The biochemical constituents of edible plants can be determined in the laboratory. With this information the paleoethnobotanist can estimate if the identified food plants will satisfy the basic food needs of a reference individual. These models are invaluable for estimating the quantity of plant food needed to satisfy basic nutrition. Deficiencies may be attributed to unrecognized or undiscovered archaeological plants (keeping animal input constant). A reconstruction of the plant environment (discussed below) will suggest whether the proposed floral dietary item would have been available. A botanical reason or probability estimate may be advanced to explain the absence of plants from the archaeobotanical record, assuming that they were culturally acceptable.

In addition to modeling of human diets a second frequently explored problem in paleoethnobotany is plant environmental reconstruction. If one begins with wood used for fuel, it must be recalled that each culture has a classification or folk taxonomy for firewood. Some woods in the environment are rejected while others may be overrepresented relative to their natural frequencies in a forest. Still other taxa are functional equivalents, depending upon their availability. The result is that quantifications of charcoal may reflect only the culturally preferred woods but not all of the wood taxa that were available. Further, it would not be assumed that the taxonomic summations reflect the actual frequency of taxa in the environment, a point considered by Smart and Hoffman (chapter 10). However, the culturally excluded taxa may be discovered by analyzing botanical data sets that normally do not pass through a cultural filter for their inclusion on a site. These are pollen and plant opal phytoliths. They can reveal taxa not found in the charred wood from a site. Even with the addition of these data, a frequency rank order of the prehistoric forest is difficult without reference to modern flora and the production of pollen and phytoliths within these forests.

A word of caution is in order when one is reconstructing the woody vegetation of a site area. Humans not only select wood differently, but their actions may also establish forests without modern analogues. Environmental reconstruction is further complicated at sites where farming was practiced or herd animals were kept. Any of these activities may change the configuration of plant succession and create plant frequencies unlike those studied by modern ecologists.

Qualification

Paleoethnobotany recognizes the cultural bases of archaeological plant assemblages. The cultural bases invariably derive from reading ethnographic accounts about how a particular taxon is used in the non-Western world. Such information is the source of hypothesis generation or the assertions made to explain the presence of an archaeological plant. While ethnographic analogy is valid as a starting point for paleoethnobotanical research, it cannot be the only font for ideas about plants in society. After all, the ethnographic record is very incomplete and is flawed by gender bias, poor plant taxonomy, and cultural ignorance. By modern standards it is a normative account, and traditionally it is devoid of processual description or a cultural understanding of why plants are useful. This record must be amplified with botanical studies of the chemistry and plant biology of available taxa.

More attention to botany provides information unknown either to anthropologists or to the people under their observation. Correct plant systematics forms the basis of all paleoethnobotany. To understand the process of plant manipulation, however, human intervention in the life cycle of a plant for any purpose, plant genetics, anatomy, physiology, reproductive strategies, and phenology must be researched. Plant biology is the study of process; missing or inadequately published information can be determined by scientific experimentation.

Paleoethnobotany lacks a coherent synthetic theory linking culture and botany. There are many problems of fundamental interest to science that only paleoethnobotany can answer, as many of these papers reveal. Two of the most fundamental are still plant domestication and environmental perturbation.

The most important variable paleoethnobotanists have is time. Human-plant interactions examined in the past are the basis of the field. The genetic changes in plants leading to the reproductive dependence upon humans is an exciting topic for investigation. When one realizes that in the last 10,000 years, virtually the only new plants on earth are domesticates, it is obvious that the cultural selection of plant genotypes requires more study. At the same time that native species have become extinct or reduced in range, numerous varieties of domesticated plants have expanded over the earth's surface. Natural selection is much slower than cultural selection. The quantitative description of the morphological changes leading to plant domesticates or cultivated varieties is a truly remarkable contribution by paleoethnobotanists. However, the cultural basis for these changes beyond functional explanations continues to defy explication.

The second critical variable paleoethnobotanists have is rates of environmental alteration. Ecological studies of floristic changes have provided a description of the processes. In nature these are constrained by biological and environmental parameters; the rate of change is relatively slow by human (not geological) standards. Under the hand of humans the rate can be very fast. Humans have sped the destruction of vegetation with fire, hand tools, domestic animals, and complex machines. Paleoethnobotanists must go beyond their static statistical methods to describe the environment, and must develop differential equations to explore the rates of change that best reveal how human behavior has altered the plant world and has even created new communities unknown in nature. Gardens, pastures, and farmland are configurations on the landscape outside the natural order. Paloethnobotanists have discovered these; now they must explain their evolution.

Conclusions

Scientific inquiry has advanced from metaphysics to observation to experimentation. The methods of science have progressed from the visual description of macroscopic objects to the analysis of microscopic phenomena and now to their elemental constituents. Paleoethnobotany parallels these developments. The cigar box of plant fragments from past excavations has been replaced by millions of charred macrofossils from a single site. Archaeological plants no longer are examined with the naked eye or a hand lens. Today identifications are based on anatomical features discovered with the scanning electron mircoscope (SEM). Numerical descriptions of seeds have moved from length, width, and thickness coordinates to allometric configurations produced by computer. The next stage, the biochemical assessment of charred plant remains, has already arrived. In paleoethnobotany as in other sciences, statistical analysis has lagged behind technological innovation. This volume has successfully addressed the modern field methods that yield quality data, the traditional laboratory procedures that underlie observation, and the advances and deficiencies in the quantitative methods of paleoethnobotany. Programs for future experimentation are outlined as well. The reader of this book quickly realizes that these little plant remains mean a lot. Statistical analyses have demonstrated the cultural importance of large samples of tiny plant fragments. Qualitative assessments based on ethnographic analogy, experimentation, and plant biology have revealed the significance of even single seeds. Progress in paleoethnobotany has been astronomical in the past decade. As the field moves from the observation of events to the development of a synthetic theory of culture and plant science, it will stand alone and receive the recognition it has been denied in both anthropology and biology.

References Cited

Bumsted, Mary Pamela. 1984. *Human variation: ^{13}C in adult bone collagen and the relation to diet in an isochronous C_4 (maize) archaeological population.* Los Alamos: Los Alamos National Laboratory.

Dove, Donald E. 1984. Prehistoric subsistence and population change along the lower Aqua Fria River, Arizona: A model simulation. *Arizona State University, Anthropological Research Paper* no. 32.

Keene, Arthur S. 1981. *Prehistoric foraging in a temperate forest: A linear programming model.* New York: Academic Press.

Munson, Patrick, Paul Parmalee, and Richard A. Yarnell. 1971. Subsistence ecology at Scovill, a terminal Middle Woodland village. *American Antiquity* 36:410-31.

Reidhead, Van. 1979. Linear programming models in anthropology. *Annual Review of Anthropology* 8: 543-78.

Scarry, Clara Margaret. 1986. Change in plant procurement and production during the emergence of the Moundville chiefdom. Ph.D. diss., Department of Anthropology, University of Michigan. Ann Arbor: University Microfilms.

Tukey, John W. 1977 *Exploratory data analysis.* Reading, Mass: Addison-Wesley.

13

Commentary: Recent Directions in Paleoethnobotanical Research

William H. Marquardt

I am delighted to have been invited to discuss the papers in this book, since I owe a debit of gratitude to archaeobotanists in general and to several of the authors in particular, because over the years their insights and analyses have helped me to understand and interpret archaeological data in the Southwest, Midwest, and Southeast. Although I profited from the colleagueship of Debby Pearsall at the University of Missouri in the late seventies, I guess I learned the most about fieldwork in archaeobotany from Gail Wagner, who analyzed the plant remains from the Kentucky shell mound project, which I codirected with Patty Jo Watson (Marquardt and Watson 1983). I was not always a quick learner, however. I recall one occasion on the banks of the Green River in which I was grazing on what I thought was goosefoot and complained to Gail, "I don't see how prehistoric people ate this stuff; it tastes terrible." Gail looked up from her work and replied calmly, "That's because you're eating jewelweed, you idiot."

My general impression of this book is that in the past decade archaeobotanists have made significant strides in the production of reliable results because of increased sophistication in field and laboratory procedures and more explicit concern with the process of inference. This advancement has been augmented by attention to the pathways by which plant remains both enter and are reclaimed from the archaeological record. I wish to make a few comments about the chapters, and then I will discuss two issues that I perceive among them.

First, Wagner makes some very important points about data recovery. To those of us for whom flotation has become a part of archaeological life, Gail's careful differentiation of dry screening from water screening from flotation may seem elementary, but I can tell you from my travels that there are many practicing archaeologists who still think they are doing flotation when in fact they are water screening. Of course there are differences from region to region and from research design to research design, but some dos and don'ts have emerged. Do not dry screen before floating. Do not confuse water screening with flotation. Do test your system for contamination. To ensure even the possibility of comparability, you must specify how your data were sampled and collected and make clear the characteristics of the raw data.

Toll is also very realistic and commonsensical when she indicates that different interpretations are obtained when different screen sizes are used. Realistically, we can't treat the whole data set with the same rigor, so why not scan for general information while also doing some detailed analysis, in order to ensure the inclusion of low-frequency, small-dimension seeds? Her emphasis on the regional perspective is very important, and here one can draw an analogy with archaeological site surveys. In surveys, learning where sites are not found is often as edifying as learning where sites are found. Even the notion of site must be given critical attention. For example, in a survey in eastern France our crews recorded the presence of scattered pre-Roman, Gallo-Roman, and medieval ceramics, even when there was insufficient integrity to the deposits to grace them with the term site. The scatters made little sense at a local scale, but when viewed at a broader (more macro) scale, at which ceramic scatters were plotted in relation to certain geological features and known road networks, comprehensible patterns began to emerge (Crumley, Marquardt, and Leatherman 1987:131-32, 138-48, 152-53). My point is that in paleoethnobotany, as in archaeological surveys, often a multiscalar regional perspective provides more interesting results than a uniscalar one.

Popper reviews the various time-honored quantification techniques: presence/absence, counts, ranks, and diversity indexes. There is no a priori best quantification technique any more than there is one best lithic analysis technique or one best seriation technique. Again, the questions we are asking should dictate our descriptive statistical choices.

Miller takes a closer look at ratios and notes that the choice of analytical categories can seriously affect the archaeobotanist's interpretations. Like Popper, Miller sees different kinds of ratios as relevant to identifying different processes. Her examples from several field contexts speak eloquently to the importance of such decisions.

Asch and Sidell point out that a very valuable role is filled by archaeobotanists in a common archaeological pursuit: basic stratigraphic analysis. Their argument is compelling, and their emphasis on using archaeobotanical data to complement other stratigraphic data is very well placed. We had a very similar experience in our Kentucky project. In interpreting shell middens of the third millennium B.C., we found that a combination of botanical, gastropod, and soil-chemical data was better than relying on so-called diagnostic artifacts alone.

Pearsall's chapter represents a very important consideration: reliability of interpretation is directly dependent on understanding the processes leading to deposition, preservation, and recovery of materials. She considers the type of source and the type of excavation context. The Panaulauca rock shelter provides an appropriate example of the importance of contexts of origin. These truly basic questions, such as Is it fuel or is it food? seem terribly important to me, and I'm happy to see such a reflexive and critical approach to the archaeological record.

Hastorf explores the information content of archaeological collections and suggests that more and better ethnographic studies on plant "production, processing, and storage" undertaken by paleoethnobotanists would be very beneficial. More replicative experimentation would undoubtedly help too, and in this pursuit we are probably far behind our British colleagues.

Also in Hastorf's chapter is the sentiment that paleoethnobotanists ought to be more involved in the planning and excavation of sites and in the anthropological interpretation of results. Hastorf emphasizes the potential role of paleoethnobotany in contributing to both economic and cultural anthropology. Hastorf and Asch and Sidell (see above) are saying that paleoethnobotanists (or archaeological botanists, which is the term Asch and Sidell prefer) should be not merely consumers, but active producers of archaeological knowledge.

Johannessen considers the role of plant remains in the interpretation of cultural change. Her case study from the Midwest is one in which changes in plant usage can be demonstrated with some certainty because of the thorough examination of many samples. It is a convincing analysis indeed, and its success reinforces a recurrent theme in this book. Simply put, that theme is that while many samples are generally better than few samples, the reliability of the end result depends heavily on an analysis that is carefully executed, standardized across sites, and integrated into a comprehensive research plan.

Smart and Hoffman are concerned with environmental reconstruction by means of ancient plant remains. We want to know how the physical environment conditioned cultural development and how human activities in turn affected that same environment. In doing so, we must be aware of possible biases introduced by field, laboratory, and analytical practices, and analogies with modern-day plant communities must be carefully evaluated as well.

The main issue that emerges from all the papers is the importance of reliability and representativeness of archaeobotanical data. Another important issue, perhaps most explicitly stated by Asch and Sidell and Hastorf, is the complaint that paleoethnobotany is not yet fully integrated into the planning, recovery, and interpretation phases of archaeological projects. What I am hearing, to paraphrase the American comedian Rodney Dangerfield, is that "We [archaeobotanists] don't get no respect!"

I now comment briefly on the two issues. It is clear to me that archaeobotanists have come a long way. In this book there is ample proof that archaeobotanists are really more competent than they were, say, ten or fifteen years ago, at dealing with such problems as the representativeness and reliability of their data. They have concentrated more on the processes of data acquisition and representativeness than on the development of interpretive statistics. Perhaps this simply reflects caution on their part, and an admirable one to be sure. I can only second Joseph Kadane's suggestion that the time is right for increased collaboration between statisticians and paleoethnobotanists. A decade or two ago, the latter were not really ready to ask statisticians intelligent questions; today they most assuredly are.

Today there is much greater awareness of the processes of extraction, use, storage, preparation, consumption, discarding, and postdepositional movements of materials than ever before, and the increased awareness of data reliability has already been mentioned as salutary. However, I feel that archaeobotanists as paleoethnobotanists, and paleoethnobotanists as anthropologists, have not yet realized their potential. [1]

Few authors in the book make much mention of interregional or even intraregional perspectives; Toll is an exception. The authors say much about method and very little about cultural interpretation; here Pearsall, Hastorf, and Johannessen are exceptions. Now granted, the emphasis of this book is on methodology, and I hope that my appreciation of recent advances in method is clear. But as we begin to feel more and more confidentthat we understand the processes by which the archaeobotanical record is produced, I hope that archaeobotanists as paleoethnobotanists will begin to move more actively into the realm of theory production.

1. Following Ford (1979:299), I distinguish between archaeobotany, which "refers to the *recovery* and *identification* of plants by specialists regardless of discipline," and paleoethnobotany, which "implies their *interpretation* by particular specialists."

The role of plants ought to be but one focus in a broad concern with the production and reproduction of human societies. Paleoethnobotanists have much to contribute to the resolution of such matters as migration, exchange and commerce, and the emergence of estate, caste, and class relations. I would make the same argument to zooarchaeologists too. Both zooarchaeologists and archaeobotanists have experienced data productivity revolutions in the past decade. Archaeobotanists, with their better flotation machines and multiscale sampling and analytic methods, and zooarchaeologists, with the recent advances made through the use of fine-screen samples and better allometric studies, are now for the first time in a position to contribute actively to important theoretical debates. To paraphase a contemporary television commercial, archaeobotany and zooarchaeology aren't just for the appendix anymore.

To the authors of this book I say again that my respect for what you have accomplished is genuine, and my gratitude for what you have taught me is real. But I also want to suggest that the potential of your contributions to the production of anthropological knowledge has yet to be realized. In part this is a matter of the liberation of paleoethnobotanists from the common perception that they are service personnel rather than bona fide members of anthropological research teams. But paleoethnobotanists must take an active role in their own liberation. Paleoethnobotanists as anthropologists must begin to participate more directly in the production of anthropological, not just botanical, knowledge. I am confident that such contributions will be seen increasingly, and that paleoethnobotanists at last will begin to get the respect that they so richly deserve.

References Cited

Crumley, Carole L., William H. Marquardt, and Thomas L. Leatherman. 1987. Certain factors influencing settlement during the later Iron Age and Gallo-Roman periods: The analysis of intensive survey data. In *Regional dynamics: Burgundian landscapes in historical perspective*, ed. by Carole L. Crumley and William H. Marquardt, pp. 121-72. San Diego: Academic Press.

Ford, Richard I. 1979. Paleoethnobotany in American archaeology. In *Advances in archaeological method and theory,* vol. 2, ed. Michael B. Schiffer, pp. 285-336. New York: Academic Press.

Marquardt, William H., and Patty Jo Watson. 1983. The Shell Mound Archaic of Western Kentucky. In *Archaic hunters and gatherers of the American Midwest,* ed. James L. Phillips and James A. Brown, pp. 323-39. New York: Academic Press.

List of Contributors

David L. Asch
Department of Anthropology
Smithsonian Institution
Washington DC

Richard I. Ford
Museum of Anthropology
University of Michigan,
Ann Arbor, MI 48109

Christine A. Hastorf
Department of Anthropology
University of Minnesota
Minneapolis, MN 55455

Ellen S. Hoffman
Museum of Anthropology
University of Michigan
Ann Arbor, MI 48109

Sissell Johannessen
Department of Anthropology
University of Minnesota
Minneapolis, MN 55455

Joseph B. Kadane
Department of Statistics
Carnegie Mellon University
Pittsburgh, PA 15213-3890

William H. Marquardt
Department of Anthropology
Florida State Museum
University of Florida
Gainesville, FL 32611

Naomi F. Miller
MASCA
University Museum
33rd and Spruce Streets
University of Philadelphia
Philadelphia, PA 19104

Deborah M. Pearsall
American Archaeology Division
Department of Anthropology
University of Missouri
Columbia, MO 65211

Virginia S. Popper
1135 Via de la Paz
Pacific Palisades, CA 90272

Nancy Asch Sidell
RFD no. 1, Box 376
Littlefield
Springvale, ME 04083

Tristine Lee Smart
Museum of Anthropology
University of Michigan
Ann Arbor, MI 48109

Mollie S. Toll
Paleoethnobotany Laboratory
Botany Department
University of New Mexico
Albuquerque, NM 87131

Gail E. Wagner
Center for American Archeology
Box 246
Kampsville, IL 62053

Index